SEASONS COME TO PASS

A POETRY ANTHOLOGY

FOR SOUTHERN AFRICAN STUDENTS

COMPILED BY

Es'kia Mphahlele
and Helen Moffett

Cape Town
Oxford University Press

OXFORD UNIVERSITY PRESS
Walton Street, Oxford OX2 6DP, United Kingdom

Oxford New York

Athens Bangkok Calcutta Cape Town Chennai
Dar es Salaam Delhi Florence Hong Kong
Istanbul Karachi Kuala Lumpur Madrid Melbourne
Mexico City Mumbai Nairobi Paris Singapore
Taipei Tokyo Toronto

and associated companies in
Berlin Ibadan

OXFORD is a trademark of Oxford University Press

SEASONS COME TO PASS: A POETRY ANTHOLOGY FOR SOUTHERN AFRICAN STUDENTS

ISBN: 0 19 570 955 1

Second impression 1996
Third impression 1997

Editor: Allison Murphy
Research: Donald Reid
Designer: Graham Arbuckle
Cover design: Mark Standley
Cover illustration: detail from a design by Alexander Podlashut

Published by Oxford University Press Southern Africa,
PO Box 12119, N1 City 7463, Cape Town, South Africa

Set in Sabon by RHT desktop publishing cc, Durbanville

Printed by ABC Book Printers, 21 Kinghall Avenue, Epping II

'. . . indeed, it is a dry white season
but seasons come to pass.'
— Mongane Wally Serote

This anthology is dedicated to all our students, who have taught us more than they can ever know.

Contents

Preface

South African students and scholars often pose the legitimate question: why should they study the poetry, written in the language of a former colonial power, and telling of centuries of foreign history and culture, that comes from a small island thousands of kilometres away?

This question is not easily answered, and most poetry anthologies available to local students do not provide much guidance. Those which give comprehensive overviews of English poetry from early medieval through to modern times are mostly published in, and imported from, the United States or Britain. These cannot be sensitive to the specific needs and concerns of a South African audience. They also demonstrate an understandably Western bias; most poets included are from North America and the British Isles, and poetry written in English by poets from Africa, Latin America and Asia is hardly represented. South African poets are almost never featured.

On the other hand there are excellent locally produced anthologies, which provide access to the wealth of poetry produced by South Africans of all colours, creeds and language backgrounds. However, these do not necessarily provide much guidance to the student who has chosen to study English literature, and who needs to comes to grips with the panoply of poetry written by English writers; who is mystified by Chaucer, intimidated by Shakespeare, alienated by the Romantic poets, and confused by Yeats and Eliot. Nevertheless, these and other English poets have much to offer, and South African students are often pleasantly surprised to discover how much enjoyment they can gain from coming to grips with the so-called 'classics' of mainstream English poetry. However, the complaint by many students that they find English poetry both boring and irrelevant requires some consideration.

One explanation is the tendency in many South African educational institutions to teach English poetry, and indeed English literature, as if it is the pinnacle of all civilization, and the hallmark of all that is universally good and beautiful. It is certainly useful to stress the rich aesthetic and cultural value of studying English poetry, with all its beauty, subtlety and complexity, its broad historical sweep and fascinating commentary on the human condition. However, to take one language and present its literature, history and culture as if these are somehow inherently superior to all others, and as if its particular standards of beauty and morality are universal, no matter how unconsciously this is done, is not only intellectually dishonest, but disabling to South African students. It is unfair to expect students who have never seen a daffodil in their lives to swoon over Wordsworth's 'I wandered lonely as a cloud', or, even worse, to somehow convey the message that appreciation of the imagined sight of unfamiliar flowers in a foreign climate implies a praiseworthy literary sensitivity. The very real and physical differences in climate, geography and surroundings mean that much that is particularly beautiful in English poetry — such as the tradition of lyric and love poetry which celebrates the advent of spring in the northern hemisphere — needs to be decoded for a South African audience.

One way of challenging the traditional baggage that often accompanies the teaching of literature is to expand the notion of what is meant by the rather vague term 'English poetry'. Above, we have largely used it to refer to poetry written by poets from the British Isles during the past eight or so centuries. However, it should be clear from the contents list of this anthology that 'poetry written in English' is a far more inclusive category than 'poetry from England'. The English language is not simply an all-powerful colonial force which has spread its tentacles all over the globe; different communities have brought their own interaction and contributions and fused these with the colonial language to form new, lively and distinctive versions of English. Some which spring to mind are the kinds of English used in the Caribbean (see John Agard's 'Poetry Jump-Up', p. 255, for example) and parts of the Pacific, as well as the various South African brands of English, which are often mingled with other languages (see Rushdy Siers' 'Sets of Two and their Silence', p. 253, for an effective example of how 'formal' English is combined with a distinctively Cape Muslim brand of Afrikaans slang). South African students are well aware of their ability to create Englishes of their own, and of the distinctive dialects that are characteristic of their own communities. There is currently a worldwide debate on the status of 'standard' English, with many asking whether there is any such thing. To see English, and therefore English poetry, as something that is neither fixed nor exclusive can be most liberating for South African students, who may have previously picked up the unspoken message that English is set in stone at the top of some kind of linguistic and literary hierarchy.

However, introducing students to the larger 'family' of poetry written in English, or kinds of English, across the globe still does not alleviate the problem of a student who is dismayed by a Shakespearian sonnet. Here we have found that providing appropriate contextual material can transform the situation. This does not mean adding a list of indigestible historical and social facts to an already unfamiliar poem. It is vital to provide information that enables the student to make connections between her or his own context, and that of the work with which she or he is presented. Almost everyone who has taught Shakespeare's 'My Mistress' Eyes are Nothing Like the Sun' (see p. 27) will be familiar with the glorious moment when it occurs to students that the unrealistic standards of physical beauty set for women, which Shakespeare both attacks and overturns, are as immediate (and oppressive) in today's world of anorexia and skin-lighteners as they were in sixteenth-century England. In fact, South African students are struck by the racism implied in choosing Caucasian characteristics (white skin, blue eyes and golden hair) as a superior standard of beauty, and find the poet's rejection of these criteria particularly powerful.

Contextual material should thus focus both on bringing the poem alive to a contemporary student audience, and on those historical, political and social aspects that apply directly to modern people. This may seem limiting, but it is not hard to do with good poetry, as what endures in literature tends to be that which provides memorable insight into the human condition. This method is often more honest than a teaching approach which assumes or pretends objective detachment. The enthusiasm with which students respond to sensitively handled Marxist, feminist or post-colonial readings of literary works testifies to the value of raising questions of class, gender, sexuality, race and religion with regard to poetry. Here one must be careful not to lay down strict rules; students are most comfortable evolving their own set of concerns to bring to a poem, and they should be strongly encouraged to do so. Moreover, to simply replace an outdated set of literary criteria with a more fashionable formula does not free students to think originally and creatively about poetry. Nevertheless, they need a good deal of contextual direction in order to feel the same confidence in handling a metaphysical poem by Donne or Herbert as they would a poem by a well-known South African author.

Another helpful means of establishing connections between modern concerns and those issues dealt with by long-dead poets, is by comparing contemporary poems (especially those by South African authors) with much earlier poems from the northern hemisphere. Students are often intrigued to find that poets from different continents and different centuries, using language and style that differs dramatically, can express very similar feelings or convictions. We have suggested comparisons and comparative exercises wherever we think this might be fruitful. Students and teachers may notice other pairings of poems which might be worthwhile to compare or contrast.

It has been particularly exciting putting this anthology together at such a momentous period in the history of South Africa. We were fascinated and thrilled to see how some of the South African poems chosen were transformed from contemporary critique into history overnight after the country's first democratic elections. Reading poems such as Serote's 'A Dry White Season' (from which the title of this anthology is taken) and Mattera's 'Remember' is now an altogether different experience.

We sincerely hope that students and teachers alike will find this anthology both useful and stimulating. It is intended to be a workbook, and we hope that its users will add to it, alter it and adapt it for their own purposes. We would welcome comment, criticism and suggestions for future editions. These can be sent to the authors c/o Oxford University Press Southern Africa, PO Box 12119, N1 City, 7463.

HELEN MOFFETT
ES'KIA MPHAHLELE
1994

How to Use this Book

We suggest that you read the introductory notes carefully, and discuss these either in tutorials or with friends who are doing the same course as you. These notes are divided into two parts; the first section is designed to give you a very brief overview of the historical backdrop against which the English language and its literature evolved. This is not intended as a list of facts you need to study and digest in order to come to grips with poetry; rather, it will hopefully give you a broad time-frame into which you can fit the poems you will study. It will give you a sense of how poems from various periods in history fit together, as well as sketching how scientific, religious, philosophical, geographical, political and cultural shifts over time affected the development of literature. A very rough outline of how English assumed its present shape will also shed some light on both the infuriating inconsistencies and rewarding richness of the English language.

The second part of the introduction gives some very basic indications, with examples, of how to go about 'analysing' a poem. Treat these as guidelines, and refer back to them at regular intervals, as you become more practised and confident in your dealings with poetry. Bear in mind that in learning to read and analyse poetry you are acquiring a skill, not learning a syllabus. Developing sensitivity to the language used around you, and evolving a set of personal critical skills, will stand you in good stead in your future studies, work and recreation, and can add to your self-confidence and communication skills. It is important not to gloss over this section, even if it seems strange at first. Giving written instructions on how to approach poetry is never quite satisfactory, as it needs to be practically demonstrated; it is rather like trying to teach someone to swim by writing them a letter! This is why you will need to go back to this section once you have become immersed in the poems themselves, and to discuss the suggestions given with other students and your teachers on a regular basis.

You will find that some of the poems are accompanied by suggestions for workshops (in the form of questions and discussion points). You and your teacher may decide to use these in the classroom; you also have the option of working through them in a study group, informally (by just chatting with a friend), or alone. Your teacher might also like to set some of these workshops as written exercises. You could also draw up your own workshops, using some of ours as examples.

As we explained in the Preface, it is vital that you have the necessary contextual information to gain the maximum enjoyment from a poem. Where necessary, we have provided brief contextual notes. You will also notice that certain words have been marked with an asterisk (*). This indicates that a short definition of that term can be found in the Glossary at the back of the book. However, you might also like to seek further information, either about the context of a poem, or a literary concept, from a library. In this case, it can be a bit daunting to leaf through books crammed with detailed information, or you might struggle to find specific books. A good starting place is the reference section of a library, with an encyclopedia or companion to English literature. By looking up the name of a specific poet, or a type of poem (sonnet, ballad, and so forth), or a historical period (Renaissance, for example), you should be able to find well-written, reliable and short pieces which should explain the facts in a clear and accessible manner.

Finally, we have suggested that you compare certain poems to others. This is because we believe that although it is necessary to present poems in chronological order to prevent historical confusion, by far the most exciting way of reading poetry is to look at how poems interact with each other, and add to our understanding of specific themes and issues. Poems that look very different might communicate the same basic message or emotion; or poems on similar topics might provide very different viewpoints — which can spark interesting classroom debates.

Poetry can be an adventure; we hope you enjoy it.

A Brief Note on Sources

With the exception of the poems by Rossetti and the previously unpublished poems, which were drawn from manuscript sources, all the poems in this anthology were drawn from published collections. Wherever possible, poems were checked against a number of authoritative sources. In the case of modern poems, we asked the copyright holders, and in some cases the poets themselves, to check our versions of the poems. Nevertheless, there remained a number of minor discrepancies (usually confined to punctuation, the use of capital letters, and line indentations) between the various sources we used, particularly in the case of poems written before the twentieth century.

In some instances, the debates concerning which version of a certain poem was 'correct' demanded a far more specialist level of scholarship than was appropriate for a student anthology. In cases of uncertainty, we turned for guidance to the major anthologies of English poetry used in undergraduate teaching in South Africa. We did this for the practical reason that many South African students (and their teachers) are already familiar with the versions of poems found in these, rather than because we were always convinced of their correctness. This anthology therefore makes no claim to provide a definitive version of poems that erudite scholars are still debating. Postgraduate students or researchers are encouraged to turn to original or variorum collections of the works of poets that interest them (or even manuscript collections, if practical) for more insight into the fascinating and complex issues concerning the provenance of works of literature.

However, in view of the fact that this anthology is geared towards undergraduate students for whom English is a second language, we have taken certain liberties with some poems. We have followed the lead of other anthologies in modernizing the spelling of some of the earlier poems, to prevent the necessity of glossing almost every word; and (where copyright holders have permitted) we have anglicized the spelling of poems by North American writers. It is also worth noting that because of our obligation to copyright holders, we have been unable to avoid certain small inconsistencies within the text, and even the appearance of what might seem like errors (such as unusual spacing in the poems by E.E. Cummings).

H.M. 1997

Introductory Notes

English History and Literature: A Contextual Time-frame

Few small islands have been as repeatedly invaded, pillaged, ransacked, and finally assimilated as a colonial domain, as the damp and green British Isles off the west coast of Europe. At a time when the pyramids of Egypt had been standing guard over the tombs of the Pharaohs for over 2 000 years, four centuries after the armies of the young Greek general Alexander the Great had established their sway as far as India, and about 100 years after the birth of Jesus in occupied territory in the Middle East, the first conquerors established their outposts on British soil.

These were the Romans, whose military power and sophisticated civilization easily overwhelmed the crude resources of the British peoples. However, there was no notion of British identity or nationhood at this early stage; the inhabitants of the British Isles were made up of relatively isolated and often warring units, who were fiercely tribal, deeply superstitious and possessed of a rich folklore. The languages they spoke bore no resemblance whatsoever to the English that is spoken today; they were drawn from a language pool broadly identified as Celtic. Few Celtic languages have survived till the present day, although various forms still persist in Ireland, Wales and the remoter parts of Scotland. Traces of the Celtic languages are hard to find in English today, although some words and sounds can still be found. For example, the Scottish word for lake, 'loch', has the last two letters pronounced as a soft 'g' (a gentler version of the way the letter 'g' is pronounced by Afrikaans and German speakers). This derives from Celtic origins, and is a sound that has since fallen away in modern English usage. Speakers of Celtic languages stress the beauty and musical qualities of these ancient dialects, and they are associated with poetry, story-telling, the singing of songs, and prayer. The attempts to keep these languages alive in present-day Britain are linked with nationalist movements, particularly in Ireland, which has a longer history of colonization by the British than any other territory in the world. (Northern Ireland is still regarded by some as a region under British occupation.)

It is not surprising that Celtic languages persist only in the western and northern corners of the British Isles, when we consider that most invasion and subsequent settlement came from the south and the east. The clans which resisted the conquerors retreated to the more inaccessible and mountainous parts of the country. Even trained Roman troops could not penetrate into present-day Scotland, and in fact they experienced so much harassment from aggressive local tribes that they built a defensive wall across the northern boundary of the conquered territory. (See Auden's 'Roman Wall Blues', p. 163.)

The Roman conquest meant that Latin became the language of education, law, commerce and administration. Over a period of time, many Roman settlers blended their culture with that of their new home. Nevertheless, Britain was not considered a particularly useful or strategic colony, and with the final collapse of the Roman Empire the occupying militia returned home, leaving behind the legacy of their language, architecture and engineering. Those who stayed behind were absorbed into the local population. However, the same Germanic tribes whose aggression had contributed to the downfall of the power of Rome, now threatened the inhabitants of the British Isles as well.

From about the fourth century CE, Britain's eastern shores were battered by wave after wave of marauding Angles and Saxons, tribes from what is today central Germany. Further north, the eastern shores of Scotland were also under attack from Norse or Viking tribes from the Scandinavian regions of northern Europe (see 'The Viking Terror', p. 3). Many of these Germanic tribes had developed superior seafaring skills to those of their neighbours, and were therefore easily able to mount raids on the unfortunate British. It is tempting to speculate that the xenophobia (fear or hatred of foreigners) with which the British are often charged might date from these bitter times, when the sight of an alien sail or sails on the horizon usually meant that the local men could expect to be killed or enslaved, the women raped, their dwellings burned or wrecked, their livestock slaughtered and their crops stolen. Still deeply fragmented along tribal lines, the British could put up no sustained resistance to the invaders, and by the seventh century Britain was almost entirely subject to Anglo-Saxon rule. As centuries passed, the settlers became increasingly identified with their new home, and their languages took their turn in further submerging the already Latinized Celtic languages.

Within a few centuries Britain was relatively stable, with original inhabitants and descendants of settlers well integrated. No matter how brutal their invasion practices were, the Germanic tribes had no interest in ruling a conquered land as a dominion (as the Romans did), but preferred to make it their new home, both assimilating the native inhabitants and themselves being assimilated. The country was fragmented, however, as the earlier arrivals, the Anglo-Saxons, found themselves wrestling with the later Danish invaders for control of the island. Meanwhile, both groups of settlers were to come under threat from a different quarter.

The ruler of the province of Normandy in France laid claim to the throne of Britain, and in 1066 his Norman troops invaded England, defeated the Saxon king, and instituted their own fresh brand of administration, law, customs and leadership, as well as yet another language: Norman French. The English, already a polyglot nation, were once again subject to alien rule, and once again the invaders slowly became assimilated into the melting pot of English culture. To further complicate matters, medieval Latin was introduced as an official language in order to cope with the difficulties of administering a multilingual nation. So the forceful, heavy and sombre language of the Anglo-Saxons met and married with the graceful, colourful and musical French of the Normans, with a good dash of the formality of Latin stirred in.

It is only once we understand this history that we can appreciate both the richness and the inconsistencies of the English language. The many languages which fed into it have created an almost bewildering array of synonyms — different words with the same meaning — and this gives English literature its complex texture and extraordinary powers of description. On the other hand, there is an equally bewildering range of differing pronunciations, spellings, idiomatic expressions and grammatical quirks which are all exceptions to the rules of the language. A recent cartoon showed a crowd of panicked foreign students stampeding out of an English language class on pronunciation: the puzzled lecturer, who had just written the words 'rough', 'through', 'plough' and 'trough' (pronounced 'ruff', 'throo', 'plow' and 'trof' respectively) on the board, was asking, 'What did I do wrong?'

To move on, the centuries that elapsed after the Norman conquest eventually led to the development of a literature, during the later Middle Ages, which is accessible to modern English speakers. English was slowly shaping into the form in which we know it today. Medieval English (known as Middle English by scholars, to distinguish it from Modern English) usually seems foreign to the first-time reader — but it can be recognized and read. Of course, there was no official adoption of a national language; the English spoken throughout the Middle Ages was made up a host of broadly similar, but regionally influenced dialects, which differed in some important respects. The English spoken today is the descendant of the south-eastern dialect used by Chaucer, and it came into predominance partly because it centred on the capital city, London, and the River Thames, along which international and local shipping and commerce flowed, and partly because of the invention of the printing press. The first books to be printed were written in the south-eastern dialect, and thus entrenched its status.

Printing made books and written material available to ordinary people for the first time. Up till then, books could only be laboriously copied by hand. Printing was to have a profound impact on literacy, which gradually moved out of the preserve of the church and a few aristocrats. Literature of this time still relied heavily on oral roots, however; poems and stories were largely passed on by reading or reciting aloud. Chaucer's *Canterbury Tales* (see p. 4), for example, are cast as the stories told for entertainment in a pub by a rowdy band of pilgrims travelling towards Canterbury, and many medieval lyrics were songs which were learnt by heart and passed on, with the names of their original creators left behind and lost.

The literature from medieval England speaks of a rural, farming nation, superstitious in spite of the all-encompassing hold the Catholic church exercised on every aspect of life, deeply rooted in and dependent on the cycle of nature. Society was organized along feudal lines, with the land-owning classes believed to have a God-given nobility and charge to rule over the 'common' people. It was only the gradual rise of an affluent and urban middle class, which had access to education, that finally weakened the hierarchical structure of society.

People were down-to-earth and lacking in modern squeamishness about birth, sex, and death; these were part of everyday experience in a society in which privacy was a luxury afforded only hermits in their cells. For example, a dead body would not have been an unusual sight. Women were openly second-class citizens, considered the property of either male relatives or their husbands. They had no legal rights, and little or no say in whom they married. Most marriages were arranged for economic or political reasons, rather than romantic ones, and a wife was valued for her ability to work hard and her fertility.

Blatant anti-Semitism was considered normal and acceptable, and attacks on Jewish communities were among the more unsavoury aspects of medieval life. This was also the time of the Crusades; these were pilgrimages by European Christians to the Holy Land (present-day Israel), many of which involved making war on the 'infidels' or 'heathens' who lived in these sacred territories. The contact with Arab culture proved advantageous to Europeans, however; many of the great libraries of the Islamic empire (which spread from the Middle East through North Africa) held the writings of the ancient Greek scholars, whose work had been largely lost to Europe during the Dark Ages that followed the barbarian invasions. The system of numbering we follow today is called 'arabic', and comes from the principles of mathematics developed by Arab scholars.

Two central shifts in European cultural and religious life brought the Middle Ages to a close, and led to the transformation of the colourful, cyclical, simple, and occasionally violent way of life of most medieval folk living in Britain. These were the Renaissance — a flowering of new scientific and literary knowledge which began in Italy and spread through Western Europe — and the Reformation, which split the Christian church down the middle, with complex political and social results which were to reverberate for centuries.

The Renaissance had its roots in, among other things, the rediscovery of the scientific, literary and philosophical writings of the ancient Greeks and Romans by various brilliant Italian scholars. This coincided with a rise in status of vernacular languages and with the corresponding development of vernacular literatures. New forms of writing were being experimented with, and new scientific, geographical and astronomical discoveries were being made, which banished the precepts of the medieval world for good. A new emphasis and value was placed on education and culture, with secular scholars moving into what had for centuries been the domain of the church.

The Renaissance came to the island fortress of Britain a little late, but there it enjoyed a particularly rich flowering, sometimes called the 'Golden Age'. After nearly a century of destructive civil war between different contenders for the throne of England (known as the Wars of the Roses) during the fifteenth century, the Tudor dynasty was securely established, with first Henry VIII and then Elizabeth I on the throne. The preceding century had been a barren period in literary terms, apart from the first comprehensive effort to weave the many legends of King Arthur and his knights into one coherent work, and the development of the lyric poem. Now, however, literature and the arts flourished, and rapidly reached new heights.

Dramatists such as Jonson, Marlowe and Shakespeare were producing plays of extraordinary wit, wisdom and impact; in their hands, as well as in those of a host of other gifted poets such as Spenser and Sidney, language was being used with new flair. There were new innovations in poetry, at first tentatively borrowed from classical writers, then developed with growing confidence and vigour. (You might want to look at some Renaissance sonnets as an example of the kind of poetic innovations of these times; see pp. 17, 20, 25–27.) Meanwhile, sailors such as Sir Francis Drake and Sir Walter Raleigh were sailing round the globe, establishing Britain's seafaring power for the first time. Many exploratory voyages were little more than glorified raiding parties, but these nevertheless brought great prestige to the monarchy of England.

This apparently golden age was nonetheless a bloody one, largely because of the Reformation referred to above. In 1517, a German monk named Martin Luther made public his objections to the practice of selling indulgences (crudely put, the forgiving of sins and guaranteed admission into heaven in exchange for money — see the notes to Chaucer's 'The Pardoner's Prologue', p. 7, for more details), and began a process of rebellion against the Catholic church which was to change the face of Western Europe. At the time, Catholicism was the only form of the Christian religion. What began as an attempt to reform the church and purge it of its excesses led to a split or schism. The various Protestant groupings (so named because of their protest against the various failings of the Catholic church) broke away and formed new religious denominations of their own. The results were sometimes tragic, as communities were divided against each other, political allegiances shifted and civil wars broke out. For several centuries, Catholic and Protestant monarchies in various countries battled for power. The succession of a Protestant monarch often meant persecution for Catholics, and vice versa. Rebellions were often planned on religious grounds, with invariably violent results. (See p. 23 for an example of a poem by a young man condemned to death for his part in a Catholic plot against the Protestant queen Elizabeth I.)

The Tudor king Henry VIII began the process of the English Reformation by declaring himself to be the head of both church and state in England, establishing new bishops (who promptly gave him permission to divorce his first wife and marry his mistress), breaking up the monasteries, and distributing the lands and wealth of the church among his nobles. After his death, his daughter Elizabeth embarked on her long and successful reign which established the sway of the new Protestant church of England. The great writers mentioned above (Spenser, Sidney, Shakespeare and Marlowe) are mostly associated with her reign, which was a period of exploration, cultural development, and glamour. Elizabeth herself was a distinguished scholar, whose work included poetry and translations. She died childless, and was succeeded by her cousin James, already king of Scotland.

James's successor, Charles I, was to run into trouble. During the seventeenth century, a new movement began among those who wished to extend the power of parliament. (This was not the same as a modern, democratically elected parliament, as members inherited their seats rather than being voted in. Nevertheless, laws were debated and voted on; this obviously had the potential to restrict the authority of the king.) Many parliamentarians, fuelled by a desire to carry the Reformation to further and stricter extremes, wished to curtail the privileges and powers of the monarchy, and legislate their own brand of religious Puritanism, an austere type of Calvinism which frowned on secular pleasures. (The first colonies in North America were established during this period by Puritans who wished to be free to practise their religion without interference.)

The growing tension between the two factions led inevitably to civil war between supporters of the monarchy (the Cavaliers) and the parliamentary forces (the Roundheads). This ended with the defeat and execution of Charles I, and the establishment of parliamentary rule under Oliver Cromwell. Culturally, this was a repressive time; strict rules governed dress, entertainment, and so forth. One of the first steps taken by the Puritans was to close the theatres; after a century and a half of brilliance, the golden age of English drama finally went into eclipse. However, after 11 years, popular pressure led to the restoration of the monarchy, with the return of Charles II from exile.

Against the backdrop of this political and religious upheaval, and in spite of the blow to drama with the banning of plays, this was a fruitful period in English literature, especially for poetry. The great poets of this era were ranged on all sides of the political spectrum; Carew, Vaughan and Herrick were supporters of the monarchy (and are still referred to as Cavalier poets); Anne Bradstreet was a Puritan; Milton and Marvell supported parliamentary rule and used their talents in government service. Nevertheless, these poets are not necessarily remembered for their political allegiances, but for the brilliance of their wit and for their contributions, together with Donne and Herbert, to the original and intellectually challenging school of what was later termed Metaphysical poetry. (See p. 30 for further notes on this type of poetry.)

Compared with the passion of the preceding centuries, the eighteenth century may seem a little tame to scholars. Sometimes called the Enlightenment, or the age of reason, this was an era in which extreme religious and political beliefs gave way to a more sceptical and rational public morality. New scientific discoveries by scientists such as Isaac Newton gave rise to a belief in an organized and ordered universe, and writings by philosophers such as Descartes and Voltaire preached tolerance and the importance of rational thought. This was very much a time of 'the head rather than the heart'.

In literary terms, the first half of the eighteenth century was to see the rise of the novel, with earlier writers paving the way for the skilled novels that Jane Austen was writing by the end of the century. This was also the great age of satire; poets such as Pope ridiculed the follies and excesses of their contemporaries in long and technically skilful works. The popularity of satire was perhaps a reflection of the real concern for responsible and prudent behaviour on the part of the land-owning upper classes; see, for example, Samuel Johnson's 'A Short Song of Congratulation' (p. 53). Johnson also compiled the first dictionary of the English language, with typical eighteenth-century enthusiasm for classifying and ordering information. This played a vital role in finally stabilizing and standardizing English.

The emphasis by thinkers such as the French philosopher Rousseau on the rights and dignity of humankind was to plant one of the fundamental seeds of the Romantic movement, which was also an inevitable reaction against the detachment of much Enlightenment thinking. Romanticism, which in England bridged the late eighteenth and early nineteenth centuries, emphasized the importance of emotion, and preached a return to Nature as a source of moral and creative guidance. Beauty was especially valued for its ability to instruct, comfort and inspire. With the beginnings of the Industrial Revolution, with its tremendous physical impact on English landscape, the recognition that natural loveliness was under threat was combined with a growing movement towards democracy, as well as indignation at the conditions in which the new urban labouring classes worked. Most of the early Romantic poets, most notably Wordworth and Coleridge (see pp. 63–69 for further details) were initially supporters of the French Revolution, with its rallying-cry 'liberty, equality and brotherhood'.

The rise of Romanticism meant a completely new direction for poetry. Although some Romantic poems, with their passionate and unselfconscious pouring forth of emotion in response to beauty, may sometimes seem alien to modern readers, we are all post-Romantics to some degree: the Romantic vision of poetry as a vessel for passing on beauty and truth has left an indelible mark on the way we read literature. Another interesting shift was in the perception of the role of the poet; the Romantics saw themselves as visionaries, with a mission to search for higher truths, and a responsibility to challenge orthodoxy. The later Romantic poets especially considered it their moral duty to rebel against society's norms. (See the biographical information on Byron and Shelley, for example; pp. 70 and 71.)

Romanticism blended into the Victorian age in 1830, when Victoria ascended the throne of Britain and began a long and relatively stable reign. This was the great age of empire; European nations were staking their claims to territorial ownership all over the globe, and Britain led the race. This was propelled in part by the need for raw materials for the factories of England, now in full swing. Legislation scrambled to keep up with the social impact and ensuing problems of industrialization and urbanization. Social reform and scientific progress rubbed shoulders with extreme poverty and often appalling working conditions. Slavery was abolished, but child labour went a fair way towards taking its place.

This era marked the burgeoning of an educated middle class with leisure and money to spend on books, entertainment and consumer goods. Fundamental issues were being brought into question: Karl Marx's economic theories and Darwin's theories of evolution (which challenged the biblical creation myth) cast doubts on previously unchallenged assumptions. One of the results was considerable nostalgia for a mythical and less complex past; Victorian artists and writers turned to legends, myths, an idealistic vision of rural life, and the distant past for more comforting sources of inspiration.

The nineteenth century also marked the beginnings of the struggle for legal and political representation by women. This was met by a flurry of writing advocating the home and domesticity as women's natural and ordained sphere. Nevertheless, women's activities and contributions to all spheres of life increased; Florence Nightingale established nursing as a respectable profession for women; charity work by middle-class women and governessing by their less affluent sisters slowly developed into social work and teaching; and female writers flourished as never before. In general, this was a period of considerable richness in literature: poets such as Lord Tennyson, Matthew Arnold, Elizabeth Barrett Browning and Robert Browning provided a feast of lyrical, narrative, epic and reflective poetry. Likewise, novelists such as Charles Dickens, the Brontë sisters, George Eliot (the pseudonym of Mary Ann Evans) and others were at the height of their powers.

The latter half of the nineteenth century saw the rise of the Pre-Raphaelite movement, a reaction against the values of the bourgeoisie, and a rather unrealistic attempt to return to medieval values. It produced not only a colourful and sometimes sentimental school of painting, but also poets such as

Christina Rossetti. Their emphasis on the value of nostalgic beauty and mysticism was to influence the aesthetic principles of both artists and writers well into the twentieth century.

It was also during the Victorian age that the literature of the colonies and of North America became known. American philosophers such as Thoreau and writers such as Longfellow, Hawthorne and Edgar Allan Poe were popular on both sides of the Atlantic. The waning of the century saw an increase in 'empire' literature, with the works of colonial officials and travellers such as Rudyard Kipling becoming part of the body of English literature. In South Africa, the writings of Olive Schreiner and Pauline Smith received acclaim.

At the time of Queen Victoria's death, the British empire ('on which the sun never set') was at its height of power; however, there were rumblings of discontent. The Anglo-Boer War at the turn of the century, fought over the establishment of Boer republics where gold had been discovered, led to eventual victory but considerable loss of prestige for the British. However, what finally destroyed all remnants of the Victorian way of life and 'blew a hole in the face of civilization' was the First World War, or the Great War (1914–1918). Most of Europe and its colonies were involved in this protracted and bloody war, which cost the lives of millions, and which was to sow the seeds of the next world war. (For more details, and some examples of poets of the Great War, see pp. 131 and 144.)

It is hard to draw a dividing line between the late Victorians and the early Modernists in literature. The poetry of Hopkins, for example, who falls into the Victorian period, is strikingly modern in its style and effect; whereas the work of several great twentieth-century poets (such as Yeats, and even later, Dylan Thomas) draws heavily on the traditions of nineteenth-century poetry.

Modernism refers, among other things, to the breakdown of 'realism' in art. This meant that, for example, a painter no longer necessarily represented subjects as they would appear to the naked eye. Writers, musicians and artists reinvented the rules, developing sometimes astonishing and provocative new techniques. The notion that art could shock, disturb and challenge as well as entertain, educate and inspire became explicit for the first time. With the rise of the Freudian and Jungian schools of psychoanalysis, and the recognition of the subconscious and unconscious components of the mind, it was inevitable that creators would begin to explore their inner as well as their outer worlds. Poetry especially moved into the realm of association rather than explanation, with words being used for their evocative effect, rather than as explicit means of communication. (See, for example, the poems by T. S. Eliot, pp. 134–139.)

The issues of censorship and political alignment of literature were especially vital in the decades after the First World War, which saw the rise of fascism in Europe. Many intellectuals and activists had to flee their native countries, Germany in particular, where the rise of Nazism under Hitler was eventually to precipitate the Second World War (1939–1945). This war was to introduce two new horrors, which have haunted human consciousness since. The first was the Holocaust (the systematic segregation of Jewish people into concentration camps, where six million of them were murdered in an insane attempt to establish 'racial purity' — see p. 243 for a poem on the Holocaust); the second was the dropping of the first atomic bomb on the Japanese city of Hiroshima.

This inflicted devastation, death and long-term radioactive poisoning on a scale that had previously been unimaginable.

After the war, the countries of the northern hemisphere settled into the 'Cold War' — the state of hostility between what was then the Soviet empire, and the Western democracies. Meanwhile, independence movements were growing throughout the southern hemisphere, with various colonies demanding and achieving independence from their former colonial 'masters'. This process was often bumpy and sometimes even chaotic. However, in terms of literary output, there was tremendous growth in what came to be known as post-colonial literature and culture in various newly independent countries, particularly in Asia and Africa.

The latter half of the twentieth century has been noteworthy for the richness and complexity of critical debates which have sprung up around literature. Different theories of literary criticism have been fiercely contested, and Marxist, feminist, and post-colonial ideologies have all been brought to bear on the way we read literature and the questions we ask of it.

In particular, there has been a hotly debated and defended shift from the principles of so-called 'new criticism' to those of post-structuralism. 'New criticism' follows a system of closely scrutinizing works of literature in order to identify their moral and aesthetic values (the word 'aesthetic' implies qualities of beauty which give pleasure and inspiration). It therefore assumes a universal set of standards by which art can be assessed. Post-structuralist theories, however, are broadly concerned with the structuring of language into hierarchically ranked binary oppositions (male/female, black/white, night/day, urban/rural, society/nature) and the power dynamics which appear in texts as a result. New theories concerning the retrieval of history, as well as input from various ideologies, have also led to a more sophisticated approach to the social and historical context of literature. Certainly the myth of objective and detached criticism is now a thing of the past. Possibly the most obvious effect of these debates is that literary criticism, of whatever kind, is now considerably more self-conscious; as late-twentieth-century readers we bear in mind how our identity, assumptions, and social values determine and shape our responses to art and entertainment.

Analysing Poetry

The difference between poetry and prose. Before we can begin to analyse poetry, it is necessary to grasp what it is that makes poetry different from other forms of literature. In particular, how does it differ from prose?

To begin with, poetry is a particularly dense and concentrated form of expression. Every single word is chosen for effect, and then combined with others and shaped with a specific end in mind. Poetic language goes much further than conveying factual information; its aim is to generate strong responses, to vividly recreate a specific scene or mood. Imagery, or vivid use of language, is at the heart of poetry. It must be remembered that words are not always restricted to their specific dictionary meaning or factual content. Many words in the English language have acquired layers of meaning, and it is these implicit meanings — associations or connotations — that poetry thrives on.

There are two essential hallmarks that distinguish poetry from prose (the everyday form of writing that we find in novels, newspapers, business letters, and so forth). These are sound and shape.

If we consider sound first, we find that unlike most other forms of literature, poetry must be read aloud to be properly appreciated. Poems are designed to be heard with the ear as well as seen by the eye. Words are chosen by poets not only for their meaning and associations, but for their musical and sensuous qualities.

Rhythm and rhyme, in particular, are components that set poetry off from other forms of writing. Although modern poets have experimented freely with rhythm and rhyme, these features are often governed by complex rules similar to those found in musical composition; in certain types of poem, there will be a set number of 'beats' or stresses per line, just as a phrase of song can be broken up into bars and beats. It is not always necessary to know the technical terms used to describe these principles, but it is important to be able to identify the rhythm and rhyme scheme of a poem. For example, the rhythm can be quick, slow, smooth, monotonous, faltering, and so forth — the possibilities are endless.

The next important distinguishing feature of poetry is its shape. This refers to the distinctive appearance of poetry on the page; a poem is immediately recognizable because it is laid out in lines. This lends special emphasis to the words of a poem, as we have to consider their arrangement and layout. Just as prose might be compared to flowers growing at random in the veld, the art of poetry might be likened to the careful arrangement of flowers for effect in a vase. Placing words in a line sets them apart, and creates a little pause before the next line begins. We can see the effect that arranging words into lines has if we look at these extracts from 'The Abandoned Old Woman' by Stephen Watson (from *Return of the Moon*):

> Our mother, old, unable to walk,
> lay there, incapable,
> alone in her old grass and reed hut.
> . . .
> It was none of our fault;
> we were all of us starving.
> No-one could help it,
> that we had to leave her behind.

The meaning of these lines would not change if we wrote them out as prose sentences: 'Our mother, old, unable to walk, lay there, incapable, alone in her old grass and reed hut . . . It was none of our fault; we were all of us starving. No-one could help it, that we had to leave her behind.' However, the impact of these words is greatly lessened if they are presented this way. Their stark message becomes more matter-of-fact, and less poignant, when the words are run together over the full width of the page. Look at the contrast between the two ways of writing out these sentences, and note how the shaping of sentences into lines gives extra emphasis to the words at the beginning and end of lines.

It is worth checking the words chosen by the poet to start and end lines; these are often significant. The ordering of the poem into lines also sometimes creates what are called 'run-on' lines, when the flow of the words travels across a line break without a pause; for example, Delius's 'Deaf-and-dumb School' (p. 175) begins: 'On a black tarmac playground dark/ Nuns, ...'. Here the end of the line comes before we see what word the adjective 'dark' is describing. In this case, the run-on line breaks up the phrase, so that we are forced to pause and consider the implications of the words used. In other instances, this device can be used to quicken the pace of these lines, or to subtly alter or emphasize the meaning of the words concerned.

So the arrangement of words into lines in poetry is by no means arbitrary. Just as rhyme and rhythm contribute to the effect that poetry has on the ear, the shaping of words into lines gives poetry its visual impact. The following poem by Lionel Abrahams, on the difference between poetry and prose, might be helpful in consolidating these distinctions:

Note in Prosy Verse

Prose on the page
fills the space from margin to margin.
Like water or unmoulded clay it has no shape
of its own. Prose words are bodiless symbols
combining in messages which only the mind can translate,
and only then their infinite meaning begins.
Verse is shaped in its own shape
visible even before the reading begins.
The lines end where they mean to end
and the form they compose does not lie
passive on the paper but strives
to lift off, to fly free like a moth,
or rather a breath. It remembers
that once it was speech or even was song.

Poetry possibly favours verse because
a poem begins as an impassioned thought,
a felt idea so strong it has to
tell itself and end with being felt again.
The poem thus needs embodiment:
each word must ring its sound, each line its tune.
The shapes on the paper are never the poem
but only the signs that a poem has been made.
Embodied, audible, palpable,
the whole made thing is made to make
the meaning felt, not merely known.

Having identified some of the features that differentiate poetry from prose, we come a little closer to engaging with poetry itself. We have also established some useful areas to investigate when we move on to analysis.

Getting to grips with a poem: preparatory work. The next question is, how do we approach a poem? A great deal of ground needs to be covered before the actual analysis of a poem can begin. The importance of this preliminary work cannot be stressed strongly enough; thorough preparation is crucial if we are to complete a successful analysis of our chosen poem. Obviously we cannot leap in with a detailed discussion of an image used in the first line if we have not established what kind of poem we are dealing with, know little or nothing about its context or history, or if we are still not certain of the meaning in some parts.

These initial stages in the process of getting to grips with a poem can be enjoyable as well as fruitful, and are best done in your tutorial or study group. Even friends and family can be drawn into the discussion.

One suggested outline for this preparatory process could be the following:

1) Discussion
2) Dictionary
3) Context
4) Connections
5) Paraphrase.

It is extremely helpful to discuss the poem with others in an informal context. Here you will be asking questions such as 'What is the poem about?'; 'What does it mean?'; 'What sort of poem is it?'; 'What does it remind me of?'; 'What is its basic message?'; 'Does it communicate this effectively? How?' At this stage, you are sorting out your initial responses to the poem, as well as familiarizing yourself with its outline and overall meaning. You will find the questions asked will shift from the general to the specific; from 'What's it about?' to 'I don't understand what the last two lines mean — does anyone have any ideas?'

Next, you will find it worthwhile to identify and look up the meaning of all unfamiliar words. Every word in a poem counts, so it is essential to establish exactly what each one means. This is the point at which you will need to use a dictionary. It is worth double-checking words that you are fairly sure you understand; dictionaries often alert the reader to the more obscure meanings of words, and this can sometimes enrich the understanding of the poem.

However, looking up unknown words in a dictionary is not always enough to answer all the questions that arise about the meaning of a poem. This leads us to the question of context. Here we must decide what background information we need to fully understand and enjoy a particular poem. This is one of the more important areas to investigate before beginning an analysis; many poems from past centuries may seem rather pointless, or even slightly ridiculous to the modern reader if their historical and political context is not known. Blake's 'And Did Those Feet' (p. 61) is an example of a poem that seems at best eccentric and at worst incomprehensible unless its specific background is understood. And some poems by the Romantic poets can seem alien and exaggerated unless we have some understanding of the poetic creed they represent.

Here it is helpful if everyone pools their knowledge. Some of your classmates may already have done some research; or your lecturer may be able to fill in background details. The poem itself might have explanatory footnotes. If you still feel that there are gaps in your understanding of the poem and its context, you will find an encyclopedia, or guide (sometimes called a companion) to English literature a welcome resource. These can be found in the reference section of your local or university library. Use them to look up poets, literary periods or genres, which will be listed alphabetically.

A rewarding way of carrying any discussion of context further is to work out whether there are any points of contact between the history and circumstances of the poem under discussion, and your own present-day situation. For example, Elizabeth Barrett Browning's indictment of her country's political complacency and lack of compassion (see 'A Curse for a Nation', p. 78) has an astonishingly modern feel to it — the poem's criticisms apply as much to many twentieth-century democracies as they once did to nineteenth-century England. Likewise, many women married within traditional or conservative communities today will be able to identify with Lady Mary Chudleigh's seventeenth-century poem, 'To the Ladies' (p. 48). And in the case of many poems by South African or African writers, any discussion of their work would be pointless without some understanding of the history of colonialism or apartheid; this history will have powerfully affected the day-to-day lives of most readers of this anthology.

A note of caution here: establishing the parallels between your own situation and that of a long-dead poet can be extremely exciting, but it is not a substitute for analysis. Unless you are specifically asked to do so in an assignment, do not use a poem as a launching pad for telling your own personal or political history. Nevertheless, establishing links across centuries or cultures (or both) is a valuable part of the preparation for analysis.

To consolidate the ground covered in your discussion and research, it often helps to paraphrase the poem. This means retelling it in your own words. It is worth stressing that this is an extremely helpful exercise if done before attempting an analysis, but it cannot take the place of analysis itself — a common error made by students.

One way of illustrating the difference between the two procedures is to imagine two different ways of looking at a painting. An initial approach might be to list the different components found in this imaginary painting; noting, for example, that it contains the colours green and blue with small amounts of yellow, and that it shows tall trees, a cloudless sky, and a winding road. The second response, by comparison, would go further by describing how these components work together to suggest a certain mood. It might read: 'The use of the cool blue and green colours conveys a calm and natural atmosphere, which is given a hint of warmth by the slight touches of yellow which brighten the landscape. The height of the trees gives a sense of loftiness and vertical direction to the composition; the cloudless sky suggests unbroken tranquillity (there are literally no clouds on the horizon); and the winding curves of the road enhance the sense of natural harmony. No harsh colours or jagged lines disrupt the symmetry of this painting. This is clearly a nostalgic recreation of an idyllic and idealized rural scene.'

The first approach is similar to paraphrase, the stage in which the 'ingredients' of the poem (or this case, a painting) are listed, sorted and clarified. However, it is the second process, which reflects on the effect of these components combined, that constitutes analysis.

Another way of demonstrating the difference between the two processes is to look at the following accounts (adapted from actual essays) of the first two lines of Christina Rossetti's 'A Birthday': 'My heart is like a singing bird/ Whose nest is in a watered shoot.'

> 'The speaker's organ of circulation is like a small melodious feathered creature which has made a place of rest in a plant which has a plentiful water supply.'
>
> 'By beginning with the word "my", the speaker makes the description of her joy personal. She uses the image of a singing bird to convey a sense of natural and spontaneous delight. The fact that the bird has a nest adds a sense of security; the word "nest" has connotations of safety and warmth. The "watered shoot" also suggests something that is growing and flourishing in a fertile environment. One conclusion might be that the speaker has secure emotional grounds for her happiness; perhaps a new relationship is developing; the word "shoot" (which suggests new or fresh growth) might refer to this.'

The first extract is clearly a rather exaggerated illustration of paraphrase, whereas the second is an example of close analysis. (While it is not necessarily an ideal example of analysis, the contrast between this approach and that of paraphrase should clearly illustrate the differences.)

This suggested programme of preparatory work on a poem need not be followed in the order described. For example, you might like to do research on the context of the poem and look up new words in the dictionary before the class discussion takes place; and the discussion itself might centre on the connections the poem suggests to you and your fellow students. Your teacher might also suggest that you paraphrase the poem as a written exercise either before the tutorial, or as an initial stage before moving on to an essay analysing the poem.

Critical analysis: a definition. By now, you have no doubt formed an impression of the process of analysis, which has been repeatedly referred to above. However, a fuller definition is necessary, as is some discussion of the more problematic aspects of this process. Critical analysis (sometimes referred to as practical criticism or close reading) is a contested, but nevertheless valuable tool when beginning critical reading, and a rewarding skill which can be applied in a variety of different situations. It involves reading something (in this case, a poem) very carefully and closely, word by word and line by line (usually in chronological order) in order to identify the parts that make it up and evaluate their effectiveness. The next step is to describe the mood and tone (or resonance) created by this particular blend of words, images, visual shapes and sound effects. (This is one of the features that distinguishes critical analysis from paraphrasing; see the examples given above.) Finally, critical analysis sometimes ends with an assessment of the value of the poem or its message.

Critical analysis has inherent limitations; it stems from a school of literary criticism referred to as 'new criticism', which has come under fire for its assumption that all readers have access to a set of absolute and universal values or criteria that can be used as yardsticks to measure a piece of art (see p. xxviii above). This is clearly a debatable issue. For example, most Westerners might find the symphonies of Beethoven or Mozart exquisitely beautiful, and claim that such beauty is universal; yet to a Tibetan monk, whose chants are sung according to an entirely different tonal scale, they might sound like the most hideous cacophony. (This is not too hard to imagine — different generations within the same family often find each other's choice of music unbearable!)

Furthermore, some scholars have pointed out that it is not always appropriate or even possible to judge whether art is 'good' or not (which evaluation is implicit in the principles of new criticism), as this raises the thorny questions of what constitutes 'good' or 'bad' art, and who gets to define and decide what is 'good' and 'bad'. Recent trends in literary criticism have focused instead on what art reveals about society, what power relations it describes, the ideological and political shifts and stances represented in cultural expression, and the extent to which a literary or artistic work can act to subvert the status quo.

However, it is unrealistic to try to entirely avoid making value judgements in assessing any piece of art, including a poem. A glance at the film reviews in any newspaper will reveal the extent to which we rank culture and entertainment according to a graded scale of values — a 'five-star' film is one with a superb script and performances, together with a serious message, one with 'three stars' is considered to be fairly entertaining, and a 'one-star' film is a piece of trash to be avoided at all costs. So to a degree, the tendency to evaluate art and entertainment according to a broad set of 'standards' is embedded in our culture. Perhaps the important thing to bear in mind is that the question 'Is this a good poem?' is not the only one to ask; there are other questions that might reveal rewarding insights.

Nevertheless, in spite of its limitations, critical analysis remains a valuable 'first stage' in acquiring critical skills. Many students find it useful in their everyday work and study; its principles can be applied when reading newspapers, magazines, advertisements and business letters; when watching films, television or plays; even when listening to the radio or to music. It can be of practical use when querying material you suspect of being less than honest or straightforward; propaganda, for example, or simply the small print in a document you are asked to sign. If you are interested in alternative theoretical or ideological approaches to literature, you will find that close reading remains a useful tool to have in your stock of critical skills. The ability to critically analyse poetry also remains an important part of most English poetry courses at tertiary educational institutions, and it is a skill that you will most likely be required to demonstrate in your poetry essays and exams.

Guidelines for analysing a poem. Once you have completed the preliminary stages, you have reached the point of plunging into the poem itself. The following steps are very basic and flexible guidelines for carrying out an analysis; as you gain more confidence, you will be able to refine this list, add pointers of your own, and shuffle the order around to suit your approach.

First of all (bearing in mind the distinguishing aspects of poetry discussed above), familiarize yourself with the sound and shape of the poem. Remember that poetry is created to be heard and seen, not just understood. If you have not already done so, begin by reading the poem aloud, or asking someone to read it to you. Listen as if it were a piece of music. This will alert you to various important aspects of the poem; its rhyme scheme, pace and rhythm, the specific sounds of its words. Does the poem sound lulling and soothing? Brisk and quick? Harsh and jarring? Racy and breathless? Or do contrasting sounds follow one another to change the effect on the ear? Hearing the poem also gives an initial impression of those poetic devices which are used to create specific sound effects, such as alliteration or onomatopoeia (see below for definitions and examples).

Next, look at the overall shape and structure of the poem. Note whether it is divided into stanzas, and where these breaks fall. It is also worth counting the number of lines, especially in shorter poems: this is often the easiest way to spot a sonnet (which always has fourteen lines). The shape will often help us to identify the type of poem; repeating choruses, for example, usually point to a song or ballad. Check for lines that are repeated, or that stand alone (these are usually significant).

At this stage, you should have enough material to draft brief introductory notes, if you are planning to turn your analysis into an essay. By now you know what kind of poem you are dealing with, understand its general meaning, and have some sense of its context and atmosphere. You might want to leave your introductory paragraph till later, when you have finished working your way through the poem; on the other hand, jotting down your overall sense of the poem at this stage might help you to deal with the most intimidating stage of an analysis: getting started.

What follows forms the 'meat' of the analysis; the examination of the poem line by line and word by word. It is best to proceed chronologically, and work your way through from beginning to end without skipping sections or backtracking.

Begin with the title, if the poem has one. (Poems without titles are usually identified by their first line, which is used as a heading under which the poem stands.) Some titles simply state the topic, but more often they contain essential additional information which illuminates the poem that follows. They can also establish an aura or atmosphere before the poem itself starts; the French title of Keats' 'La Belle Dame Sans Merci' (p. 74) helps to create a mysterious and exotic mood even if we are not certain what it means. Bear in mind that even short, simple titles can make a profound contribution to the poem as a whole; the title of Wilfred Owen's poem 'Futility' (p. 144) expresses the poet's opinion of war with a bitterness that is largely absent from the poem itself.

Now examine the poem line by line, keeping an eye open for any words or phrases you find striking. As you proceed, bear the following checklist in mind. The pointers and questions it suggests are not meant to be prescriptive, and should not be followed rigidly, as each poem will present slightly different challenges. Nevertheless, it will provide you with options for making your analysis as thorough and rewarding as possible.

- Identify significant words, and note where they are placed in the structure of the poem. Do they fall at the beginning of lines or stanzas? Do they stand alone? Are they repeated? Is our attention drawn to them because they 'jar' or 'jump out' of an otherwise smoothly flowing line? Is there anything else unusual about where they are placed?

- Look more carefully at any repeated words or lines. What effect does the repetition have? Does it lend special emphasis? Does it act as a chorus? Is the effect that of a lullaby or song? If a line or phrase is repeated at intervals throughout the poem, check whether the impact of the words remains the same. If any changes are made to a repeated line, what effect does this have?

- Check punctuation, which becomes particularly expressive in poetry. Dashes, colons, semi-colons, exclamation and question marks will have obvious effects on the meaning of the poem; also investigate the placing of commas and full stops. Do any of these fall in unusual places? How do they contribute to the pace of the poem; do they hurry it along, or break it up? (See Tennyson's *In Memoriam* poems [pp. 84–87] for examples of how punctuation can underline the message contained in words.)

- If you are really stuck, you could break the poem down into its grammatical components. This can be surprisingly revealing. A poem crammed with verbs will be punchy, full of action, brisk and swift; one that uses many adjectives and adverbs is more likely to be descriptive, flowery and slow-paced. It is also often rewarding to look at the pronouns used; the third-person pronoun ('one') is associated with a style that is formal, detached and even cold; the second-person pronoun ('you') is much more immediate and informal in its effect, but still indicates a degree of distance; and the first-person pronoun ('I', 'we') is intimate, personal, and confessional. The use of 'I' can also indicate power, as the speaker then 'owns' the words spoken, and has control over any description that follows.

- Pay attention to word-music. This draws on the earlier stage of listening to the poem to gauge its sound effects. Two common poetic devices or techniques which specifically affect how poetry sounds are onomatopoeia and alliteration. Knowing how to spell these terms is not as important as being able to recognize them! Onomatopoeia involves using words that sound like the action or object described; some examples are 'the *hissing* of waves on sand'; 'the *clip-clop* of hooves'; 'the *clashing* cymbals'. Alliteration is the repetition of the same letter or sound in several successive words; for example, 'the grass grows green and golden.' (The first stanza of 'Binsey Poplars' by Hopkins [p. xli below] features alliteration in almost every line; read it for further examples.) Sometimes both alliteration and onomatopoeia can appear together in the same phrase: 'the mournful moan of doves'. It should be clear that these are often very evocative or sensuous aspects of a poem, which can add colour and texture.

- Rhythm and rhyme scheme have been mentioned above. Now is the time to note where and how the rhythm of a poem changes, and to ask why that specific change takes place. (Marvell's 'To his Coy Mistress' on p. 45 is an excellent example of how changes in rhythm reinforce the argument of the poem.) Also consider the rhyme scheme; how many rhyming sounds are there, and in what pattern do they occur? What do these sounds suggest to you? The rhyme scheme is often important in that it contributes control and structure to the poem. A poem governed by a strict sense of rhyme and rhythm will often come across as complex and carefully crafted, whereas a poem in free verse (no rhyme scheme) tends to be loose and informal.

Also consider how the rhythmic and rhyming features of a poem contribute to or amplify its meaning. Usually, they intensify the message of the words (see, for example, Wyatt's 'My Lute, Awake!' [p. 14], Tichborne's 'Elegy'[p. 23], and Tennyson's 'Mariana'[p. 89]). However, there is sometimes a deliberate contrast between the argument of the poem and its rhythm and rhyme scheme; see Millay's 'I, Being Born a Woman and Distressed' (p. 141) for an example of sharp contrast between the elegant formality of the strict rhythm and rhyme scheme (and equally elegant vocabulary), and the humorous, cynical and bawdy message of the poem.

- One of the more important (and enjoyable) parts of analysis is the examination and assessment of the images, or 'word-pictures', that appear in the poem. Broadly speaking, images refer to anything described in particularly vivid and picturesque language. However, most imagery involves a comparison (either explicit or implicit) of some kind. Comparisons involve a transfer of associations between two different things which nevertheless share a specific quality or have some features in common. In other words, if we wish to suggest that someone is courageous we can either say so directly, or we could describe them as a 'lion'. This does not mean that they have literally changed species; instead, everything we associate with the word 'lion' (courage, majesty, power and so forth) is transferred momentarily to that person. The power of comparisons to illuminate and illustrate should be obvious; it is far more dramatic to greet a brave friend with the words 'You are a lion!' than to state 'You are brave'.

  Comparisons can be found in two forms in literature: as metaphors and as similes. In the case of a simile, the comparison is made explicit by the linking words 'as' or 'like'; for example, 'she is as brave as a lion' or 'he sings like an angel'. Metaphors collapse the comparison into a single image; for example, 'She is a lion'; 'His song is angelic'. Metaphors and similes are often found in everyday speech ('politicians should get off the gravy train'; 'the price of meat is daylight robbery'; 'it's like taking sweets from a baby' and so forth), and can be quite commonplace. Your task is not simply to identify the metaphors and similes in the poem, but to judge their effectiveness. Are they ordinary? Vivid? Unusual? You will also need to 'unpack' the associations involved; to return to our 'lion' example, it is obviously not enough to say: 'In this metaphor, the person is compared to a lion.' You would need to list the qualities suggested by the image of a 'lion', and to link these associations with the person being described.

  In a poem, imagery can be used in an accumulative way. One image often builds on another, weaving different associations together into a united whole. This means that you should not study the images in the poem in isolation. Check to see if they are linked to one another, or whether you can trace any development between them. (The suggestions for discussion on Mtshali's poem 'Men in Chains' [p. 225] provide practical questions on metaphor and simile.)

- It is essential to bear mood or tone in mind. These are very difficult qualities to define or pin down. One way of clarifying mood and tone might be to refer to the emotional resonance of the poem; what feelings does it evoke? If you struggle to express these, the following questions might help (use them to identify your responses, not as part of a formal analysis): what flavour does the poem have? If you had to illustrate it, what colours would you choose? Would they be bright, warm, murky or cool? If you had to choose music to match the poem, what kind of music and instruments would you pick? Ominous drums, 'laid-back' jazz saxophones, a brisk march, a dreamy waltz?

  It is also important to track the shifts in tone; do you notice any abrupt changes? Are there parts where it is more intense? One way of monitoring these often subtle changes is to ask what effect is being created at various stages in the poem. At this point, our guidelines may seem frustratingly vague; it might help to turn back to the examples of paraphrase and analysis above. Here, one of the features that distinguishes the written samples of analysis from those of paraphrase is that the former include descriptions of mood and tone. As you read and analyse more poetry, you will develop your own 'mood thermometer', but this aspect of analysis takes practice at first.

- Finally, it is extremely important to keep asking the questions how and why: *How* was this effect achieved, and *why*? (Analysis demands endless curiosity.) These questions are essential to prevent our analysis from reverting to a catalogue of parts. It is all too easy to reduce our findings to a mechanical list, which might run something like this: 'this poem features a metaphor in line 4, alliteration in line 5, use of the first person throughout, three semi-colons, and the repetition of the last line of each stanza'. At all costs, we must engage with each poem that we analyse and remain alert to the shifts and transformations within the tiny landscape it seeks to create; repeated questioning will aid us in this task. The 'how' question also acts as a reminder that in written analysis it is vital to quote from the poem to support our arguments.

Once we have worked our way through the poem armed with our checklist, we are likely to see new connections and relationships between the different parts. As the poem is put back together again, a message may emerge that was not clear before. If the analysis has been successful, you will find that you have gained a new appreciation of the poem, or developed a more sophisticated critique of it. You might like to use these discoveries as the basis for concluding remarks, if you are planning to turn your analysis into an essay. This is also the stage at which you might find it interesting to swop findings with fellow students, noting the differences and similarities between your efforts.

Above all, it must be remembered that the task of analysis is an individual process. This is because our response to poetry is extremely personal. Each reader will interact with the text in a different way; individual taste, differing value systems and cultural heritages, and so forth will all determine our responses to some degree. Life would be very boring if we all liked identical clothing, food and music, and indeed the value of diversity has become a catch-phrase for South Africa in recent years. This principle is a valuable one in the development of critical skills; you should be encouraged to make personal choices and express preferences when engaging with poetry. (A revealing exercise would be for you and several classmates each to list your favourite five or ten poems from this anthology, and state your reasons for choosing them. You will find the wide range of choices that is bound to result most enlightening.) However, remember that you will seldom be examined on whether or not you like a poem and why!

It must also be stressed that there are no right or wrong answers when analysing a poem, although there might be weak and strong answers. Strong answers are those which reflect a sensitivity towards the language and intention of the poem, and which provide evidence from the poem for each conclusion drawn. Remember that two different interpretations of the same poem might be equally valid, even if they contradict each other. If both arguments are clear, logical and well supported, both should be equally worthy of praise.

Writing a draft essay. If you are asked to write a critical analysis of a poem, then to some extent the shape of that poem will determine the shape of your essay. Begin with some broad introductory statements; these should arise out of your pre-analysis preparations (described above). If there is vital contextual information that shapes your reading of the poem, now is the time to set it out. Next, collate the notes you have made on the poem itself (following the guidelines for analysis suggested above), and organize them so that the individual points are clear as you write, and the line of discussion flows easily. Remember to proceed chronologically through the poem; do not hop from discussing line 11 to line 22 and then back to something you have noticed in line 17. However, if the poet is developing a particular image which is subtly changing, then refer back to the points you have already established, but without repeating yourself. (For example: 'The description of the house, which was presented as a warm, cosy environment in the second stanza, has become increasingly eerie and threatening by the time we reach stanza four.')

It is extremely important to support your opinions by quoting from the text, even if only a few words are used. Turn back to the hypothetical analysis of a painting on p. xxxii, and imagine that it reads 'This painting has a cool, calm and natural feel, with touches of warmth. It has a sense of vertical height and loftiness, and conveys a tranquil atmosphere of harmony.' This leaves us with a description of the onlooker's personal feelings and responses rather than an analysis. Yet these claims become perfectly valid if they are supported with evidence. Vague statements (such as 'this poem has a good feeling') are not much use, so ensure that your responses to the poem are firmly grounded in the text. It is a good idea to quote those words or images which trigger a specific response.

Finish by drawing some kind of conclusion, or by summarizing your findings: this is a good place to restate the message of the poem. Some sample endings: at the end of an analysis of an anti-war poem, for example, you might write something along the lines of:

> 'This bitter catalogue of the brutality and destructive power of warfare spells out the message that war is both immoral and futile';

or, at the end of a poem about township life, you might conclude:

> 'This poem combines a celebration of the liveliness and resourcefulness of township dwellers with a stinging indictment of the apartheid policies (in particular, the Group Areas Act) which led to the creation of these slums.'

This is probably the best point at which to include your own personal response to the poem, but be careful to focus on summing up the essence of the poem itself, rather than ending with a mini-essay on your own beliefs and views.

If you are asked a specific question that also involves a close reading of the poem, the process may become a little more complicated, but the essential procedure remains the same. In these cases, you are analysing the poem in search of specific evidence. For example, if you are asked to write an essay on the use of irony in a poem, you will need to tease out all aspects of the poem that contribute to this feature. Try to establish exactly what is expected of you. Begin by 'analysing' the question; break it down into its component parts, and ensure that you understand what these mean; use the dictionary if necessary. Later, when you have finished the rough draft of your essay, go back to the question, and check that every aspect of it has been covered.

Close critical analysis is extremely useful if you are asked to compare two or more poems in an essay, as the closer the scrutiny of each poem, the richer the level of contrasts and parallels between them.

Bear in mind that it is vital to write all your essays in draft form before beginning the final copy. You should now edit your draft with a critical eye. By all means ask friends and fellow students for their comments. (This is quite different from asking them to do the work for you; get as much feedback as possible at this stage.) Your lecturer might also be willing to comment on your draft before you submit your final essay. Your writing can only benefit from reworking and polishing.

How much should you rely on critical works when planning and writing a critical analysis? We feel that during the initial stages of learning this skill, you should not place too much reliance on the works of commentators and critics. Rather read up more about the background of the poem, or read further poems by that poet. It is easy to be intimidated by critics who are experts in their field, and tempting to submit your opinions to theirs. There is also a tendency to feel that because their assessment of a poem or poet is in print, it must necessarily be correct and of more value than anything you can offer. This means that you run the risk of turning your analysis into a patchwork of other people's ideas and interpretations. It also detracts from the pleasure and sense of exploration of establishing your own personal response to a poem. Bear in mind that your goal is to develop your own critical skills, rather than to defer to the opinions of others.

To provide some practical help with the process of moving from analysing a poem to writing a formal essay on it, we have given some examples of poems ('Binsey Poplars' by Gerard Manley Hopkins and 'For Albert Luthuli (21.7.67)' by Jennifer Davids) which have rough notes scribbled all over them. It helps enormously to begin by jotting down your analysis all over the poem itself; this process of 'dissection' makes the poem less daunting, and means that you are less likely to leave out important points. We have also provided some samples

Binsey Poplars

newspaper headline?

FELLED 1879

date of 'death' - gravestone?

1st person pronoun

personal, possessive

loving

My aspens dear, whose airy cages quelled,°
Quelled or quenched in leaves the leaping sun,
All felled, felled, are all felled;
Of a fresh and following folded rank
Not spared, not one
That dandled a sandalled
Shadow that swam or sank
On meadow and river and wind-wandering
weed-winding bank.

alliteration: rustling leaves?

death knell

suggests soldiers?

no mercy

lazy, relaxed images

words suggest shape of river: slow and curving

shift: from description of trees to 'sermon' on environmental concerns

O if we but knew what we do
When we delve or hew—
Hack and rack the growing green!
Since country is so tender
To touch, her being só slender,
That, like this sleek and seeing ball
But a prick will make no eye at all,
Where we, even where we mean
To mend her we end her
When we hew or delve:
After-comers cannot guess the beauty been.
Ten or twelve, only ten or twelve
Strokes of havoc únselve
The sweet especial scene,
Rural scene, a rural scene,
Sweet especial rural scene.

1-4: move from harmless words to language of torture

delicacy; feminization of nature

image of extreme vulnerability: makes us wince!

words look similar, but opposite in meaning

Most NB point of poem (irony: the beauty lost has been recreated in the poem)

repetition: emphasis on how little it takes to create devastation

repetition: chanting, mourning

harsh, strong word

of written analysis, to demonstrate how your rough notes can be transformed into a formal essay, or at least the first draft of one.

Below are two possible beginnings for a written critical analysis of this poem, based on the notes made on 'Binsey Poplars'. Both are equally valid interpretations. Although you might find one or the other more convincing, both support their conclusions with evidence drawn from the poem itself.

Essay 1: This poem is one of mourning for the loss of a group of trees which were an integral part of a beautiful country scene. The title resembles the headstone of a grave, with the date and manner of death ('Felled 1879') written below the name. This immediately strikes us as unusual, as it suggests that these trees are being commemorated in the same way that we mourn loved ones who have died.

This provides evidence that the poplar trees are extremely important to the speaker, who speaks of them as if they were humans he loved very much. This is confirmed by the first words of the poem: '*My aspens dear*'. The use of endearments and the first person implies that he had a personal relationship with the trees, and strengthens the impression that this poem is an elegy. The first two lines reveal both the speaker's love and the beauty of the trees. The words 'airy cages' give a strong visual impression of the shape of the trees, with the branches and leaves forming the bars of the 'cage'. This image looks like an apparent contradiction (or paradox); the sense of freedom and light conveyed by the word 'airy' dissolves the sense of enclosure that the 'cage' gives. The music of the words 'quelled,/Quelled or quenched in leaves the leaping sun' tries to imitate the sound of rustling leaves, as we find repetition of both words ('quelled,/Quelled') and sounds ('que' and 'lea'). The images also suggest the constant interplay of light and shade caused by the movement of branches and trees.

Essay 2: This poem traces the intense emotional involvement of the speaker with a specific place of natural beauty, and charts his passionate response to the destruction both of this particular spot and the countryside in general.

The title makes one think of an obituary column in a newspaper, with the name of the deceased and the date of their death laid out as a headline. In this case the 'dead' are the poplar trees near Binsey (a village outside Oxford, where Hopkins studied). Obituaries are often written by someone close to the person who has died, and in this case the speaker feels personally involved.

We know this because the first word of the poem is the first-person possessive pronoun 'My'. This suggests that the speaker 'owns' the aspens, or feels extremely possessive of them. The use of the first person tells us that the speaker is no detached onlooker; he is personally affected, and feels he has the right to describe and

date of death

implies gift or memorial

For Albert Luthuli (21.7.67)

You a fragment of the sun — *light, warmth*
go turn the world — *world revolves around sun*; *also means change*
in the long strength
of your fingers — *famous for 'knocking on a door'*

Bounded
you gave me
knowledge of freedom

paradox

Silenced
you taught me
how to speak

developed further

Luthuli was killed in a train accident; also metaphor for a journey

Somewhere a train
has reached a destination
and tonight
the cold fist of winter — *contrast to sun*; *contrast to fingers (line 4): a fist is closed, potentially violent*
clenches around the world — *effect of Luthuli's death*

But beyond it
the endless pulsations of space — *freedom, no limits*
grow louder
and stars breaking the dark — *traditional image of hope*
grow large

Walk now father — *close relationship: personal, loving*
unchecked — *significant as Luthuli was banned: death grants him freedom*
from sun to sun — *takes his place in the universe*

> define both the beauty of the trees and the extent of his bereavement. The sheer loveliness of the trees (described in the first and second lines) makes way for the death knell in the third line: 'All felled, felled, all are felled.' Here the swift, light rhythm of the first two lines, which suggests the rapid and graceful movements of poplar leaves in the wind, is displaced by a slow and repetitive beat, like the tolling of a bell to announce a death. The word 'felled' both looks and sounds like the word 'knell'.

'For Albert Luthuli (21.7.67)' is a good example of a poem which needs a fair amount of contextual background filled in before any analysis can begin. As this was written on the occasion of Albert Luthuli's death, it is important to know who he was and something about his life. At the very least, we need to know that he was one of the great leaders of the ANC during the 1950s and 60s, a chief, and a Nobel Prize winner. He was constantly harassed by the apartheid regime, and eventually placed under a banning order. This restricted his movements, forbade political involvement, and attempted to isolate him. Luthuli is perhaps best remembered for a speech in which he spoke of 'knocking on a door', a metaphor for his life's engagement in the struggle against apartheid. He died in a train accident, on the date mentioned in the title of the poem. This information sheds light on several of the references in the poem.

Here we have provided some examples of how imagery might be analysed. (Note that this is not a complete essay; there is no introduction and conclusion, and not all the images in the poem are discussed. The intention is to demonstrate how interlinking imagery in a poem might be approached.)

> One set of images traced throughout this poem are those of the world, the sun and the stars in space ('fragment of the sun'; 'world'; 'endless pulsations of space'; 'stars breaking the dark'; 'sun to sun'). These are significant because they suggest absolute freedom. The universe is infinitely huge, and there are no boundaries in space. Chief Luthuli was restricted throughout his life — first by the discriminatory laws of apartheid, and then later by his banning order, which placed him under house arrest and tried to end his political activism. The choice of images of freedom is thus particularly telling.
>
> The first and last lines of the poem both use the sun as a metaphor, which links into this theme, but also operates on other levels. By describing Luthuli as a 'fragment of the sun' at the beginning of the poem, the speaker immediately conveys the sense that he is a source of warmth, light and inspiration. At the end of the poem, however, the image has changed slightly; now it is suggested that Luthuli takes his place in the universe as a sun among suns ('Walk now father . . . from sun to sun'). This could mean, first of all, that even after his death, he remains a source of light and guidance; it also gives a sense of his stature and dignity. Finally, it could also mean his death has given him the freedom of the entire universe, in sharp contrast to the restrictions he endured in life.

Another image that is developed involves hands. The speaker describes the 'long strength' of Luthuli's fingers; later we read that the 'cold *fist* of winter/ clenches around the world'. These images remind us of Luthuli's famous phrase 'knocking on a door'. We use our hands to knock, and so the power of Luthuli's words, which constantly 'knocked' at apartheid's door, are translated into an image of hands and strong fingers. The speaker considers the power of Luthuli's words/hands to be so great that they can 'turn' (or change) the world. This image of 'fingers' contrasts with the later image of a fist, which is used to describe the immediate impact of Luthuli's death. Unlike fingers, which can hold, point, guide or knock, a fist is closed, potentially violent and unable to give or receive. One interpretation of the 'cold fist of winter' is that it is a metaphor for apartheid; without the guiding light and warmth ('fragment of the sun') of Luthuli's leadership to combat it, apartheid 'clenches around the world' like a fist. This image also suggests the experience of being 'gripped' by grief and loss.

Writing poetry exams. A final word needs to be added about poetry exams. Many good students underperform simply because they reproduce prepared material in the exam, instead of answering the specific questions asked. Just as in the essay, it is vital that you read the question carefully, break it down into parts, and analyse it. For essay-type questions, you should spend the first five minutes of your allotted time for that question doing this. Next, work on a very short rough draft of your essay. Scribble down any thoughts you might have and see if you can organize them into a logical sequence. This is particularly important if you have been asked to present an argument, or to explain whether you agree or disagree with a criticism of a poem. Now is the time to draw a skeleton structure for your answer; this will help if your mind goes blank, or if you run out of ideas halfway through your essay.

It is vital to allow yourself time for planning in an exam. Do not be daunted by the sight of your fellow students around you scribbling as fast as they can; you will benefit from taking a few extra minutes to plan your answer. Now work through the poem chronologically. If you are writing about the first stanza, and you suddenly get a fresh idea about an image in the fifth stanza, quickly jot this down on your rough structure, so that you will remember to include it once you are further along in your essay. The same rule applies to exam questions as to essays; try not to skip backwards and forwards in the poem. Leave plenty of space between paragraphs in case you think of something you want to add to an argument you have already made. Remember to add a conclusion, even if this is only one sentence summing up your point of view or your response to the poem. If you have time at the end of the exam, read through your answer to check for errors and to satisfy yourself that your meaning is clear.

Working through your exam question according to this system can help to control anxiety. More important, it increases your chances of doing justice to your careful preparation. Remember that you are being asked to demonstrate a skill which you have mastered, rather than to repeat factual information contained in a syllabus. **Good luck!**

Li Ho (791 – 817)

Li Ho was an innovative contributor to the 'golden age' of Chinese poetry (which reached its height during the eighth and ninth centuries), and was famous in his lifetime for his often unorthodox poems. Although he died young, he established a reputation for sensual and pessimistic poetry which explored the themes of transience and death.

On the Frontier

A Tartar[1] horn tugs at the north wind,
Thistle Gate shines whiter than the stream.
The sky swallows the road to Kokonor.
On the Great Wall,[2] a thousand miles of moonlight.

The dew comes down, the banners drizzle,
Cold bronze rings the watches of the night.
The nomads' armour meshes serpents' scales.
Horses neigh, Evergreen Mound's[3] champed° white. *chewed by horses*

In the still of autumn see the Pleiades.[4]
Far out on the sands, danger in the furze.° *bushes*
North of their tents is surely the sky's end
Where the sound of the river streams beyond the border.

1 *War-like nomadic tribes which threatened the borders of the old Chinese empire.*
2 *Long, fortified wall built as a defence against the Tartars. It stretched for thousands of kilometres, and much of it still stands today.*
3 *Grave of a royal mistress and Tartar empress. According to legend, grass always grew on her grave.*
4 *Constellation of stars; their flickering was seen as an omen of Tartar attack.*

Tu Mu (803 – 852)

Tu Mu spent time wandering between monasteries in the lovelier parts of his country, and his work closely observes and celebrates the natural beauty of the Chinese landscape. He was particularly admired for his brief four-line poems (called chueh-chu*), of which two examples have been given here.*

The Gate Tower of Ch'i-an City[1]

The sound grates on the river tower, one blast of the horn.
Pale sunlight floods, sinking by the cold shore.
Pointless to lean on the balcony and look back miserably:
There are seventy-five post-stations from here to home.

To Judge Han Ch'o at Yang-chou

Over misted blue hills and distant water
In Chiang-nan at autumn's end the grass has not yet wilted.
By night on the Four-and-Twenty Bridges, under the full moon,
Where are you teaching a jade girl to blow tunes on your flute?

Contextual notes

China, ruled by the Tang dynasty, was at this time the largest empire in the world. Its flourishing and rich civilization was constantly under threat of invasion by land-hungry and nomadic tribes from Mongolia and inner Asia, who were feared for their swiftness of attack and brilliance on horseback (a significant military advantage). This is why the reference to horses in 'On the Frontier' conveys especial menace.

Some historians argue that it was pressure on the eastern borders of Europe by these same tribes that led to the westward spread of the Germanic peoples. As in Europe, the force of the invaders (often referred to as Tartars or Mongols) eventually proved too much, and China was conquered and itself colonized.

1 *Presumably an outpost on the Great Wall of China.*

Anonymous (eighth or ninth century)

The Viking[1] Terror

Fierce is the wind tonight,
It ploughs up the white hair of the sea
I have no fear that the Viking hosts° — *bands of fighting men*
Will come over the water to me.

Contextual notes

Although composed two continents away, this short Irish poem (found written on the margin of a religious manuscript) expresses the same anxiety that we see in 'On the Frontier', p.1.

1 *Seafaring warriors from northern Europe (Scandinavia); among the Germanic tribes which repeatedly raided (and eventually conquered) the British Isles.*

Geoffrey Chaucer (*c.* 1343 – 1400)

Chaucer's fascination with the class structure of England, which he explores in his works, is hardly surprising considering his own upwardly mobile career. Born into the new middle class that was changing the face of feudal medieval society, he travelled to Europe as a soldier, established links with three successive royal courts, married into the aristocracy, and held a number of increasingly prestigious civil, diplomatic and political posts. Nevertheless he was often in debt, and was once charged with rape.

In an uncertain and hectic age Chaucer produced a significant amount of great writing. His works are extraordinary for their ability to capture the language and idiom of their time, while remaining open to contemporary interpretation and enjoyment.

From THE CANTERBURY TALES

The Pardoner's Prologue *(extracts)*

Lordinges° — quod° he — in chirches whan I preche, *sirs / said*
I paine me° to han an hautein° speeche, *take pains / loud*
And ringe it out as round as gooth a belle,
For I can° al by rote that I telle. *know*
My theme is alway oon,° and evere° was: *the same / always*
Radix malorum est cupiditas.[1]
First I pronounce whennes° that I come, *from where*
And thanne my bulles[2] shewe I alle and some:
Oure lige lordes seel on my patente,[3]
That shewe° I first, my body to warente,° *show / protect*
That no man be so bold, ne° preest ne° clerk, *neither / nor*
Me to destourbe of Cristes holy werk.[4]
And after that thanne telle I forth my tales —
Bulles° of pope and of cardinales, *letters*
Of patriarkes° and bisshopes I shewe, *church fathers*
And in Latin I speke a wordes fewe,
To saffron with° my predicacioun,° *spice up / preaching*
And for to stire hem° to devocioun. *them*

1 *Avarice (or love of money) is the root of all evil (1 Timothy: 6).*
2 *Letters of authorization from a bishop.*
3 *The papal ('lige lorde' refers to the Pope) seal on my licence.*
4 *Try to stop me doing Christ's holy work.*

Thanne shewe I forth my longe crystal stones,° *glass jars*
Ycrammed ful of cloutes° and of bones — *rags*
Relikes[5] been they, as weenen° they eechoon.° *suppose / each one*
Thanne have I in laton° a shulder-boon° *metal case / shoulder-bone*
Which that was of an holy Jewes sheep.
'Goode men,' I saye, 'take of my wordes keep:°.... *notice*
Goode men and wommen, oo° thing warne I you: *one*
If any wight° be in this chirche now *person*
That hath doon sinne horrible, that he
Dar nat for shame of it yshriven[6] be,
Or any womman, be she yong or old,
That hath ymaked hir housbonde cokewold,[7]
Swich° folk shal have no power ne no grace *such*
To offren° to my relikes in this place; *make offerings*
And whoso findeth him out of swich blame,
He wol come up and offre in Goddes name,
And I assoile° him by the auctoritee° *forgive / authority*
Which that by bulle ygraunted was to me.'
By this gaude° have I wonne, yeer by yeer, *trick*
An hundred mark° sith° I was pardoner. *pounds / since*
I stonde lik a clerk in my pulpet,
And whan the lewed° peple is down yset,° *simple / sitting*
I preche so as ye han herd bifore,
And telle an hundred false japes° more. *jokes*
Thanne paine I me to strecche forth the nekke,
And eest and west upon the peple I bekke[8]
As dooth a douve,° sitting on a berne;° *dove / barn*
Mine handes and my tonge goon so yerne° *quickly*
That it is joye to see my bisinesse.
Of avarice and of swich cursednesse
Is al my preching, for to make hem free
To yiven hir pens,° and namely unto me, *pennies, money*
For myn entente is nat° but for to winne,° *nothing / gain*
And no thing for correccion of sinne:
I rekke° nevere whan that they been beried° *care / buried*
Though that hir soules goon a-blakeberied.[9]
For certes, many a predicacioun° *good sermon*
Comth ofte time of yvel entencioun:°.... *evil intention*
Thus spete° I out my venim under hewe° *spit / disguise*
Of holinesse, to seeme holy and trewe.

5 *Relics supposed to have belonged to holy figures were very popular in medieval times; this led to widespread manufacture and sale of fake relics.*

6 *Confess and be forgiven.*

7 *Made her husband a cuckold (i.e. been unfaithful to him).*

8 *Nod my head.*

9 *Even if their souls go black-berrying (i.e. go to hell).*

But shortly myn entente° I wol devise:°   *intention / describe*
I preche of no thing but for coveitise;[1]
Therfore my theme is yit and evere was
Radix malorum est cupiditas.
    Thus can I preche again° that same vice   *against*
Which that I use, and that is avarice.
But though myself be gilty in that sinne,
Yit can I make other folk to twinne°   *turn*
From avarice, and sore to repente —
But that is nat my principal entente:°   *intention*
I preche no thing but for coveitise.
Of this matere it oughte ynough suffise.°   *to provide enough*
    Thanne telle I hem ensamples° many oon°   *moral stories / ones*
Of olde stories longe time agoon,
For lewed° peple loven tales olde —   *simple*
Swiche thinges can they wel reporte° and holde.°   *repeat / remember*
What, trowe ye° that whiles I may preche,   *do you think*
And winne gold and silver for° I teche,   *because*
That I wol live in poverte wilfully?
Nay, nay, I thoughte° it nevere, trewely,   *considered*
For I wol preche and begge in sondry° landes;   *many*
I wol nat do no labour with mine handes,
Ne make baskettes and live therby,[2]
By cause° I wol nat beggen idelly.°   *because / in vain*
I wol none of the Apostles countrefete.°   *imitate*
I wol have moneye, wolle,° cheese, and whete,   *wool*
Al were it yiven of the pooreste page,[3]
Or of the pooreste widwe° in a village —   *widow*
Al sholde hir children sterve for famine.[4]
Nay, I wol drinke licour of the vine
And have a joly wenche in every town.
But herkneth,° lordinges, in conclusioun,   *hark*
Youre liking° is that I shal telle a tale: *wish*
Now have I dronke a draughte of corny ale,°   *beer*
By God, I hope I shal you telle a thing
That shal by reson been at youre liking;
For though myself be a ful vicious man,
A moral tale yit I you telle can,
Which I am wont° to preche for to winne.   *likely*
Now holde youre pees,[5] my tale I wol biginne.

1 *I preach for no reason except greed.*
2 *Nor make a living from weaving or handiwork (basket-making).*
3 *Even if it was given by the poorest child.*
4 *Even if her children died of hunger.*
5 *Now keep quiet.*

Contextual notes

This extract from the prologue (or introduction) to a tale told by the Pardoner (a character in Chaucer's *Canterbury Tales*) shows Chaucer's concern with the abuses of the medieval church. Pardoners were minor members of the clergy who were licensed to travel from place to place, granting people absolution. In the Catholic faith (the only Christian religion in western Europe until the 1520s), this was the practice whereby people confessed their sins, and were given some form of penance to do to prove genuine contrition. Unfortunately, money sometimes changed hands; the penitent might be urged to make a financial contribution to a holy cause, for example. This, combined with the sale of relics and the practice of paying for prayers to be said for the souls of the dead, led to widespread corruption and even extortion by some representatives of the church.

In the figure of the Pardoner, Chaucer launches a stinging attack on these practices. What is interesting is that he did so at a time when the church had enormous political, secular and even legal power, and practised strict censorship. Its critics could even be executed for heresy (the religious equivalent of treason).

(If the unfamiliar spelling makes this extract difficult to understand, read it aloud, pronouncing the words as they are spelt; Middle English spelling [in an age of many dialects and no dictionaries] is rather inconsistent, but much more phonetic than Modern English. So 'preche' is 'preach', 'beried' is 'buried', 'trewe' is 'true', and so on. Also check whether any unfamiliar words resemble Afrikaans words you might know; because of the shared Germanic heritage, the meaning is often the same; 'sterve', for example, means to die in both Middle English and Afrikaans — and is obviously related to the English 'starve'.)

Suggestions for discussion

1. Given the above information, what literary and narrative techniques does Chaucer use to 'get away with' his attack on the abuses within the church? In what ways does this extract differ from a pamphlet or letter he might have written making exactly the same criticisms?
2. If you have correctly identified irony* as one of the ways in which Chaucer gets his point across without explicitly attacking the institution, try working through the extract, identifying exactly where irony is located and how it operates. You might like to start by drawing up a list, from the extract, of all the ways in which a compassionate and self-sacrificing member of the clergy might be expected to act, especially towards the poor; next, list all the acts of the Pardoner which contradict

these. The irony becomes even richer when the tale that follows the prologue is read. You might like to consult a modern translation; Neville Coghill's version of *The Canterbury Tales* is a racy and easy read.

3. The Pardoner is an unforgettable study of an utterly corrupt and cynical human being. Some critics argue that he is a supreme hypocrite; others say that he at least recognizes his own depravity. What kind of emotional blackmail does he use? Are there modern equivalents of the Pardoner? You might remember the American 'tele-evangelists' of the late 1980s (now largely discredited), whose promises of prayers answered were often accompanied by demands for donations. Corruption is of course not limited to religious figures; all professions which involve power (whether psychological, spiritual, political or economic) over other people involve this risk. How can people like the Pardoner be prevented from abusing their power?
4. You might also like to consider the effect of censorship on culture generally; were there similar levels of irony and satire* in resistance art during South Africa's period of state censorship?

Anonymous (fifteenth century)

Western Wind

Western wind, when will thou blow,
    The small rain down can rain?
Christ, if my love were in my arms
    And I in my bed again!

Anonymous (fifteenth century)

I Sing of a Maiden

I sing of a maiden
    That is makéles;° *matchless, mateless*
King of alle kingés
    To her son she ches.° *chose*
He cam also stillé
    Ther His moder was,
As dew in Aprìlle
    That falleth on the gras.
He cam also stillé
    To His moderes bowr,° *room or garden*
As dew in Aprìlle
    That falleth on the flowr.
He cam also stillé
    Ther His moder lay,
As dew in Aprìlle.
    That falleth on the spray.
Moder and maiden
    Was never none but she;
Wel may swich° a lady *such*
    Godés moder be.

Contextual notes

This is a lovely example of a lyric.* It uses simple, repetitive language and has a regular and musical rhythm. If you read it aloud, you will find it easy to imagine this poem being sung.

The poem takes the form of a prayer to Mary, the mother of Jesus (during the Middle Ages, the practice of honouring Mary was at its height, and was expressed in a variety of cultural forms — poetry, music, sculpture, tapestry and even architecture). However, it also closely resembles much of the secular love poetry typical of this time, which reflected the values of 'courtly love'. This began as an aristocratic game of manners, and set women up on pedestals as objects of adoration. The poet-lover (always male), following a strictly observed script, would praise his beloved extravagantly, claiming to suffer greatly as a result of his love for her, and begging her to return his love, or at least show some sign of her favour. (Later on, as Renaissance values replaced medieval ones, many poets were to subvert or satirize the tradition of courtly love; see

Wyatt's 'My Lute, Awake!' [p. 14] for a chilling example of how an apparently conventional courtly love poem is turned into a series of threats. Some of Shakespeare's sonnets [see pp. 25–27] also poke fun at the more formal and artificial features of courtly love poetry.)

Nevertheless, as an influence on art, culture and social relations, the underlying attitudes of courtly love persist to this day. Concepts such as 'courtesy', 'chivalry' and 'gallantry' all stem from it, as do many traditional ideas concerning the roles and behaviour of women and men. The belief that men are active and direct in romantic affairs, whereas women are passive and perhaps manipulative, still persists. Many societies continue to endorse the convention that men should court and women should be courted.

You will notice that the simple but effective imagery of spring used in this poem refers, of course, to the northern hemisphere. The coming of spring in England must have seemed like a miracle after the darkness, hunger and often life-threatening cold of winter, and it is not surprising that its symbolism was used in religious poetry, usually to refer to the resurrection of Jesus from the dead, or the hope of life after death.

Anonymous (fifteenth century)

The Unquiet Grave

'The wind doth blow today, my love,
    And a few small drops of rain;
I never had but one true-love,
    In cold grave she was lain.

'I'll do as much for my true-love
    As any young man may;
I'll sit and mourn all at her grave
    For a twelvemonth, and a day.'

The twelvemonth and a day being up,
    The dead began to speak,
'Oh who sits weeping on my grave,
    And will not let me sleep?'

' 'Tis I, my love, sits on your grave
And will not let you sleep,
For I crave one kiss of your clay-cold lips
And that is all I seek.'

'You crave one kiss of my clay-cold lips,
But my breath smells earthy strong;
If you have one kiss of my clay-cold lips
Your time will not be long:

' 'Tis down in yonder garden green,
Love, where we used to walk,
The finest flower that e're° was seen *ever*
Is withered to a stalk.

'The stalk is withered dry, my love,
So will our hearts decay;
So make yourself content, my love,
Till God calls you away.'

Contextual notes

This poem has many of the hallmarks of a ballad;* it tells a story, making use of dialogue, that resembles a folk-tale or fable, and involves a supernatural element. It also has a lilting rhythm and can be sung (the folk-singer Joan Baez has recorded a version); however, it does not have the 'chorus' or set of repeating lines that is typical of most ballads.

Comparison

Once you have read through this poem, turn to Christina Rossetti's 'Song' (p. 103). At first the poems may seem to have only superficial similarities; both deal with the separation (or potential separation) of lovers, one of whom is alive and mourning, the other dead and buried.

However, in 'The Unquiet Grave', it is clear that the conventions of elegy* are being gently mocked. The young lover is determined to behave in an appropriate (but not necessarily sincere) manner, and to do all the right and proper things: 'I'll do as much ... As any young man may'. His dead girlfriend is far more realistic and sensible, and points out that life must go on without her. 'Song', meanwhile, comes across at first as a sweet, but rather sentimental and morbid love poem.

If you consider the following questions, you may find that your view of Rossetti's poem changes, and that you also see 'The Unquiet Grave' in a new light.

1. What do you think of the fact that both the speakers 'from the grave' are women? Is it usual to hear women's voices in love poems? What do you make of the fact that both women are dead or dying? Do you think that the poets are perhaps using the grave as a platform from which women can 'answer back'?
2. In real life, the dead cannot respond to the elegies that are said over their graves. Could both poets be making a point about sincerity? In Rossetti's poem, is there a harsher message? Whereas the young woman in 'The Unquiet Grave' has plenty of sensible advice for her melodramatic lover, Rossetti's speaker seems to underline the sheer indifference of the dead to the living, and warns that once she is dead, the whole drama of mourning will be irrelevant to her. If you read this poem again, do you pick up any darker overtones?
3. Why do you think Rossetti's poem has such a conventional form? You will notice she uses imagery that is so traditional it is almost clichéd. Could this be deliberate? Do you think that poets sometimes use conservative and conventional techniques as a form of camouflage? Why would they do this? Under what kind of circumstances are subversive messages disguised?
4. Look at 'The Unquiet Grave' again. Would you now agree that it shares the same basic message as 'Song'? However, its tone in expressing this message is quite different. Which is the more humorous poem? Which is the more subtle?
5. Now compare these two poems with the elegiac poems from Tennyson's *In Memoriam* (see p. 84). It should be clear that there is a significant difference between the two sets of poems. Tennyson's are elegies in every sense of the word; do you agree that the other two are poems which look like elegies, but which are actually anti-elegy in intention?

John Skelton (*c.* 1460 – 1529)

Skelton was known as a learned eccentric, and was one of Henry VIII's tutors. A witty poem mocking of one of the king's ministers landed him temporarily in jail. His wide range of often comic poetry was known (and sometimes mockingly imitated) for its distinctive style of short rhyming lines and quick rhythms.

To Mistress Margaret Hussey

Merry Margaret,
As midsummer flower,
Gentle as falcon
Or hawk of the tower:
With solace and gladness,
Much mirth and no madness,
All good and no badness;
So joyously,
So maidenly,
So womanly
Her demeaning° — *demeanour, behaviour*
In every thing,
Far, far passing
That I can indite,° — *express*
Or suffice to write
Of Merry Margaret
As midsummer flower,
Gentle as falcon
Or hawk of the tower.
As patient and still
And as full of good will
As fair Isaphill,
Coriander,° — *fragrant spice*
Sweet pomander,° — *scented bag or ball*
Good Cassander,[1]
Steadfast of thought,
Well made, well wrought,
Far may be sought

1 *This list of names from classical literature lends glamour and stature to the description of Margaret.*

Ere that ye can find
So courteous, so kind
As Merry Margaret,
    This midsummer flower,
Gentle as falcon
Or hawk of the tower.

Contextual notes

This is another courtly love poem. Note that in literature from the Middle Ages until about the eighteenth century, the word 'mistress' (used here as a respectful form of address) does not necessarily imply a sexual relationship; both 'mistress' and 'lover' usually mean 'girlfriend' or 'beloved' when used in poems from this period.

Sir Thomas Wyatt (1503 – 1542)

Thomas Wyatt was educated at Cambridge University and served as a diplomat in various European countries including Italy, where he began translating Petrarch's sonnets. His career at the court of King Henry VIII was placed in jeopardy when his mistress, Anne Boleyn, became Henry's queen. This, together with rumours of treason, resulted in periods of imprisonment. His style (especially in his love poems) marks a distinct shift away from the conventions of medieval verse to new, innovative and sometimes cynical kinds of poetry.

My Lute, Awake!

My lute, awake! Perform the last
Labour that thou and I shall waste,
And end that I have now begun;
For when this song is sung and past,
My lute, be still, for I have done.

As to be heard where ear is none,
As lead to grave° in marble stone, *engrave*
My song may pierce her heart as soon.
Should we then sigh or sing or moan?
No, no, my lute, for I have done.

The rocks do not so cruelly
Repulse the waves continually
As she my suit° and affection. *courtship*
So that I am past remedy,° *curing, saving*
Whereby my lute and I have done.

Proud of the spoil° that thou hast got *prizes, loot*
Of simple hearts, thorough° love's shot; *through*
By whom, unkind, thou hast them won,
Think not he hath his bow[1] forgot,
Although my lute and I have done.

Vengeance shall fall on thy disdain
That makest but game on earnest pain.
Think not alone under the sun
Unquit° to cause thy lovers plain, *unrequited*
Although my lute and I have done.

Perchance thee lie withered and old
The winter nights that are so cold,
Plaining° in vain unto the moon. *complaining*
Thy wishes then dare not be told.
Care then who list,° for I have done. *likes*

And then may chance thee to repent
The time that thou hast lost and spent
To cause thy lovers sigh and swoon.
Then shalt thou know beauty but lent,
And wish and want as I have done.

Now cease, my lute. This is the last
Labour that thou and I shall waste,
And ended is that we begun.
Now is this song both sung and past;
My lute, be still, for I have done.

Suggestions for discussion

1. Read the notes on courtly love poetry on p. 9. Do you agree that 'My Lute, Awake!' looks like a courtly love poem? How does it outwardly resemble one?

1 *Cupid, god of love (referred to in line 17), who shoots his victims with a bow and arrow.*

2. In what ways is it an attack on the conventions of courtly love? How would the 'beloved' feel on hearing the speaker's words?
3. Identify the specific threats made in this poem. Does it still come across as a love poem? What emotions are being expressed by the speaker? Does this help you to identify the tone of the poem?
4. Look closely at the structure of the poem. Note how the rhyme scheme operates; you will notice that the sound of the word 'done' echoes through the entire poem, and that most of the words at the end of the lines have one syllable only. How does this support the tone and meaning of the poem? You will also notice that the last line of each stanza acts as a kind of chorus. How do the small changes in each one shift the meaning? Line 5 and the last line of the poem are identical; yet the meaning has been transformed. What is the difference in the last line?

Whoso List to Hunt

Whoso list° to hunt, I know where is an hind,° *likes / female deer*
But as for me, helas,° I may no more. *alas*
The vain travail° hath wearied me so sore, *struggle*
I am of them that farthest cometh behind.
Yet may I by no means my wearied mind
Draw from the deer, but as she fleeth afore
Fainting I follow. I leave off therefore
Since in a net I seek to hold the wind.
Who list her hunt, I put him out of doubt,
As well as I may spend his time in vain.
And graven° with diamonds in letters plain *engraved*
There is written her fair neck round about:
'*Noli me tangere*[2] for Caesar's° I am, *the king's*
And wild for to hold though I seem tame.'

Contextual notes

The new fascination with Italian literature that was a characteristic of the Renaissance led to a rebirth of the sonnet,* which was to flower in the hands of poets such as Sidney, Spenser and Shakespeare. Wyatt was responsible for bringing the sonnets of the medieval Italian poet and philosopher Petrarch to England,

2 *'Touch me not.' The last two lines probably refer to Wyatt's relationship with Anne Boleyn.*

and early attempts to master this new form were mostly adaptations or translations of his poems. Both 'Whoso List to Hunt' and Spenser's 'Like as a Huntsman' are versions of sonnets by Petrarch.

Edmund Spenser (*c.* 1552 – 1599)

Although Spenser's origins were not aristocratic, he was educated at Cambridge University and worked his way up in noble circles. He was rewarded with a post as a colonial official in Ireland where, during a rebellion, his castle was burnt down. He is best known for his work The Faerie Queen, *an allegory* of Queen Elizabeth I's reign. His writing borrows from both the Chaucerian tradition and classical* works, and reflects his belief that poetry should demonstrate moral idealism.*

Sonnet: Like as a Huntsman

Like as a huntsman after weary chase,
Seeing the game from him escaped away,
Sits down to rest him in some shady place,
With panting hounds beguilèd° of their prey: *tricked, enchanted*
So, after long pursuit and vain assay,° *attempt*
When I all weary had the chase forsook,
The gentle deer returned the self-same way,
Thinking to quench her thirst at the next brook:
There she, beholding me with milder look,
Sought not to fly, but fearless still did bide;° *stay*
Till I in hand her yet half trembling took,
And with her own good-will her firmly tied.
 Strange thing, meseemed,° to see a beast so wild, *it seemed to me*
 So goodly won, with her own will beguiled.

Contextual notes

This sonnet is from *Amoretti,* a series of sonnets celebrating Spenser's love for and courtship of his wife. The image of the hunt became a popular metaphor for courtship in Renaissance poetry (see also Wyatt's 'Whoso List to Hunt'. Consider what these images of hunting imply about the social relations between men and women during this period.

Sir Walter Raleigh (*c.* 1552 – 1618)

The legend of how Raleigh laid his cloak in a puddle for Queen Elizabeth I to step on has given him a rather romantic image. In reality, like many Renaissance heroes, he combined sophisticated scholarship with exploits of war and colonization. He made a marriage considered unwise in an era when choice of spouse had significant political implications, and had to undertake daring missions to regain favour at court. He was thus one of the first Europeans to sail to both South and North America, carrying out a number of raids. Elizabeth's successor, King James I, nevertheless imprisoned Raleigh on false charges of treason. He was eventually freed to go back to South America in search of gold. The trip was a disaster, and he was executed on his return.

His writing (much of which was done in prison) included his scholarly History of the World. *Few of his poems survive; those that do demonstrate wit, intelligence, and a calm awareness of impending death.*

The Nymph's Reply to the Shepherd[1]

If all the world and love were young,
And truth in every shepherd's tongue,
These pretty pleasures might me move
To live with thee and be thy love.

Time drives the flocks from field to fold,
When rivers rage and rocks grow cold,
And Philomel[2] becometh dumb;
The rest complain of cares to come.

The flowers do fade, and wanton fields
To wayward winter reckoning yields;
A honey tongue, a heart of gall,° *bitter liquid*
Is fancy's spring, but sorrow's fall.

1 *Written in response to Christopher Marlowe's 'The Passionate Shepherd to his Love'* *(see p. 21).*

2 *Classical name given to the nightingale. In legend, Philomel was a princess who was turned into a bird after being raped, so as to escape her assailant.*

The gowns, thy shoes, thy beds of roses,
Thy cap, thy kirtle,° and thy posies *skirt*
Soon break, soon wither, soon forgotten,
In folly ripe, in reason rotten.

Thy belt of straw and ivy buds,
Thy coral clasps and amber studs,[3]
All these in me no means can move
To come to thee and be thy love.

But could youth last and love still breed,
Had joys no date nor age no need,
Then these delights my mind might move
To live with thee and be thy love.

3 *Coral is a hard reddish substance formed by sea-creatures; amber is gold-coloured fossilized plant sap; both are used in making jewellery.*

Sir Philip Sidney (1554 – 1586)

Sidney belonged to a generation of Renaissance scholar-soldiers who prided themselves on being equally skilled with both the pen and sword. Born into a noble family, he was a polished diplomat who travelled and studied in Europe. He was a respected and learned literary patron, and his own writings included the critical work Defence of Poetry, *as well as poetry which, while experimenting with classical* forms, established a unique English identity that was to influence both Shakespeare and Spenser. Sidney died young after being wounded in battle, and is supposed to have gallantly handed his water bottle to a dying man as he was carried off the battlefield.*

Sonnet: Who Will in Fairest Book of Nature Know

Who will in fairest book of Nature know
How virtue may best lodged in beauty be,
Let him but learn of love to read in thee,
Stella, those fair lines which true goodness show.
There shall he find all vices' overthrow,
Not by rude force, but sweetest sovereignty
Of reason, from whose light those night birds[1] fly,
That inward sun in thine eyes shineth so.
And, not content to be perfection's heir
Thyself, dost strive all minds that way to move,
Who mark° in thee what is in thee most fair. *notice*
So while thy beauty draws the heart to love,
As fast thy virtue bends that love to good.
'But ah,' Desire still cries, 'give me some food.'

Contextual notes

This poem is taken from the sonnet sequence *Astrophel and Stella* ('star-lover' and 'star'), supposedly inspired by Sidney's thwarted love for a woman he considered marrying, but who eventually married someone else. It deals with an age-old problem for lovers:

1 *Symbols of wickedness.*

the tension between chaste love and lust. This theme was inventively explored by many later poets, especially the generation that followed on immediately after the sixteenth century. You might like to read Andrew Marvell's 'To His Coy Mistress' (see p. 45), which takes the complaint in Sidney's sonnet and gives it a marvellous twist. How many other poems in this anthology deal with this topic?

Christopher Marlowe (1564 – 1593)

Marlowe was educated at Cambridge University and was widely admired for his powerful dramatic tragedies, which strongly influenced Shakespeare's plays. His life was surrounded by intrigue of the shadier kind; it is likely that he was involved in espionage and fraud. He was also mixed up in a street fight in which a man died. He himself was killed (at the age of 29) in suspicious circumstances, shortly before he was due to be tried on mysterious charges.

The Passionate Shepherd to His Love[1]

Come live with me and be my love,
And we will all the pleasures prove
That valleys, groves, hills and fields,
Woods, or steepy mountain yields.

And we will sit upon the rocks,
Seeing the shepherds feed their flocks
By shallow rivers, to whose falls
Melodious birds sing madrigals.° *songs*

And I will make thee beds of roses
And a thousand fragrant posies
A cap of flowers, and a kirtle° *skirt*
Embroidered all with leaves of myrtle;° *evergreen shrub*

1 *This poem inspired a response by Sir Walter Raleigh (see p. 18). Other poets who wrote humorous replies were John Donne and, more recently, Cecil Day-Lewis (father of the actor Daniel Day-Lewis).*

A gown made of the finest wool
Which from our pretty lambs we pull;
Fair linèd slippers for the cold,
With buckles of the purest gold;

A belt of straw and ivy buds,
With coral clasps and amber studs:[2]
And if these pleasures may thee move,
Come live with me and be my love.

The shepherds' swains° shall dance and sing *lovers*
For thy delight each May morning:
If these delights thy mind may move,
Then live with me and be my love.

Contextual notes

This poem is an excellent example of the classical pastoral* tradition revived by Sidney and other Renaissance poets. Pastoral poetry was based on a highly stylized and utopian view of rural life, in which shepherds, shepherdesses and their unrealistically docile flocks gambolled together against a backdrop of perennial spring. The poet was concerned with the creation of beauty, rather than with realism.

Comparison

Although this poem can stand alone (and lends itself very well to close analysis), it is probably more enjoyable when compared with Raleigh's 'The Nymph's Reply to the Shepherd' (see p. 18). Perhaps your class or study group could split into two groups, one to discuss and analyse each poem. After twenty minutes or so, each group could then report back to the other to 'combine' the debate, and to see how the conclusions reached about one poem enrich the understanding of the other. You might also like to try to find the other 'replies' to this poem (by John Donne and Cecil Day-Lewis) in a library.

2 *See footnote 3, p. 19.*

Chidiock Tichborne (*c.* 1568 – 1586)

We know almost nothing about Tichborne other than the fact that he was Catholic, and became involved in a plot to assassinate the Protestant queen Elizabeth I. He was arrested and sentenced to a gruesome death along with the other conspirators.

Tichborne's Elegy

Elegy Written with His Own Hand in the Tower before His Execution

My prime of youth is but a frost of cares,
    My feast of joy is but a dish of pain,
My crop of corn is but a field of tares,° *weeds*
    And all my good is but vain hope of gain;
The day is past, and yet I saw no sun,
And now I live, and now my life is done.

My tale was heard, and yet it was not told,
    My fruit is fall'n, and yet my leaves are green,
My youth is spent, and yet I am not old,
    I saw the world, and yet I was not seen;
My thread is cut, and yet it is not spun,
And now I live, and now my life is done.

I sought my death, and found it in my womb,
    I looked for life, and saw it was a shade,
I trod the earth, and knew it was my tomb,
    And now I die, and now I was but made;
My glass° is full, and now my glass is run, *hourglass*
And now I live, and now my life is done.

Contextual notes

The only poem that Tichborne is known to have written is this elegy he wrote for himself the night before his execution. Although poetry is not necessarily autobiographical, the force of this poem comes from the honesty with which the poet writes about his own desperate situation. It has an impact that is quite different from any of the other elegies in this anthology (see Jonson's two poems [pp. 34–35]; Tennyson's *In Memoriam* poems [pp. 84–87]; Roethke's 'Elegy for Jane' [p. 168]; Jack Cope and Sally Bryer's poems in memory of Ingrid Jonker [pp. 171 and 239]; and Jennifer

Davids' 'For Albert Luthuli (21.7.67)' [analysed on p. xli].) This is no doubt because this elegy was written by the doomed man himself. He was only eighteen at the time; one critic has noted that there is one line of poetry for each year of his life.

In twentieth-century South African terms, Tichborne would have been a 'political prisoner' facing the death penalty for taking part in an 'armed struggle' or 'revolutionary violence'. Can you find any poems, speeches, letters or stories by South Africans in similar situations?

William Shakespeare (1564 – 1616)

Little is known about Shakespeare's life. He did not receive much formal education, married and had three children, and joined a theatrical company in London in the 1590s. He had a flourishing career as an actor, poet and dramatist; he wrote, directed and acted in his own plays (over 35 in all), which included histories, comedies, tragedies* and romances.* Because they were produced directly for the stage, his plays were often not published until much later and the sometimes uncertain status of their scripts remains a subject of lively debate.*

Shakespeare was recognized while he lived as the best dramatist of his age; his memorable characters, unrivalled skill with language, and ability to entertain all spheres of society mark him as the most famous playwright in the English language. His output of poetry was also considerable, and his sonnets are ranked among the finest examples of their kind. Ben Jonson described him (prophetically) as 'not of our age, but of all time'.

Sonnet: Let Me Not to the Marriage of True Minds

Let me not to the marriage of true minds
Admit impediments. Love is not love
Which alters when it alteration finds,
Or bends with the remover to remove.
O, no! it is an ever-fixèd mark
That looks on tempests and is never shaken;
It is the star to every wand'ring bark,° *ship*
Whose worth's unknown, although his height be taken.[1]
Love's not Time's fool, though rosy lips and cheeks
Within his bending sickle's[2] compass come;
Love alters not with his brief hours and weeks,
But bears it out even to the edge of doom.
    If this be error and upon me proved,
    I never writ, nor no man ever loved.

1 *Reference to the measurements of a ship, in particular the height of the mast.*

2 *Curved knife used for harvesting or cutting crops.*

Contextual notes

The image of the ship and star in lines 7 and 8 is significant, given that this was written at a time of renewed exploration by sea and increasingly sophisticated navigation. Without modern radar, sixteenth-century sailors relied heavily on the position of stars and constellations to guide them to safety. (Find out if any of your friends know how to work out the position of the South Pole by looking at the stars, or check in an encyclopedia. If you can imagine being on a boat in the middle of the ocean without any landmarks to indicate where you are, or what direction you are going, you can appreciate the security that stars offer sailors!)

The reference to Time in lines 9 and 10 draws on the common medieval and Renaissance personification of both death and time as a reaper who uses his sickle to harvest souls (or, in the case of time, youth) rather than crops. This image of the 'grim reaper' has become popular in recent fantasy writing, including the humorous books by Terry Pratchett.

Sonnet: Shall I Compare Thee to a Summer's Day?

Shall I compare thee to a summer's day?
Thou art more lovely and more temperate:° *moderate*
Rough winds do shake the darling buds of May,
And summer's lease hath all too short a date;
Sometime too hot the eye of heaven shines,
And often is his gold complexion dimmed;
And every fair from fair sometime declines,
By chance or nature's changing course untrimmed:
But thy eternal summer shall not fade
Nor lose possession of that fair thou ow'st;° *own*
Nor shall Death brag thou wand'rest in his shade,
When in eternal lines to time thou grow'st;
So long as men can breathe or eyes can see,
So long lives this, and this gives life to thee.

Sonnet: My Mistress' Eyes are Nothing Like the Sun

My mistress' eyes are nothing like the sun;
Coral[1] is far more red than her lips' red;
If snow be white, why then her breasts are dun;° *yellowish-brown*
If hairs be wires, black wires grow on her head.
I have seen roses damasked,° red and white, *mixed, patterned*
But no such roses see I in her cheeks;
And in some perfumes is there more delight
Than in the breath that from my mistress reeks.
I love to hear her speak, yet well I know
That music hath a far more pleasing sound;
I grant I never saw a goddess go;
My mistress when she walks treads on the ground.
And yet, by heaven, I think my love as rare
As any she belied° with false compare.° *lied about / comparisons*

Contextual notes

Both of these sonnets undermine the Petrarchan tradition in which extravagant and unrealistic comparisons were made between a woman's appearance and a list of beautiful objects; for example, eyes were like 'sapphires', teeth were like 'pearls', hair was 'spun gold'; necks were 'ivory towers', and so on. The first sonnet simply takes one comparison and turns its failure to adequately describe the beloved into a serious and serene love poem. The second is far more irreverent, pragmatic and humorous. However, they both use the same logical reasoning.

Suggestions for discussion

1. In 'My Mistress' Eyes', what word in the first line alerts us to the fact that this poem is not going to follow the conventional line?
2. A careful reading of this sonnet gives two very different pictures: one of the ideal Petrarchan woman, and one of Shakespeare's lover. Work through the poem, sorting out their different sets of characteristics. How does the poet feel about

1 *See footnote 3, p. 19.*

the Petrarchan criteria for beauty in women? Do any of these criteria still exist? Where would you find these and similar standards of beauty advertised? How do you feel about them? Is there still a difference in value between the descriptions 'blonde' and 'brunette'? What about 'fat' and 'thin'? Why do you think this is so?

3. At times the poet's picture of his girlfriend seems quite cruel, even if funny. How do we know that this is a love poem? In sonnets, the last two lines usually sum up the message underlying the whole poem. What happens to this poem if we leave the last couplet out?

Song: Full Fathom Five Thy Father Lies

Full fathom[1] five thy father lies;
    Of his bones are coral[2] made;
Those are pearls that were his eyes:
    Nothing of him that doth fade,
But doth suffer a sea-change
Into something rich and strange.
Sea-nymphs hourly ring his knell:
                    Ding-dong.
Hark! now I hear them, — Ding-dong, bell.

Contextual notes

In the play *The Tempest*, the spirit Ariel sings these words to a prince who believes that his father has been drowned at sea. Unknown to the prince, his father has survived. Critics argue as to whether the words are cruel or strangely comforting, given the beauty of the images used.

1 *Measurement used to judge depth of water.*

2 *See footnote 3, p. 19.*

John Donne (1572 – 1631)

John Donne (pronounced Dun) came from a Catholic family and was thus not allowed to graduate from Oxford University, where he studied. Ambitious and brilliant, he trained further as a lawyer and established contacts in powerful circles. He was much in demand socially, and conducted a string of affairs. On the brink of a prestigious career as an MP, he fell deeply in love, and married secretly, a politically unpopular step which forced him to retire from public life. In the meantime, he made a sincere conversion to the Anglican church, and became a celebrated preacher. He was eventually made Dean of St Paul's, the biggest church in London.

He was one of the first great metaphysical poets, and his poems are typically witty and rich in their inventive use of comparisons. He is especially known for his passionate expression of both secular and sacred love.*

The Sun Rising

Busy old fool, unruly sun,
Why dost thou thus,
Through windows and through curtains, call on us?
Must to thy motions lovers' seasons run?
Saucy pedantic wretch, go chide
Late school-boys, and sour prentices,° *apprentices*
Go tell court-huntsmen that the King will ride,
Call country ants to harvest offices;
Love, all alike, no season knows, nor clime,° *climate*
Nor hours, days, months, which are the rags of time.

Thy beams, so reverend and strong
Why shouldst thou think?
I could eclipse and cloud them with a wink,
But that I would not lose her sight so long:
If her eyes have not blinded thine,
Look, and tomorrow late, tell me,
Whether both th' Indias of spice and mine[1]
Be where thou left'st them, or lie here with me.
Ask for those kings whom thou saw'st yesterday,
And thou shalt hear, All here in one bed lay.

1 *Reference not just to India, but also South-east Asia, which was seen as a mysterious and exotic source of spices, jewels and precious metals.*

She's all states, and all princes, I,
Nothing else is.
Princes do but play us; compared to this,
All honour's mimic; all wealth alchemy.[2]
Thou, sun, art half as happy as we,
In that the world's contracted thus;
Thine age asks ease, and since thy duties be
To warm the world, that's done in warming us.
Shine here to us, and thou art everywhere;
This bed thy centre is, these walls, thy sphere.

Contextual notes

Donne's poems are full of references to the new inventions and sciences of his age, including a cosmopolitan awareness of the newly explored globe. In this poem, he makes use of the belief that the sun revolved around the earth (although astronomers were discovering for the first time that it happened the other way round) as the central metaphor or 'conceit' of this poem. A 'conceit' is a particular kind of image used by the metaphysical poets, and refers to a comparison that is striking because it is original or unusual, rather than accurate.

Suggestions for discussion

1. Both the title and the first line are fairly unusual, given that this is a love poem. What tone is established in the first line? Why is it so surprising? Does it make more sense once you have read through the entire poem?
2. Throughout the poem, the speaker sets himself and his lover apart from other inhabitants of the world. What tone is used to refer to others 'out there', and who exactly are these people? Could this possibly be related to Donne's own experience of love and marriage? Even if the answer can only be speculative, do you agree that the poem has a sincere and personal quality, and that this is partly what makes it so moving?
3. As is typical of metaphysical poetry, the poet establishes an image, and then transforms it, or 'stretches' it to even more

2 *The medieval art, part chemistry, part magic, of trying to create gold; widely discredited by Donne's time.*

inventive limits. In this poem, the two lovers are first set apart from the world; they then become the world itself, effectively replacing the globe! Trace the exact development of these images throughout the poem; where does the change take place?

4. Look closely at how the poet structures his lines and syntax. For example, read the first two lines of the third stanza, and check the positioning of the pronouns as well as the nouns to which they are linked. How does this emphasize the message that the first-person speaker and his lover are the whole world to each other?

Holy Sonnet: Batter My Heart, Three-personed God[3]

Batter my heart, three-personed God; for, you
As yet but knock, breathe, shine, and seek to mend;
That I may rise, and stand, o'erthrow me, and bend
Your force, to break, blow, burn, and make me new.
I, like an usurped° town, to another due, *overthrown*
Labour to admit you, but O, to no end;
Reason, your viceroy° in me, me should defend, *surrogate ruler*
But is captivated, and proves weak or untrue.
Yet dearly I love you, and would be loved fain,° *gladly*
But am betrothed° unto your enemy.[4] *married*
Divorce me, untie, or break that knot again,
Take me to you, imprison me, for I
Except you enthrall° me, never shall be free, *captivate*
Nor ever chaste, except you ravish me.

To His Mistress Going to Bed

Come, madam, come, all rest my powers defy,
Until I labour, I in labour lie.
The foe oft-times, having the foe in sight,
Is tired with standing though they never fight.
Off with that girdle, like heaven's zone[5] glistering,
But a far fairer world encompassing.
Unpin that spangled breastplate which you wear,
That the eyes of busy fools may be stopped there.

3 *Reference to the Christian belief in the Trinity.*

4 *Sin or Satan.*

5 *Probably the Milky Way (a broad, dense band of stars).*

Unlace yourself, for that harmonious chime
Tells me from you that now 'tis your bed time.
Off with that happy busk,° which I envy, *corset, undergarment*
That still can be, and still can stand so nigh.
Your gown's going off such beauteous state reveals,
As when from flowry meads° the hill's shadow steals. *meadows*
Off with that wiry coronet° and show *head-dress*
The hairy diadem° which on you doth grow: *crown (of hair)*
Off with those shoes, and then safely tread
In this love's hallowed temple, this soft bed.
In such white robes heaven's angels used to be
Received by men; thou, Angel, bring'st with thee
A heaven like Mahomet's° Paradise; and though *Mohammed's*
Ill spirits walk in white, we easily know
By this these angels from an evil sprite:° *spirit*
Those set our hairs, but these our flesh upright.
License my roving hands, and let them go
Behind, before, between, above, below.
O my America! my new found land,
My kingdom, safeliest when with one man manned,
My mine of precious stones, my empery,° *empire*
How blest am I in this discovering thee.
To enter in these bonds is to be free;
Then where my hand is set, my seal shall be.
Full nakedness, all joys are due to thee.
As souls unbodied, bodies unclothed must be
To taste whole joys.[6] Gems which you women use
Are like Atalanta's balls,[7] cast in men's views,
That when a fool's eye lighteth on a gem,
His earthly soul may covet theirs, not them.
Like pictures, or like books' gay coverings made
For laymen, are all women thus arrayed;
Themselves are mystic books, which only we
Whom their imputed grace will dignify
Must see revealed. Then, since I may know,
As liberally as to a midwife, show
Thyself: cast all, yea, this white linen hence,
Here is no penance, much less innocence.[8]
To teach thee, I am naked first; why than,° *then*
What needst thou have more covering than a man?

6 *Donne suggests that nudity is, literally, heavenly.*

7 *Goddess, who in classical legend was distracted in an important race by golden balls dropped in her path.*

8 *Wearing white usually signified innocence or repentance.*

Comparison

The poems on the previous two pages, together with 'The Sun Rising', demonstrate Donne's ability to write love poems that differ dramatically in style, tone and content. 'Batter my Heart, Three-personed God' uses sexual imagery to convey religious fervour, whereas 'To His Mistress Going to Bed' is a frankly erotic and funny seduction poem, completely different once again from 'The Sun Rising'. Yet Donne uses a similar set of images in the latter two poems; can you identify these?

If you have difficulty pinning down exactly what is meant by tone, a comparison of all three poems might be a useful way of seeing how tone can differ dramatically in works that might seem to deal with similar topics, and even use the same images.

Ben Jonson (1572 – 1637)

Jonson's life was a colourful one. He was well educated, distinguished himself as a soldier, and then joined a company of travelling entertainers both as an actor and a writer. His part in a slanderous play landed him in jail and he narrowly avoided execution after killing a fellow actor in a duel. Shakespeare acted in his first play, and his career blossomed until another defamatory play got him into trouble with King James I. However, the king eventually granted him a pension, which made him the first Poet Laureate (i.e. someone officially employed by the court to write poetry). His friends included Donne and Shakespeare, as well as several younger poets who called themselves the 'sons' or 'tribe of Ben'. His work, which included poetry as well as plays, together with his forceful personality, made him one of the foremost literary figures of his time.

On My First Daughter

Here lies, to each her parents' ruth,° *sorrow, pity*
Mary, the daughter of their youth;
Yet, all heaven's gifts being heaven's due,
It makes the father less to rue.
At six months' end she parted hence
With safety of her innocence;
Whose soul heaven's Queen (whose name she bears),
In comfort of her mother's tears,
Hath placed amongst her virgin train;° *company*
Where, while that severed doth remain,
This grave partakes the fleshly birth;[1]
Which cover lightly, gentle earth.

1 *Reference to the belief that the body would eventually be physically resurrected ('fleshly birth') from the grave and reunited with the soul.*

On My First Son

Farewell, thou child of my right hand,[2] and joy;
My sin was too much hope of thee, loved boy.
Seven years thou wert lent to me, and I thee pay,
Exacted by thy fate, on the just day.
Oh, could I lose all father now! For why
Will man lament the state he should envy?
To have so soon 'scaped world's and flesh's rage,
And, if no other misery, yet age?
Rest in soft peace, and, asked, say here doth lie
Ben Jonson his best piece of poetry;
For whose sake, henceforth, all his vows be such,
As what he loves may never like too much.[3]

COMPARISON

In an age of high infant mortality, it was certainly not unusual to lose more than one child. Here it is interesting to compare, first of all, the poems that Jonson wrote on the deaths of his daughter and son. Try to establish what similarities there are, as well as what differences. What lies behind the differences?

Now turn to De Kok's 'Small Passing' (p. 248) and read it closely. At first it may seem very different to Jonson's poems; how do you think the gender of the poets shapes these differences? Can you find any similarities? Are there aspects of the tragedy of losing a child that transcend gender and historical period, and can you identify these in the poems? Interestingly enough, all three poems deal with the moral implications of mourning, and whether this is selfish or not. What different conclusions do Jonson and De Kok reach? Can you identify with both positions?

2 *This is the literal meaning of the name 'Benjamin', shared by father and son.*

3 *The poet seems to be hoping that he will never love selfishly.*

Robert Herrick (1591 – 1674)

Initially an apprentice goldsmith, Herrick studied at Cambridge University and moved in literary circles in London, coming under the influence of Ben Jonson. He was eventually ordained and took charge of a rural parish in Devon. No conventional priest, he kept a pet pig and regularly escaped to London, where he had a mistress 27 years his junior. He is remembered for his delightful secular lyrics, concerned mostly with the sweetness and shortness of life.

To the Virgins, to Make Much of Time

Gather ye rosebuds while ye may,
Old Time is still a-flying:
And this same flower that smiles to-day
Tomorrow will be dying.

The glorious lamp of heaven, the sun,
The higher he's a-getting,
The sooner will his race be run,
And nearer he's to setting.

That age is best which is the first,
When youth and blood are warmer;
But being spent, the worse, and worst
Times still succeed the former.

Then be not coy, but use your time,
And while ye may, go marry:
For having lost but once your prime
You may for ever tarry.° *wait*

Contextual notes

This is one of the most famous of the *carpe diem* poems. This Latin phrase, first used by the Roman philosopher Horace, literally means 'seize the day', and urges that pleasure should never be postponed, given the brevity of life. This theme was skilfully developed by several seventeenth-century poets; see, for example, Marvell's 'To His Coy Mistress' (p. 45). The *carpe diem* philosophy was recently popularized by Hollywood in the film *Dead Poets' Society*.

George Herbert (1593 – 1633)

Herbert was born into a prominent family and performed brilliantly at Cambridge, becoming public orator of the university. Initially worldly and ambitious, he was tempted to follow a career in politics. However, towards the end of his short life he experienced a deep religious calling, and was ordained in the Anglican church. He brought great humility and sincerity to his spiritual duties, and wrote what is widely recognized as some of the finest devotional poetry in the English language.*

Redemption

Having been tenant long to a rich lord,
  Not thriving, I resolvèd to be bold,
  And make a suit° unto him, to afford° — *plea / grant*
A new small-rented lease, and cancel the old.

In heaven at his manor° I him sought; — *mansion*
  They told me there that he was lately° gone — *recently*
  About some land, which he had dearly bought
Long since on earth, to take possessiön.

I straight returned, and knowing his great birth,
  Sought him accordingly in great resorts;
  In cities, theatres, gardens, parks, and courts;
At length I heard a ragged noise and mirth
  Of thieves and murderers; there I him espied,
  Who straight, *Your suit is granted,* said, and died.

Contextual notes

In style this sonnet deliberately imitates the parables told by Jesus and recorded in the New Testament, although the story it tells is the poet's own invention. It is obviously intended to function as a parable, or religious allegory*.

Note the accents in lines 2 and 8 which ensure that the metre (number of rhythmic stresses in each line) is regular. The double dots over the 'o' in 'possession' mean that it should be pronounced with four syllables: poh-ze-shee-on, with the last syllable rhyming with 'gone' in line 6.

Virtue

Sweet day, so cool, so calm, so bright,
The bridal° of the earth and sky: *marriage, union*
The dew shall weep thy fall tonight,
For thou must die.

Sweet rose, whose hue, angry° and brave,° *red / bright*
Bids the rash gazer wipe his eye:
Thy root is ever in its grave,
And thou must die.

Sweet spring, full of sweet days and roses,
A box where sweets° compacted lie: *perfumes*
My music shows ye have your closes,[1]
And all must die.

Only a sweet and virtuous soul,
Like seasoned timber, never gives;
But though the whole world turn to coal,[2]
Then chiefly lives.

The Flower

How fresh, oh Lord, how sweet and clean
Are thy returns! even as the flowers in spring;
To which, besides their own demean,° *demeanour*
The late-past frosts tributes of pleasure bring.
Grief melts away
Like snow in May,
As if there were no such cold thing.

Who would have thought my shrivelled heart
Could have recovered greenness? It was gone
Quite underground; as flowers depart
To see their mother-root, when they have blown° *bloomed*
Where they together
All the hard weather,
Dead to the world, keep house unknown.

1 *Musical term for conclusions.*
2 *Reference to the burning end of the world, as described in the Bible.*

These are thy wonders, Lord of power,
Killing and quickening,° bringing down to hell — *bringing to life*
And up to heaven in an hour;
Making a chiming of a passing-bell[3]
We say amiss
This or that is:
Thy word is all, if we could spell.

Oh that I once past changing were,
Fast in thy Paradise, where no flower can wither!
Many a spring I shoot up fair,
Offering° at heaven, growing and groaning thither; — *aiming*
Nor doth my flower
Want a spring shower,
My sins and I joining together.

But while I grow in a straight line,
Still upwards bent, as if heaven were mine own,
Thy anger comes, and I decline:
What frost to that? what pole is not the zone
Where all things burn,
When thou dost turn,
And the least frown of thine is shown?

And now in age I bud again,
After so many deaths I live and write;
I once more smell the dew and rain,
And relish versing. Oh, my only light,
It cannot be
That I am he
On whom thy tempests fell all night.

These are thy wonders, Lord of love,
To make us see we are but flowers that glide;
Which when we once can find and prove,
Thou hast a garden for us where to bide;
Who would be more,
Swelling through store,° — *wealth*
Forfeit their Paradise by their pride.

3 *Church bell tolled to announce a death.*

Comparison

You might find it interesting to compare this poem to Hopkins' 'No Worst, There is None' (p. 110). Both deal with depression and spiritual alienation, but whereas Hopkins' poem is written from the depths of misery, Herbert's speaks of surviving the ordeal and experiencing a 'rebirth'. Herbert's skill here lies in his ability to use ordinary and natural imagery to describe a common human experience in fresh and accessible terms, in sharp contrast to the vivid, almost nightmarish images Hopkins packs into his tortured poem. Yet both describe similar emotional conditions.

Both poems lend themselves very well to close critical analysis; here again, you might like to split into two groups, each discussing and analysing one poem, and then combining to report back. You will discover that both poems are extremely rich in possible meanings (the Herbert poem is deceptively simple!) and should provoke some interesting debates. Although both poets explore their relationship with God in explicitly religious and Christian terms, the power of both poems is that the emotional territory they chart is familiar to people of all faith traditions, as well as agnostics.

Thomas Carew (*c.* 1594 – 1640)

Trained in law at Oxford, Carew (pronounced Carey) served as a diplomat in Europe. He was favoured by King Charles I, and given a post at court. Here he established himself as the most gifted of the 'Cavalier' poets. This was a group of poets loyal to the monarchy, who specialized in elegant lyrics and gallant love poems. Influenced by both Donne and Jonson, Carew's poetry is invariably polished and sophisticated.

The Spring

Now that the winter's gone, the earth hath lost
Her snow-white robes; and now no more the frost
Candies° the grass, or casts an icy cream *sugars*
Upon the silver lake or crystal stream:
But the warm sun thaws the benumbèd° earth, *numb, frozen*
And makes it tender; gives a sacred birth
To the dead swallow;[1] wakes in hollow tree
The drowsy cuckoo and the humblebee.
Now do a choir of chirping minstrels° bring, *singers*
In triumph to the world, the youthful spring.
The valleys, hills, and woods in rich array
Welcome the coming of the longed-for May.
Now all things smile; only my love doth lower;° *frown, glower*
Nor hath the scalding noonday sun the power
To melt that marble ice, which still doth hold
Her heart congealed,° and makes her pity cold. *frozen*
The ox, which lately did for shelter fly
Into the stall, doth now securely lie
In open fields; and love no more is made
By the fireside; but in the cooler shade
Amyntas now doth with his Chloris sleep[2]
Under a sycamore,° and all things keep *species of tree*
Time with the season: only she doth carry
June in her eyes, in her heart January.

Contextual notes

This graceful poem combines the pastoral* traditions of the previous century (see notes to Marlowe's 'The Passionate Shepherd to His Love', p. 22) with the lover's traditional complaint.

1 *Swallows were believed to hibernate and reawaken in Spring.*

2 *Classical names for a shepherd and shepherdess.*

John Milton (1608 – 1674)

Milton was educated at Cambridge University. A learned and serious young man, he studied further to prepare himself for a career either as a poet or a priest, and soon gained a reputation as a writer of vivid imagination and skill. He travelled in Europe, meeting intellectuals and scientists such as Galileo, before returning to find England in a state of civil war between supporters of the monarchy and Cromwell's parliamentarians. Milton was an ardent supporter of the new Puritan regime under Cromwell, and worked hard publishing pamphlets and tracts in favour of the new government, even though this contributed to his going blind. After the restoration of the monarchy, he returned to writing poetry and produced his most famous work, the monumental Paradise Lost, *in which he set out to 'justify the ways of God to man'. His use of blank verse (poetry with no end-rhymes, previously found only in drama) was to influence the course of English poetry; he is also recognized for his contribution to the art of sonnet-writing.*

On His Blindness

When I consider how my light is spent,° *wasted*
Ere half my days, in this dark world and wide,
And that one talent which is death to hide[1]
Lodged with me useless, though my soul more bent
To serve therewith my Maker, and present
My true account, lest He returning chide;
'Doth God exact day-labour, light denied?'
I fondly° ask. But Patience, to prevent *foolishly*
That murmur, soon replies, 'God doth not need
Either man's work or his own gifts. Who best
Bear his mild yoke, they serve him best. His state
Is kingly: thousands at his bidding speed
And post° o'er land and ocean without rest; *travel*
They also serve who only stand and wait.'

1 *Reference to the parable of the talents told by Jesus (Matthew 25: 14-30). This warned that it was spiritually essential to make use of the gifts granted to one.*

Anne Bradstreet (*c.* 1612 – 1672)

Bradstreet was born in England, but emigrated to the new colony of Massachusetts in North America at the age of eighteen, together with her father (who became governor of the colony) and her husband. Her family were among the first Puritan settlers who left for the 'New World' to escape religious repression at home. She had eight children, and suffered from ill-health throughout her life. Her poetry was taken to London by a relative for publication; she was subsequently acknowledged as the first poet of the North American colonies.

The Author to Her Book

Thou ill-formed offspring of my feeble brain,
Who after birth didst by my side remain,
Till snatched from thence by friends, less wise than true,
Who thee abroad exposed to public view,
Made thee in rags,[1] halting° to th' press to trudge, *limping, faltering*
Where errors were not lessened (all may judge).
At thy return my blushing was not small,
My rambling brat (in print) should mother call;
I cast thee by as one unfit for light,
Thy visage was so irksome in my sight;
Yet being mine own, at length affection would
Thy blemishes amend, if so I could:
I washed thy face, but more defects I saw,
And rubbing off a spot still made a flaw.
I stretched thy joints to make thee even feet,[2]
Yet still thou run'st more hobbling than is meet;
In better dress to trim thee was my mind,
But nought save homespun cloth i' th' house I find.
In this array 'mongst vulgars may'st thou roam;
In critic's hands beware thou dost not come,
And take thy way where yet thou are not known;
If for thy father asked, say thou hadst none;
And for thy mother, she alas is poor,
Which caused her thus to send thee out of door.

1 *Paper used to be made out of cloth and rags.*

2 *This pun refers to the metre of poetry; feet are units made up of one stressed (or 'strong') syllable together with a few unstressed syllables.*

Suggestions for discussion

1. Although today it is not so unusual for a writer to compare a book to a baby, this poem is probably one of the first to have done so. The author develops and elaborates on this central comparison in a way that is characteristically metaphysical; can you trace this development throughout the poem? (If you have not worked with a metaphysical poem before, you might like to read the contextual notes and questions for Donne's 'The Sun Rising' [p. 30] first.)
2. As you will have noticed, the poet draws on her practical experience as a parent to create effective imagery. What images are specifically maternal? You will notice that the speaker is overt about her gender; what could be the reasons for this?
3. The author struggles with two conflicting emotions throughout the poem; what are they? At times, one dominates, then the other overcomes it; can you chart this progress? How do these feelings contribute to the tone of the poem?
4. The poet makes clever use of words which have a double meaning, especially when applied separately to a book and a child; can you identify some of these words?
5. What final motive does the poet give for publication? How does this alter the conventional picture of the poet writing when inspiration strikes?

Andrew Marvell (1621 – 1678)

One of the last great metaphysical poets, Marvell graduated from Cambridge University and travelled in Europe during the English Civil War. On returning, he moved in literary circles among both parliamentarians and those loyal to the monarchy. He was friends with Milton, and the two supported each other through unsettling political changes. Marvell became the unofficial laureate to Cromwell, who ruled England temporarily after the war. During his lifetime, he had a reputation as a sharp satirist; today, he is best remembered for his lyrical poems.

To His Coy Mistress

Had we but world enough, and time,
This coyness, Lady, were no crime.
We would sit down, and think which way
To walk, and pass our long love's day.
Thou by the Indian Ganges'[1] side
Shouldst rubies find: I by the tide
Of Humber[2] would complain. I would
Love you ten years before the Flood;[3]
And you should, if you please, refuse
Till the conversion of the Jews.[4]
My vegetable° love should grow *plant-like*
Vaster than empires, and more slow;
An hundred years should go to praise
Thine eyes, and on thy forehead gaze;
Two hundred to adore each breast;
But thirty thousand to the rest.
An age at least to every part,
And the last age should show your heart.
For, Lady, you deserve this state,° *dignity*
Nor would I love at lower rate.
    But at my back I always hear
Time's wingéd chariot hurrying near;
And yonder all before us lie
Deserts of vast eternity.

1 *Holy river in the north of India.*
2 *River beside Hull, Marvell's home town in the north of England.*
3 *The great flood described in the Old Testament.*
4 *This conversion (to Christianity) would supposedly be a sign that the world was ending.*

Thy beauty shall no more be found;
Nor, in thy marble vault, shall sound
My echoing song: then worms shall try
That long preserved virginity:
And your quaint[5] honour turn to dust,
And into ashes all my lust:
The grave's a fine and private place,
But none, I think, do there embrace.
 Now therefore, while the youthful hue
Sits on thy skin like morning glew,° *glow, warmth*
And while thy willing soul transpires° *breathes*
At every pore with instant fires,
Now let us sport us while we may;
And now, like amorous birds of prey,
Rather at once our time devour,
Than languish in his slow-chapped[6] power.
Let us roll all our strength, and all
Our sweetness, up into one ball:
And tear our pleasures with rough strife
Thorough° the iron gates of life: *through*
Thus, though we cannot make our sun
Stand still, yet we will make him run.

Contextual notes

This is one of the best-known *carpe diem* poems in the English language (you might like to compare it with Herrick's 'To the Virgins, to Make Much of Time', p. 36). It is also an excellent example of the metaphysical* delight in manipulating logic. For another example of a seduction poem which shamelessly twists logical argument, you might like to try and find Donne's 'The Flea' in a library.

Suggestions for discussion

1. How exactly does the poet use (or misuse) logic in this poem? Try to paraphrase Marvell's line of argument into a short paragraph.
2. You will notice that the poem is divided into three parts. Find where these breaks occur, and note at what stage of the argument they take place. How does the rhythm and pace of the poem change from section to section? (You will need to

5 *A bawdy pun; since Chaucer's time, 'quaint' had been affectionate slang for female genitals (today degraded to the strongly vulgar 'cunt').*

6 *Chaps are jaws; time is presented as slowly consuming human beings.*

read the poem aloud at this point.) How do these changes reinforce the poet's reasoning?

3. Now examine the images used in each section. What atmosphere and tone do they conjure up, and how does this alter from section to section? What effect does the pace and tone of the last section have, coming after the first two?

Lady Mary Chudleigh (1656 – 1710)

Chudleigh married young. Most of her life was spent in solitude on her husband's country estate, but she read and corresponded with other writers, including early feminists, and formulated progressive views of her own. Several editions of her poems were published in her lifetime; her work also includes plays and translations.

To the Ladies

Wife and servant are the same,
But only differ in the name:
For when that fatal knot is tied,
Which nothing, nothing can divide,
When she the word *Obey* has said,
And man by law supreme has made,
Then all that's kind is laid aside,
And nothing left but state° and pride. *dignity*
Fierce as an eastern prince he grows,
And all his innate rigour shows:
Then but to look, to laugh, or speak,
Will the nuptial° contract break. *marital*
Like mutes,[1] she signs alone must make,
And never any freedom take,
But still be governed by a nod,
And fear her husband as her god:
Him still must serve, him still obey,
And nothing act, and nothing say,
But what her haughty lord thinks fit,
Who, with the power, has all the wit.
Then shun,° oh! shun that wretched state, *avoid*
And all the fawning flatterers hate.
Value yourselves, and men despise:
You must be proud, if you'll be wise.

1 *Those physically unable to speak.*

Contextual notes

This unusually polemic* poem was written at a time when the status of women under British law meant that women were considered the property first of their fathers, then of their husbands. They had no legal rights to land, wealth, income or even their own children (their husbands had full control over all these), and on marrying, they became legal minors. This situation persisted from the first codifying of law in England up until the late nineteenth century. Today there are still many countries in which women are, if not legally, then socially and economically rendered second-class citizens. This gives Chudleigh's poem its contemporary flavour.

Alexander Pope (1688 – 1744)

A childhood illness left Pope sickly and crippled for life, but he compensated for physical weakness with mental brilliance. His translation of Homer's Iliad *and* Odyssey *(classical Greek legends) brought him recognition and financial independence; he earned a reputation as one of the best satirists of his time, even though the accuracy of his barbs often made him most unpopular. Most of his poetry is written in rhyming couplets, an astonishing testimony to his technical skill. Today he is best remembered as the author of the mock-heroic* poem 'The Rape of the Lock'.*

A Little Learning

A little learning is a dangerous thing;
Drink deep, or taste not the Pierian spring:[1]
There shallow draughts intoxicate the brain,
And drinking largely sobers us again.
Fired at first sight with what the Muse[2] imparts,
In fearless youth we tempt the heights of Arts;
While from the bounded° level of our mind *restricted*
Short views we take, nor see the lengths behind,
But, more advanced, behold with strange surprise
New distant scenes of endless science rise!
So pleased at first the towering Alps[3] we try,
Mount o'er the vales, and seem to tread the sky;
The eternal snows appear already past,
And the first clouds and mountains seem the last:
But those attained, we tremble to survey
The growing labours of the lengthened way;
The increasing prospect tires our wandering eyes,
Hill peep o'er hills, and Alps on Alps arise!

1 *Fountain reputed to be the source of wisdom and inspiration.*

2 *Classical goddess supposed to prompt inspiration.*

3 *Highest mountain range in western Europe.*

Lady Mary Wortley Montagu (1689 – 1762)

Montagu was the daughter of a duke, and even as a young woman she moved in impressive social and literary circles. She married Edward Wortley Montagu secretly and went with him to Turkey. On her return she introduced the practice of inoculating against smallpox into England. She was a close associate of Pope's until a public quarrel ended the friendship. She spent much of her later life in Europe. Cosmopolitan and sophisticated, she is best remembered for her witty letters, although her poems are also worthy of note.

An Answer to a Love-Letter in Verse

Is it to me, this sad lamenting strain?
Are Heaven's choicest gifts bestowed in vain?
A plenteous fortune, and a beauteous bride,
Your love rewarded, and content your pride:
Yet leaving her — 'tis me that you pursue,
Without one single charm but being new.
    How vile is man! how I detest the ways
Of artful falsehood, and designing praise!
Tasteless, an easy happiness you slight,
Ruin your joy, and mischief your delight.
Why should poor pug[1] (the mimic of your kind)
Wear a rough chain, and be to box confined?
Some cup, perhaps, he breaks, or tears a fan,
While moves unpunished the destroyer, man.
Not bound by vows, and unrestrained by shame,
In sport you break the heart, and rend the fame.
Not that your art can be successful here,
Th' already plundered need no robber fear:
Nor sighs, nor charms, nor flattery can move,
Too well secured against a second love.
Once, and but once, that devil charmed my mind;
To reason deaf, to observation blind,
I idly hoped (what cannot love persuade?)
My fondness equalled, and my truth repaid:
Slow to distrust, and willing to believe,
Long hushed my doubts, and would myself deceive;
But oh! too soon — this tale would ever last;
Sleep, sleep my wrongs, and let me think 'em past.

1 *Pet monkey.*

For you, who mourn with counterfeited grief,
And ask so boldly like a begging thief,
May soon some other nymph° inflict the pain *beautiful girl*
You know so well with cruel art to feign.
Though long you've sported with Dan Cupid's dart,[2]
You may see eyes, and you may feel a heart.
So the brisk wits, who stop the evening coach,[3]
Laugh at the fear that follows their approach;
With idle mirth, and haughty scorn, despise
The passenger's pale cheek and staring eyes:
But seized by Justice, find a fright no jest,
And all the terror doubled in their breast.

Contextual notes

English poetry since the Middle Ages has included hundreds of love poems written by men urging the woman of their dreams to return their love and begin an affair with them. This poem gives us a rare glimpse of what it meant to be on the receiving end of one of these pleas. The speaker in Montagu's poem assumes that her would-be lover is completely insincere; how many love poems or seduction poems can you find in this anthology which you suspect of falling into this category?

2 *The arrow with which Cupid (the god of love) was supposed to strike.*

3 *Reference to highwaymen, who held up and robbed travelling coaches.*

Samuel Johnson (1709 – 1784)

Poverty and illness marred Johnson's early years. Although he was a good scholar, lack of funds forced him to leave Oxford University. He spent nine years writing the first dictionary in the English language, and its publication confirmed his growing status in literary circles. His writing included essays, reviews, political articles, biographies and a novel, as well as poetry. His close friend Boswell wrote an extremely popular biography celebrating Johnson's achievements, which ensured the fame of both men.

A Short Song of Congratulation

Long-expected one-and-twenty,
Lingering year at last is flown:
Pomp and pleasure, pride and plenty,
Great Sir John, are all your own.

Loosened from the minor's tether,
Free to mortgage[1] or to sell,
Wild as wind, and light as feather,
Bid the slaves of thrift farewell.

Call the Betties, Kates, and Jennies,
Every name that laughs at care;
Lavish of your grandsire's guineas,
Show the spirit of an heir.

All that prey on vice and folly
Joy to see their quarry fly;
Here the gamester° light and jolly, *gambler*
There the lender grave and sly.

Wealth, Sir John, was made to wander,
Let it wander as it will;
See the jockey, see the pander,° *pimp*
Bid them come and take their fill.

1 *Borrow money against land or property.*

When the bonny blade° carouses,[2] *young man*
Pockets full, and spirits high,
What are acres? What are houses?
Only dirt, or wet or dry.

If the guardian or the mother
Tell the woes of wilful waste,
Scorn their counsel, scorn their pother:° *bother, anxiety*
You can hang or drown at last!

Contextual notes

This poem refers to Sir John Lade, the nephew of one of Johnson's friends, who wasted the fortune he inherited. Underlying its witty sarcasm is a very real concern for the laws of inheritance which allowed such irresponsibility. During the eighteenth century, the role of the 'landed gentry' (minor aristocrats who inherited estates and lived off the income generated by farming or renting their land) came increasingly under scrutiny, and responsible management was strongly urged.

2 *Enjoys a noisy drinking-party.*

Thomas Gray (1716 – 1771)

Gray was educated at Cambridge. Apart from a tour of Europe with Horace Walpole, the Prime Minister's son, he lived the life of a recluse at Cambridge University, where he was made professor of Modern History. His few poems show evidence of his careful research, and are mostly rather solemn. His most famous work, 'Elegy Written in a Country Church Yard', was so popular that he was offered the position of Poet Laureate, which he refused. He spent the last part of his life pursuing his studies in subjects ranging from botany to Welsh poetry.

Ode on the Death of a Favourite Cat, Drowned in a Tub of Gold Fishes

'Twas on a lofty vase's side,
Where China's gayest art had dyed
    The azure° flowers, that blow;° *blue / bloom*
Demurest of the tabby kind,
The pensive Selima reclined,
    Gazed on the lake below.

Her conscious tail her joy declared;
The fair round face, the snowy beard,
    The velvet of her paws,
Her coat, that with the tortoise vies,
Her ears of jet, and emerald eyes,
    She saw; and purred applause.

Still had she gazed; but 'midst the tide
Two angel forms were seen to glide,
    The Genii° of the stream: *guardian spirits*
Their scaly armour's Tyrian[1] hue
Through richest purple to the view
    Betrayed a golden gleam.

1 *Tyre was an ancient Mediterranean city where purple dye was made from shellfish.*

The hapless nymph° with wonder saw: *beautiful girl*
A whisker first and then a claw,
With many an ardent wish,
She stretched in vain to reach the prize.
What female heart can gold despise?
What cat's averse to fish?

Presumptuous maid! with looks intent
Again she stretched, again she bent,
Nor knew the gulf between.
(Malignant Fate sat by, and smiled)
The slippery verge her feet beguiled,
She tumbled headlong in.

Eight times emerging from the flood
She mewed to every watery God,
Some speedy aid to send.
No dolphin came, no Nereid[2] stirred:
Nor cruel Tom, nor Susan heard.
A favourite has no friend!

From hence, ye Beauties, undeceived,
Know, one false step is ne'er retrieved,
And be with caution bold.
Not all that tempts your wandering eyes
And heedless hearts, is lawful prize;
Nor all, that glisters, gold.

Contextual notes

The poet here uses mock-heroic* language and imagery to mourn a drowned cat. In other words, a fairly trivial subject is described in a language and style much loftier and grander than is appropriate, for humorous effect. The poem follows in the tradition of much eighteenth-century satire*, which was greatly influenced by Pope.

2 *Sea goddess.*

William Blake (1757 – 1827)

Blake is a classic example of a genius born before his time. He had no formal education, but was trained as an engraver (book illustrator). He developed a unique artistic style, opened a print shop in London, and produced books written and illustrated by himself. These introduced his energetic and often socially critical poetry and his visionary art to the public. However, his mystic philosophies, condemnation of orthodox religion, and passion for justice meant that he was considered insane by most of his contemporaries. After his death, he was to have a growing influence on poets and artists who were inspired by his revolutionary ideas.

The Garden of Love

I went to the Garden of Love,
And saw what I never had seen:
A Chapel was built in the midst,
Where I used to play on the green.

And the gates of this Chapel were shut,
And Thou shalt not. writ over the door;
So I turn'd to the Garden of Love,
That so many sweet flowers bore,

And I saw it was filled with graves,
And tomb-stones where flowers should be:
And Priests in black gowns were walking their rounds,
And binding with briars° my joys & desires. *thorns*

London

I wander thro' each charter'd[1] street,
Near where the charter'd Thames[2] does flow.
And mark in every face I meet
Marks of weakness, marks of woe.

1 *Mapped out; also legally defined or restricted.*

2 *River running through central London.*

In every cry of every Man,
in every Infant's cry of fear,
In every voice: in every ban,[3]
The mind-forg'd manacles° I hear

chains

How the Chimney-sweeper's cry
Every blackning Church appalls,
And the hapless Soldier's sigh
Runs in blood down Palace walls

But most thro' midnight streets I hear
How the youthful Harlot's curse[4]
Blasts the new-born Infant's tear
And blights with plagues the Marriage hearse.

Contextual notes

Blake was one of the first writers to voice his horror and concern at the effect the Industrial Revolution was having on the social fabric of England. Here he addresses the problems of rapid urbanization. The new drive for industrialization, and the migration of poor people from the countryside to the cities in search of jobs, led to appalling living conditions and gross exploitation. There were no laws, for example, governing labour conditions. The 'Chimney-sweepers' in line 9, for example, were small boys (the younger the better) who were made to climb up inside chimneys to clean them; many suffocated. Forced child labour was perfectly legal. The reference to the 'hapless Soldiers' (line 11), meanwhile, possibly alludes to conscription. And the description of the 'Harlot' (prostitute) as 'youthful' (line 14) may be a reference to the fact that impoverished families sometimes sold their daughters (many of them scarcely teenagers) into prostitution.

3 *Legal prohibition or punishment; possibly also a pun on 'bann' (marriage announcement).*

4 *Swearing; also a reference to the venereal disease syphilis; babies born to infected women were often blind or deformed (see line 15).*

Comparison

Once you have read 'London' carefully, turn to Serote's 'Alexandra' and 'City Johannesburg' (pp. 234–236). Both poets, although writing from different countries and centuries, share a passionate concern for those social injustices that are highlighted or made worse by urban living.

The following questions will enable you to explore this connection further.

1. Both poets write in judgement of particular cities. However, in 'Alexandra', Serote's indictment of his home township is mixed with other emotions. Can you identify some of these?
2. Work through both 'London' and 'City Johannesburg'. What specific social and political evils are listed by each poet?
3. Now that you have established exactly what Blake criticizes in urban society, note how economically he uses serious puns and words with double meanings to get his message across. The footnotes already identify two 'double' words; can you find any others? (Look closely at line 10.) Serote, however, makes use of colourful images rather than loaded words in his poems, although there is one very clever pun in 'City Johannesburg'. (Check line 27.) What central metaphor* does he develop throughout 'Alexandra'? In what way is it unusual? In 'City Johannesburg', locate each metaphor and simile.* How does each one work, and which do you find the most effective? Debate these with your classmates. (Remember that there are no 'correct' answers.)
4. Bearing in mind your answers to the second question, can you identify any specific social and political problems or structures that were the same or similar in London in the 1790s and South African cities under apartheid?
5. Blake is particularly concerned with the problem of prostitution. Do you feel that he is giving a lecture on morality? Or is his treatment of the issue more complex? How does he present it as a social, rather than a moral problem?
6. Do you feel that the criticisms both poets make are effective? Why? How does their treatment of these issues differ from the way they might be handled by a politician or an activist? Does this suggest any further insights on the nature or role of poetry?

The Tiger

Tiger, Tiger, burning bright
In the forests of the night;
What immortal hand or eye,
Could frame thy fearful symmetry?° *regular proportions*

In what distant deeps or skies
Burnt the fire of thine eyes!
On what wings dare he aspire?
What the hand, dare seize the fire?

And what shoulder, & what art,
Could twist the sinews° of thy heart? *muscles*
And when thy heart began to beat,
What dread hand? & what dread feet?

What the hammer? what the chain?
In what furnace was thy brain?
What the anvil?[5] what dread grasp
Dare its deadly terrors clasp?

When the stars threw down their spears
And water'd heaven with their tears:
Did he smile his work to see?
Did he who made the Lamb make thee?

Tiger, Tiger, burning bright,
In the forests of the night:
What immortal hand or eye,
Dare frame thy fearful symmetry?

5 *Iron block on which metal is hammered into shape; used by blacksmiths.*

From MILTON

And Did Those Feet in Ancient Time

And did those feet in ancient time
Walk upon England's mountains green?
And was the holy Lamb of God
On England's pleasant pastures seen?

And did the Countenance Divine
Shine forth upon our clouded hills?
And was Jerusalem builded here,
Among these dark Satanic Mills?[1]

Bring me my Bow of burning gold:
Bring me my Arrows of desire:
Bring me my Spear: O clouds unfold!
Bring me my Chariot of fire!

I will not cease from Mental Fight,
Nor shall my Sword sleep in my hand,
Till we have built Jerusalem
In England's green & pleasant Land.

Contextual notes

This poem is included as an interesting piece of evidence of the extent of English patriotism. It refers to the belief that Jesus travelled to England and spent several years there before returning to Palestine to spread his teachings. Some English people (including Blake) believed, with a fervent combination of nationalism and mysticism, that a second Jerusalem, which was to herald a new order at the end of time, would be raised up on English soil. These verses — which Blake used as a preface to a long poem dealing with his vocation as a spiritual prophet — have become a popular hymn, from which the title of the film *Chariots of Fire* was taken. Note that even in a mystic poem, Blake cannot help showing his outrage at the evils of industrialism.

1 *Factories for producing cloth.*

Robert Burns (1759 – 1796)

Burns was a patriotic Scottish poet, and his birthday is still celebrated by the Scots. Raised to be a farmer, he struggled financially and was about to emigrate to Jamaica when his first book of poems, many in the Scottish dialect, was published. It was an immediate success, and guaranteed his popularity in society, which in turn led to a string of romantic affairs. He also embarked on the task of collecting and thus preserving local Scottish songs, before dying at the age of 37. His lively poems are still popular today.

John Anderson, My Jo

John Anderson my jo,° John, *dear*
    When we were first acquent;° *acquainted*
Your locks were like the raven,
    Your bonie° brow was brent;° *bonny / smooth*
But now your brow is beld,° John, *bald*
    Your locks are like the snaw;° *snow*
But blessings on your frosty pow,° *head*
    John Anderson, my Jo.

John Anderson my jo, John,
    We clamb° the hill the gither;° *climb / together*
And mony° a canty° day, John, *many / merry*
    We've had wi' ane° anither: *one*
Now we maun° totter down, John, *must*
    And hand in hand we'll go;
And sleep the gither at the foot,
    John Anderson, my Jo.

William Wordsworth (1770 – 1850)

Wordsworth was born in the Lake District, a beautiful part of England later celebrated in his poetry. After graduating from Cambridge University he spent a year in France, where he passionately supported the French Revolution, then at its height. He also fell in love with a Frenchwoman who bore him an illegitimate daughter. Back home, he was horrified when England declared war on France; he also found his radical principles challenged by the violent excesses of the revolution, and became deeply depressed. A retreat to the countryside to live with his adoring sister Dorothy, and an inspiring friendship with the poet Coleridge helped him to recover. Together with Coleridge, he produced work that was to establish the foundations of a new era in English poetry. Their concept of Nature and its beauties as a source of consolation and moral guidance was perhaps inevitable in a rapidly industrializing country; it shapes our aesthetic perceptions to this day. Later in life, Wordsworth was appointed Poet Laureate.*

Three Years She Grew

Three years she grew in sun and shower,
Then Nature said, 'A lovelier flower
On earth was never sown;
This Child I to myself will take;
She shall be mine, and I will make
A Lady of my own.

'Myself will to my darling be
Both law and impulse: and with me
The Girl, in rock and plain,
In earth and heaven, in glade and bower,° — *enclosed garden*
Shall feel an overseeing power
To kindle or restrain.

'She shall be sportive° as the fawn — *playful*
That wild with glee across the lawn
Or up the mountain springs;
And hers shall be the breathing balm,
And hers the silence and the calm
Of mute insensate° things. — *without feeling*

'The floating clouds their state shall lend
To her; for her the willow bend;
Nor shall she fail to see
Even in the motions of the Storm
Grace that shall mould the Maiden's form
By silent sympathy.

'The stars of midnight shall be dear
To her; and she shall lean her ear
In many a secret place
Where rivulets° dance their wayward round, *small streams*
And beauty born of murmuring sound
Shall pass into her face.

'And vital feelings of delight
Shall rear her form to stately° height *dignified*
Her virgin bosom swell;
Such thoughts to Lucy I will give
While she and I together live
Here in this happy dell.'° *forest clearing*

Thus Nature spake — The work was done —
How soon my Lucy's race was run!
She died, and left to me
This heath,° this calm, and quiet scene; *moor*
This memory of what has been,
And never more will be.

Contextual notes

This poem is interesting for its presentation both of Nature and the feminine. One of the basic principles of Romantic poetry was to place the poet as a first-person speaker ('I') reflecting on the comfort and inspiration of Nature — which was invariably given female characteristics. The poem would often go on to establish a relationship between the male poet and female Nature. (This meant that it was difficult at first for women to write Romantic poetry, as they found themselves in the awkward position of being both speaker [subject] and spoken about [object]. Later, however, many Victorian women poets were to ingeniously adapt the Romantic formula for writing nature poetry. You might want to look at Dickinson's 'I Taste a Liquor Never Brewed' [p.100] for an example of a startlingly unusual 'Nature poem'.)

In this poem, Wordsworth takes a female figure and Nature and describes how one is absorbed into the other; at the end of the poem we realize that it also functions as an elegy.* It is this use of natural imagery as a convention of mourning that we see Rossetti's speaker rejecting in 'Song' (p. 103). A number of poems in this anthology make powerful or innovative use of this tradition, nevertheless; see Tennyson's 'It is the day when he was born' and 'Thy voice is on the rolling air' (pp. 86–87), Hardy's 'The Voice' (p. 106), and Cope's 'The Flying Fish' (p. 171). Can you find any others?

Composed upon Westminster Bridge,[1] September 3, 1802

Earth has not anything to show more fair:
Dull would he be of soul who could pass by
A sight so touching in its majesty:
This City now doth, like a garment, wear
The beauty of the morning; silent, bare,
Ships, towers, domes, theatres, and temples lie
Open unto the fields, and to the sky;
All bright and glittering in the smokeless air.
Never did sun more beautifully steep
In his first splendour, valley, rock, or hill;
Ne'er saw I, never felt, a calm so deep!
The river glideth at his own sweet will:
Dear God! the very houses seem asleep;
And all that mighty heart is lying still!

Comparison

This poem is in sharp contrast to Blake's 'London' (p. 57). Nevertheless, together they encompass the main characteristics of much Romantic poetry; a passionate concern for justice and a deep emotional and even spiritual response to spectacles of beauty.

1 *Central bridge over the Thames river in London.*

I Wandered Lonely as a Cloud

I wandered lonely as a cloud
That floats on high o'er vales and hills,
When all at once I saw a crowd,
A host, of golden daffodils;
Beside the lake, beneath the trees,
Fluttering and dancing in the breeze.

Continuous as the stars that shine
And twinkle on the milky way,[1]
They stretched in never-ending line
Along the margin of a bay:
Ten thousand saw I at a glance,
Tossing their heads in sprightly° dance. *lively*

The waves beside them danced; but they
Out-did the sparkling waves in glee:
A poet could not but be gay,
In such a jocund° company: *jolly*
I gazed — and gazed — but little thought
What wealth the show to me had brought:

For oft,° when on my couch I lie *often*
In vacant or in pensive mood,
They flash upon that inward eye
Which is the bliss of solitude;
And then my heart with pleasure fills,
And dances with the daffodils.

Contextual notes

Although in recent times the intense romanticism of this poem has sometimes been mocked, it is a classic example of how the Romantic philosophy of beauty in Nature operates. The poet sees a vision of natural beauty which he mentally photographs and describes in a poem. This image of beauty is then recalled at later moments to induce happiness. (In order to fully appreciate this poem, it is necessary to know that the part of the stem to which the daffodil flower is attached is very flexible; the flower thus bobs and 'dances' up and down in the slightest breeze.)

Another interesting fact about this poem is that it is one which Wordsworth 'plagiarized' from his sister Dorothy's diary. She would

1 *Broad, dense band of stars.*

often write vivid prose descriptions of beautiful sights she had seen and show these to her brother; he would then sometimes rewrite her piece in the form of a poem. Scholars have recently begun to investigate the extent to which she was a 'co-author' of some of Wordsworth's more famous poems.

London, 1802

Milton! thou should'st be living at this hour:
England hath need of thee: she is a fen° *marsh, bog*
Of stagnant waters; altar, sword, and pen,
Fireside, the heroic wealth of hall and bower,° *enclosed garden*
Have forfeited their ancient English dower° *dowry, heritage*
Of inward happiness. We are selfish men;
Oh! raise us up, return to us again;
And give us manners, virtue, freedom, power.
Thy soul was like a Star, and dwelt apart;
Thou hadst a voice whose sound was like the sea:
Pure as the naked heavens, majestic, free,
So didst thou travel on life's common way,
In cheerful godliness; and yet thy heart
The lowliest duties on herself did lay.

Contextual notes

This address to Milton (see p. 42) is written as a sonnet,* perhaps in honour of Milton's mastery of that form. (After Milton's death, the sonnet form was hardly used until the Romantic poets revived it.) This poem refers not only to the morally compromised and cynical politics of the day, but attempts to link Milton's belief that the poet had a moral duty to society with the Romantic view that the poet's vocation was to reveal truth to the world.

Samuel Taylor Coleridge (1772 – 1834)

Coleridge was a gifted but tormented person. Although he was a brilliant student at Cambridge University, his academic career was wrecked by drink, involvement in revolutionary politics and turbulent affairs. Later he became addicted to opium, quarrelled with his close friends, struggled with depression, and marred his marriage by falling hopelessly in love with another woman. He was nevertheless both politically active and a prolific writer. He was one of the greatest literary critics and poets of his age. He enjoyed creative friendships with a number of other writers, including Wordsworth, under whose influence he wrote his best poetry. No matter how chaotic Coleridge's personal affairs became, he remained energetic throughout his life, and was to significantly influence a band of younger writers (including Byron).

Kubla Khan

In Xanadu did Kubla Khan[1]
A stately pleasure-dome decree:
Where Alph, the sacred river, ran
Through caverns measureless to man
    Down to a sunless sea.
So twice five miles of fertile ground
With walls and towers were girdled° round: *encircled*
And there were gardens bright with sinuous rills,° *streams*
Where blossomed many an incense-bearing tree;
And here were forests ancient as the hills,
Enfolding sunny spots of greenery.

But oh! that deep romantic chasm which slanted
Down the green hill athwart° a cedarn° cover! *across / cedar*
A savage place! as holy and enchanted
As e'er beneath a waning moon was haunted
By woman wailing for her demon-lover!
And from this chasm, with ceaseless turmoil seething,
As if this earth in fast thick pants were breathing,
A mighty fountain momently° was forced: *at intervals*
Amid whose swift half-intermitted burst
Huge fragments vaulted like rebounding hail,
Or chaffy grain beneath the thresher's flail:
And 'mid these dancing rocks at once and ever

1 *Kubla was the first Mongol ruler, or 'Khan' of China. Coleridge invents the name of the capital city, calling it 'Xanadu'.*

It flung up momently the sacred river.
Five miles meandering with a mazy motion
Through wood and dale° the sacred river ran, *valley*
Then reached the caverns measureless to man,
And sank in tumult to a lifeless ocean:
And 'mid this tumult Kubla heard from far
Ancestral voices prophesying war!

The shadow of the dome of pleasure
Floated midway on the waves;
Where was heard the mingled measure
From the fountain and the caves.
It was a miracle of rare device,
A sunny pleasure-dome with caves of ice!

A damsel with a dulcimer° *harp*
In a vision once I saw:
It was an Abyssinian maid,
And on her dulcimer she played,
Singing of Mount Abora.[2]
Could I revive within me
Her symphony and song,
To such a deep delight 'twould win me,
That with music loud and long,
I would build that dome in air,
That sunny dome! those caves of ice!
And all who heard should see them there,
And all should cry, Beware! Beware!
His flashing eyes, his floating hair!

Weave a circle round him thrice,
And close your eyes with holy dread,
For he on honey-dew hath fed,
And drunk the milk of Paradise.

Contextual notes

This extraordinary fantasy was 'revealed' to the poet during a hallucination or dream induced by opium. It is apparently only part of what was meant to be a much longer work; Coleridge himself describes how, while writing down his vision, he was interrupted by a visitor; after their business was completed, the poet tried to continue, only to discover that he could no longer recall his dream.

2 *Possible reference to Amara, supposed to be the location of paradise.*

George Gordon, Lord Byron (1788 – 1824)

Byron was one of the rare poets who achieved fame (or perhaps notoriety) in his own lifetime. While young, he established himself both as a promising politician and as the leader of the younger generation of Romantic poets, who wrote passionate poetry and cultivated defiant and glamorous images, rather like rock stars of the twentieth century. He had several theatrical affairs, but went too far when he fell in love with his half-sister. After she gave birth to a child, public outrage and his own bitterness forced him to leave England. He stayed with the Shelleys in Switzerland and travelled in Italy, continuing to write innovative and daring poetry while living as riotously as ever. He died (in appropriately dramatic circumstances) while fighting alongside Greek nationalists in their struggle for independence from the Turks.

When We Two Parted

When we two parted
In silence and tears,
Half broken-hearted
To sever° for years, *cut, separate*
Pale grew thy cheek and cold,
Colder thy kiss;
Truly that hour foretold
Sorrow to this.

The dew of the morning
Sunk chill on my brow —
It felt like the warning
Of what I feel now.
Thy vows are all broken,
And light° is thy fame; *cheap*
I hear thy name spoken,
And share in its shame.

They name thee before me,
A knell to mine ear;
A shudder comes o'er me —
Why wert thou so dear?
They know not I knew thee,
Who knew thee too well: —
Long, long shall I rue° thee, *regret*
Too deeply to tell.

In secret we met —
    In silence I grieve,
That thy heart could forget,
    Thy spirit deceive.
If I should meet thee
    After long years,
How should I greet thee?
    With silence and tears.

Percy Bysshe Shelley (1792 – 1822)

Shelley, whose poetry combines lyricism with passion, was a born rebel. He was expelled from Oxford for writing a pamphlet on the need for atheism; next he eloped with a girl of sixteen. A vegetarian and political radical, he led a nomadic life as a writer before abandoning his family to run away to Europe with seventeen-year-old Mary Godwin (daughter of the feminist writer Mary Wollstonecraft). He later married her, after his first wife committed suicide. Together with Byron, they were part of a circle of eccentric but creative artists. (Mary was the author of the famous horror novel Frankenstein.*) Because of Shelley's infidelities, his marriage became increasingly unhappy. He drowned at the age of 29, while deliberately sailing during a storm.*

Ozymandias[1]

I met a traveller from an antique land
Who said: Two vast and trunkless legs of stone
Stand in the desert . . . Near them, on the sand,
Half sunk, a shattered visage° lies, whose frown, *face*
And wrinkled lip, and sneer of cold command,
Tell that its sculptor well those passions read° *understood*
Which yet survive, stamped on these lifeless things,
The hand that mocked them, and the heart that fed:
And on the pedestal these words appear:
My name is Ozymandias, king of kings:
Look on my works, ye Mighty, and despair!
Nothing beside remains. Round the decay
Of that colossal wreck, boundless and bare
The lone and level sands stretch far away.

1 *Greek name for the Egyptian king Ramses II, who had a huge statue of himself built as a monument to his power.*

England in 1819

An old, mad, blind, despised, and dying king, —
Princes, the dregs of their dull race, who flow
Through public scorn, — mud from a muddy spring, —
Rulers who neither see, nor feel, nor know,
But leech-like to their fainting country cling,
Till they drop, blind in blood, without a blow, —
A people starved and stabbed in the untilled° field, — *unploughed*
An army, which liberticide[1] and prey
Makes as a two-edged sword to all who wield, —
Golden and sanguine° laws which tempt and slay; *bloody*
Religion Christless, Godless — a book sealed;
A Senate, — Time's worst statute° unrepealed[2], — *law*
Are graves, from which a glorious Phantom° may *spirit, ghost*
Burst, to illumine our tempestuous day.

Contextual notes

Here Shelley expresses his scorn at the political state of England, seventeen years after Wordsworth wrote a similar sonnet* (see p. 67). The 'dying king' is George III, one of the Hanoverian (German) line of kings which had been installed on the English throne in the eighteenth century. He was insane, and in the final years of his life his sons, the 'princes' (who were neither popular nor respected), had to manage the affairs of state.

1 *Destruction of liberty.*
2 *Probably the Act of Union, which legally bound Ireland under English rule.*

John Keats (1795 – 1821)

As a young man Keats studied medicine and became a licensed chemist, a career he gave up to concentrate on poetry. Although he moved in circles that included Shelley and Wordsworth, his writing was denounced by critics. In spite of financial difficulties, he continued writing significant amounts of poetry, which subsequently earned him a reputation as one of the greatest younger Romantic poets. After nursing his brother, who subsequently died of tuberculosis, Keats also contracted the disease. His deteriorating health eventually drove him to the warmer climate of Italy, where he died at the age of 26.

When I Have Fears That I May Cease To Be

When I have fears that I may cease to be
Before my pen has glean'd° my teeming brain, *harvested*
Before high piled books, in charactry,° *letters of the alphabet*
Hold like rich garners° the full ripen'd grain; *storehouses*
When I behold, upon the night's starr'd face,
Huge cloudy symbols of a high romance,
And think that I may never live to trace
Their shadows, with the magic hand of chance;
And when I feel, fair creature of an hour,
That I shall never look upon thee more,
Never have relish in the fairy° power *magic*
Of unreflecting love; — then on the shore
Of the wide world I stand alone, and think
Till love and fame to nothingness do sink.

Contextual notes

Keats wrote this in 1818, the same year that he was diagnosed as having tuberculosis. His response was to spend this year engrossed in intense creative and romantic activity, writing some of his best poetry; he also became engaged.

La Belle Dame Sans Merci[1]

O, what can ail thee, knight-at-arms,
  Alone and palely loitering?
The sedge° has withered from the lake *reed-like grass*
  And no birds sing!

O, what can ail thee, knight-at-arms,
  So haggard and so woe-begone?
The squirrel's granary is full,
  And the harvest's done.

I see a lily on thy brow,
  With anguish moist and fever dew
And on thy cheek a fading rose
  Fast withereth too.

I met a lady in the meads,° *meadows*
  Full beautiful, a fairy's child,
Her hair was long, her foot was light,
  And her eyes were wild.

I made a garland for her head,
  And bracelets too, and fragrant zone;° *belt of flowers*
She looked at me as she did love,
  And made sweet moan.

I set her on my pacing steed,
  And nothing else saw all day long;
For sidelong would she bend, and sing
  A fairy's song.

She found me roots of relish sweet,
  And honey wild, and manna° dew; *bread-like*
And sure in language strange she said,
  'I love thee true.'

She took me to her elfin grot,° *cave*
  And there she wept, and sighed full sore,
And there I shut her wild, wild eyes
  With kisses four.

1 *French for 'The beautiful woman without pity'.*

And there she lulléd me asleep,
  And there I dreamed — Ah! woe betide! —
The latest° dream I ever dreamed *last*
  On the cold hill side.

I saw pale kings, and princes too,
  Pale warriors, death-pale were they all;
They cried — 'La belle dame sans merci
  Hath thee in thrall!'° *hypnotized, enslaved*

I saw their starved lips in the gloam° *dusk*
  With horrid warning gapéd wide,
And I awoke, and found me here
  On the cold hill's side.

And this is why I sojourn° here, *stay*
  Alone and palely loitering,
though the sedge is withered from the lake,
  And no birds sing.

Suggestions for discussion

1. Here the poet sets out to create a 'medieval' atmosphere. Much Romantic (and later, Victorian) art attempted a nostalgic recreation of medieval culture. To begin with, the poem takes the form of a ballad.* How do we know this? What other 'medieval' features are used?
2. How does the question and answer format function in the poem? (Note how the tone of the poem is set by the very first question in the opening two lines. We do not expect a cheerful answer!)
3. How are natural phenomena used in the first few stanzas to suggest atmosphere or mood? What exact atmosphere is created?
4. Would you agree that while the mood of the poem is melancholy, eerie and even threatening, it cannot be described as stark or harsh? Why not? What sensual or attractive elements are found in the poem?
5. The poem clearly deals with a supernatural occurrence. What does this contribute to tone and mood?
6. The poet's description of the fatal consequences of enchantment could well be operating on two different levels. What warning signs does the mesmerized knight ignore?

Ode on a Grecian Urn° *vase*

Thou still unravish'd bride of quietness,
Thou foster-child of silence and slow time,
Sylvan° historian, who canst thus express *pastoral*
A flowery tale more sweetly than our rhyme:
What leaf-fring'd legend haunts about thy shape
Of deities° or mortals, or of both, *gods*
In Tempe or the dales of Arcady?[2]
What men or gods are these? What maidens loth°? *reluctant*
What mad pursuit? What struggle to escape?
What pipes and timbrels?° What wild ecstasy? *tambourines*

Heard melodies are sweet, but those unheard
Are sweeter; therefore, ye soft pipes, play on;
Not to the sensual ear, but, more endear'd,
Pipe to the spirit ditties° of no tone: *tunes*
Fair youth, beneath the trees, thou canst not leave
Thy song, nor ever can those trees be bare;
Bold lover, never, never canst thou kiss,
Though winning near the goal — yet, do not grieve;
She cannot fade, though thou hast not thy bliss,
For ever wilt thou love, and she be fair!

Ah, happy, happy boughs! that cannot shed
Your leaves, nor ever bid the spring adieu;
And, happy melodist, unwearièd,
For ever piping songs for ever new;
More happy love! more happy, happy love!
For ever warm and still to be enjoy'd,
For ever panting, and for ever young;
All breathing human passion far above,
That leaves a heart high-sorrowful and cloy'd,° *sickened with excess*
A burning forehead, and a parching tongue.

Who are these coming to the sacrifice?
To what green altar, O mysterious priest,
Lead'st thou that heifer° lowing at the skies, *young cow*
And all her silken flanks with garlands drest?
What little town by river or sea shore,
Or mountain-built with peaceful citadel,° *fortress, tower*
Is emptied of this folk, this pious morn?
And, little town, thy streets for evermore
Will silent be; and not a soul to tell
Why thou art desolate, can e'er return.

2 *Tempe and Arcady were places of ideal pastoral beauty in ancient Greece.*

O Attic° shape! Fair attitude! with brede° *Greek / pattern*
Of marble men and maidens overwrought,° *decorated*
With forest branches and the trodden weed;
Thou, silent form, dost tease us out of thought
As doth eternity: Cold Pastoral!
When old age shall this generation waste,
Thou shalt remain, in midst of other woe
Than ours, a friend to man, to whom thou say'st,
'Beauty is truth, truth beauty,' — that is all
Ye know on earth, and all ye need to know.

Contextual notes

There was considerable interest in classical art and 'ruins' among young artists and writers of this time. The ancient Greeks were revered for their literary and cultural achievements in much Romantic and Victorian poetry.

Elizabeth Barrett Browning (1806 – 1861)

Barrett was a childhood prodigy who learnt from reputable scholars and tutors. She was troubled by ill-health, and her invalid status meant that she was able to concentrate on her writing and studies. She established a secret romantic correspondence with Robert Browning, and eventually eloped with him, against the wishes of her tyrannical father. They lived in Italy until her death, and were extremely happy together. Although her poetry was initially so popular that she was considered for the position of Poet Laureate, she was subsequently attacked for the political and social criticism she voiced in her later poems. The subjects she dealt with in these poems (child labour, slavery, rape, prostitution, illegitimacy, politics and nationalism) were considered to be scandalously inappropriate for a woman writer.

From A Curse For a Nation

Prologue

I heard an angel speak last night,
And he said 'Write!
Write a Nation's curse for me,
And send it over the Western Sea.'

I faltered, taking up the word:
'Not so, my lord!
If curses must be, choose another
To send thy curse against my brother.

'For I am bound by gratitude,
By love and blood,
To brothers of mine across the sea,
Who stretch out kindly hands to me.'

'Therefore,' the voice said, 'shalt thou write.
My curse to-night.
From the summits of love a curse is driven,
As lightning is from the tops of heaven.'

'Not so,' I answered. 'Evermore
My heart is sore
For my own land's sins: for little feet
Of children bleeding along the street:

'For parked-up honours that gainsay° — *deny, contradict*
The right of way:
For almsgiving° through a door that is — *charity*
Not open enough for two friends to kiss:

'For love of freedom which abates
Beyond the Straits:[1]
For patriot virtue starved to vice on
Self-praise, self-interest, and suspicion:

'For an oligarchic° parliament, — *government by a few*
And bribes well-meant.
What curse to another land assign,
When heavy-souled for the sins of mine?'

'Therefore,' the voice said, 'shalt thou write
My curse to-night.
Because thou hast strength to see and hate
A foul thing done *within* thy gate.'

'Not so,' I answered once again.
'To curse, choose men.
For I, a woman, have only known
How the heart melts and the tears run down.'

'Therefore,' the voice said, 'shalt thou write
My curse to-night.
Some women weep and curse, I say
(And no one marvels), night and day.

'And thou shalt take their part to-night,
Weep and write.
A curse from the depths of womanhood
Is very salt, and bitter, and good.'

So thus I wrote, and mourned indeed,
What all may read.
And thus, as was enjoined on me,
I send it over the Western Sea.

1 *The English Channel, which separates Britain from continental Europe.*

Contextual notes

It is not certain precisely which country the speaker in the poem is being urged to curse. Barrett Browning was a passionate supporter of Italian nationalism, and its democratic movements which were then being ruthlessly suppressed, and it is possible that Italy is her target; the reference to the 'Western Sea' also suggests the United States, at that stage bitterly divided and on the verge of a tragic and brutal civil war over the issue of slavery. However, it is ultimately the indictment of England in stanzas five to eight that gives this piece its power.

Henry Wadsworth Longfellow (1807 – 1882)

An American, Longfellow studied in Europe before becoming a professor at Harvard University. His long narrative poems (such as 'The Song of Hiawatha') were hugely popular both at home and abroad, and he became the most famous American poet of his time. He was widowed twice, and his work became increasingly poignant in his old age.

Chaucer

An old man in a lodge within a park;
    The chamber walls depicted all around
    With portraitures° of huntsman, hawk, and hound, *pictures*
    And the hurt deer. He listeneth to the lark,
Whose song comes with the sunshine through the dark
    Of painted glass in leaden lattice° bound; *bars or strips of lead*
    He listeneth and he laugheth at the sound,
    Then writeth in a book like any clerk.° *scholar*
He is the poet of the dawn, who wrote
    The Canterbury Tales, and his old age
Made beautiful with song; and as I read
I hear the crowing cock, I hear the note
    Of lark and linnet,° and from every page *type of bird*
    Rise odours of ploughed field or flowery mead.

Contextual notes

This is one of a series of sonnets that Longfellow wrote celebrating the great writers (see pp. 4–8 for details of Chaucer's life and extracts from *The Canterbury Tales*.) Try to identify what aspects of Chaucer's writing Longfellow imitates to add flavour to his description.

Alfred, Lord Tennyson (1809 – 1892)

Tennyson studied at Cambridge University, where he was befriended by Arthur Hallam, a brilliant young man whose early death was to profoundly affect Tennyson. His attempts to come to terms with this loss led to his In Memoriam *poems, which were to establish his fame. He became enormously popular during his lifetime, eventually holding the position of Poet Laureate for 42 years. His public status was at odds with his melancholy nature; he delayed marriage to his fiancée for over a decade, fearing possible mental illness and experiencing religious doubts. Nevertheless, he became probably the most respected figure in Victorian literature, and was granted a title by Queen Victoria. He was particularly admired for his technically polished poetry, noteworthy for its mastery of sound (his poems must be read aloud) and often dreamlike, nostalgic quality.*

Ulysses[1]

It little profits that an idle king,
By this still hearth, among these barren crags,
Matched with an agèd wife, I mete° and dole° *give out / distribute*
Unequal laws unto a savage race,
That hoard, and sleep, and feed, and know not me.
I cannot rest from travel: I will drink
Life to the lees:° all times I have enjoyed *sediment of wine*
Greatly, have suffered greatly, both with those
That loved me, and alone; on shore, and when
Through scudding drifts the rainy Hyades[2]
Vext the dim sea: I am become a name;
For always roaming with a hungry heart
Much have I seen and known; cities of men
And manners, climates, councils, governments,
Myself not least, but honoured of them all;
And drunk delight of battle with my peers,
Far on the ringing plains of windy Troy.[3]
I am part of all that I have met;
Yet all experience is an arch wherethrough
Gleams that untravelled world, whose margin fades
For ever and for ever when I move.

1 *Roman name for Odysseus, the Greek hero of Homer's* Odyssey.

2 *Group of stars; their rising was thought to herald rain.*

3 *Scene of the Trojan War, an epic battle described in Homer's* Iliad.

How dull it is to pause, to make an end,
To rust unburnished,° not to shine in use! *unpolished*
As tho' to breathe were life. Life piled on life
Were all too little, and of one to me
Little remains: but every hour is saved
From that eternal silence, something more,
A bringer of new things; and vile it were
For some three suns to store and hoard myself,
And this gray spirit yearning in desire
To follow knowledge like a sinking star,
Beyond the utmost bound of human thought.
    This is my son, mine own Telemachus,
To whom I leave the sceptre[4] and the isle —
Well-loved of me, discerning to fulfil
This labour, by slow prudence to make mild
A rugged people, and through soft degrees
Subdue them to the useful and the good.
Most blameless is he, centred in the sphere
Of common duties, decent not to fail
In offices of tenderness, and pay
Meet° adoration to my household gods, *fitting*
When I am gone. He works his work, I mine.
    There lies the port; the vessel puffs her sail:
There gloom the dark broad seas. My mariners,
Souls that have toiled, and wrought, and thought with me —
That ever with a frolic welcome took
The thunder and the sunshine, and opposed
Free hearts, free foreheads — you and I are old;
Old age hath yet his honour and his toil;
Death closes all: but something ere the end,
Some work of noble note, may yet be done,
Not unbecoming men that strove with gods.
The lights begin to twinkle from the rocks:
The long day wanes: the slow moon climbs: the deep
Moans round with many voices. Come, my friends,
'Tis not too late to seek a newer world.
Push off, and sitting well in order smite
The sounding furrows;[5] for my purpose holds
To sail beyond the sunset, and the baths
Of all the western stars, until I die.

4 *Staff; symbol of royalty and authority.*

5 *This image refers to rowing through waves.*

It may be that the gulfs will wash us down:
It may be we shall touch the Happy Isles,[6]
And see the great Achilles,[7] whom we knew.
Though much is taken, much abides; and though
We are not now that strength which in old days
Moved earth and heaven; that which we are, we are;
One equal temper of heroic hearts,
made weak by time and fate, but strong in will
To strive, to seek, to find, and not to yield.

Contextual notes

This poem assumes some knowledge of the works of the classical Greek author Homer. The *Iliad* tells the tale of the Trojan War, topic of many Greek dramas. This was sparked off when the beautiful Helen left her husband, a Greek king, for Paris, the son of the king of Troy. The two kingdoms then fought an epic war, in which the gods actively took part, and deeds of great heroism were done. Odysseus (Ulysses in the poem) was one of generals who fought bravely in this struggle. The *Odyssey* tells of his exciting adventures and explorations on the voyage home after the war.

From IN MEMORIAM A.H.H.

LIV

Oh yet we trust that somehow good
    Will be the final goal of ill,
    To pangs of nature, sins of will,
Defects of doubt, and taints of blood;

That nothing walks with aimless feet;
    That not one life shall be destroy'd,
    Or cast as rubbish to the void,° *emptiness*
When God hath made the pile complete;

That not a worm is cloven° in vain; *cut*
    That not a moth with vain desire
    Is shrivell'd in a fruitless fire,
Or but subserves another's gain.

6 *The Greek Paradise, where the brave and the good lived after death.*

7 *The most heroic of the Greeks killed in the Trojan war.*

Behold, we know not anything;
I can but trust that good shall fall
At last — far off — at last, to all,
And every winter change to spring.

So runs my dream: but what am I?
An infant crying in the night:
An infant crying for the light:
And with no language but a cry.

LV

The wish, that of the living whole
No life may fail beyond the grave,
Derives it not from what we have
The likest God within the soul?

Are God and Nature then at strife,
That Nature lends such evil dreams?
So careful of the type° she seems, *species*
So careless of the single life;

That I, considering everywhere
Her secret meaning in her deeds,
And finding that of fifty seeds,
She often brings but one to bear,

I falter where I firmly trod,
And falling with my weight of cares
Upon the great world's altar-stairs
That slope thro' darkness up to God,

I stretch lame hands of faith, and grope,
And gather dust and chaff, and call
To what I feel is Lord of all,
And faintly trust the larger hope.

LVI

'So careful of the type?' but no.
From scarpèd° cliff and quarried stone *steep*
She cries, 'A thousand types are gone:
I care for nothing, all shall go.

'Thou makest thine appeal to me:
I bring to life, I bring to death:
The spirit does but mean the breath:
I know no more.' And he, shall he,

Man, her last work, who seem'd so fair,
Such splendid purpose in his eyes,
Who roll'd the psalm to wintry skies,
Who built him fanes° of fruitless prayer, *temples*

Who trusted God was love indeed
And love Creation's final law—
Tho' Nature, red in tooth and claw
With ravine,° shriek'd against his creed— *bloodshed*

Who loved, who suffer'd countless ills,
Who battled for the True, the Just,
Be blown about the desert dust,
Or seal'd within the iron hills?

No more? A monster then, a dream,
A discord. Dragons of the prime,
That tare° each other in their slime, *tear*
Were mellow music match'd with him.

O life as futile, then, as frail!
O for thy voice to soothe and bless!
What hope of answer, or redress?
Behind the veil, behind the veil.

CVII

It is the day when he was born,
A bitter day that early sank
Behind a purple-frosty bank
Of vapour, leaving night forlorn.

The time admits not flowers or leaves
To deck the banquet. Fiercely flies
The blast of North and East, and ice
Makes daggers at the sharpen'd eaves,

And bristles all the brakes° and thorns *thicket*
To yon hard crescent, as she hangs
Above the wood which grides° and clangs *grinds*
Its leafless ribs and iron horns

Together, in the drifts that pass
    To darken on the rolling brine
    That breaks the coast. But fetch the wine,
Arrange the board and brim the glass;

Bring in great logs and let them lie,
    To make a solid core of heat;
    Be cheerful-minded, talk and treat
Of all things ev'n as he were by;

We keep the day. With festal° cheer, *festive*
    With books and music, surely we
    Will drink to him, whate'er he be,
And sing the songs he loved to hear.

CXXX

Thy voice is on the rolling air;
    I hear thee where the waters run;
    Thou standest in the rising sun,
And in the setting thou art fair.

What art thou then? I cannot guess;
    But tho' I seem in star and flower
    To feel thee some diffusive power,
I do not therefore love thee less:

My love involves the love before;
    My love is vaster passion now;
    Tho' mix'd with God and Nature thou,
I seem to love thee more and more.

Far off thou art, but ever nigh;
    I have thee still, and I rejoice;
    I prosper, circled with thy voice;
I shall not lose thee tho' I die.

Contextual notes

These poems are taken from a series that Tennyson wrote in memory of his closest friend, Arthur Henry Hallam, who died tragically young while on a trip to Europe. Tennyson's efforts to make sense of his loss coincided with the publication of Darwin's biological theories on evolution. These argued for a natural, rather than divine origin of the human species, which caused initial consternation and even scandal, before gaining acceptance.

Suggestions for discussion

1. The original series of poems (over 130 of them) show a progression of emotions, which we have tried to reflect in this selection. What emotional shifts do you notice between the poems? What 'emotional journey' does the speaker make? (You may find it helpful to consider what emotional stages usually follow a loss or bereavement. Can you identify any of these here?)
2. The punctuation in all these poems is used simply but effectively to underscore the emotional progress of the speaker. How is this accomplished? Look at where the question marks, colons and dashes occur, and what effect they have; also check where sentences end.
3. In the third poem (LVI), the first stanza refers to cliffs and quarries, then popular sites for the new craze of fossil collecting. How does this allusion to fossilized and extinct species work in conjunction with the rest of this poem?
4. Still referring to poem LVI, who or what does the 'She' in line 3 refer to? What conclusions can you draw about the impact of evolutionary theories on the Romantic view of Nature?
5. There is a distinct shift in the way that Nature is used as a vehicle for the poet's feelings in the last three poems. What is the difference between poem LVI and poem CVII in this respect? And what has happened by the time we reach poem CXXX, which is one of the last poems in the series? Does anything in this poem remind you of Wordsworth's 'Three Years She Grew' (see p. 63)? What does this suggest about Tennyson's final resolution of his grief?
6. Although the poems express very different feelings and use contrasting language and imagery, the series as a whole has a unified and cohesive feel to it. What structural features do all the poems share?

Mariana

Mariana in the moated grange[8]
— MEASURE FOR MEASURE

With blackest moss the flower-plots
Were thickly crusted, one and all:
The rusted nails fell from the knots
That held the pear to the gable-wall.
The broken sheds looked sad and strange:
Unlifted was the clinking latch;
Weeded and worn the ancient thatch
Upon the lonely moated grange.° *country house*
She only said, 'My life is dreary,
He cometh not,' she said;
She said, 'I am aweary, aweary,
I would that I were dead!'

Her tears fell with the dews at even;° *evening*
Her tears fell ere the dews were dried;
She could not look on the sweet heaven,
Either at morn or eventide.
After the flitting of the bats,
When thickest dark did trance the sky,
She drew her casement-curtain by,
And glanced athwart° the glooming flats. *across*
She only said, 'The night is dreary,
He cometh not,' she said;
She said, 'I am aweary, aweary,
I would that I were dead!'

Upon the middle of the night,
Waking she heard the night-fowl crow;
The cock sung out an hour ere light:
From the dark fen° the oxen's low *marsh, bog*
Came to her; without hope of change,
In sleep she seemed to walk forlorn,
Till cold winds woke the gray-eyed morn
About the lonely moated grange.
She only said, 'The day is dreary,
He cometh not,' she said;
She said, 'I am aweary, aweary,
I would that I were dead!'

8 *Mariana, a character in Shakespeare's* Measure for Measure, *was abandoned by her faithless lover.*

About a stone-cast from the wall
A sluice° with blackened waters slept *ditch*
And o'er it many, round and small,
The clustered marish°-mosses crept. *marsh*
Hard by a poplar shook alway,
All silver-green with gnarlèd bark:
For leagues no other tree did mark
The level waste, the rounding gray.
She only said, 'My life is dreary,
He cometh not,' she said;
She said, 'I am aweary, aweary,
I would that I were dead!'

And ever when the moon was low,
And the shrill winds were up and away,
In the white curtain, to and fro,
She saw the gusty shadow sway.
But when the moon was very low,
And wild winds bound within their cell,[9]
The shadow of the poplar fell
Upon her bed, across her brow.
She only said, 'The night is dreary,
He cometh not,' she said;
She said, 'I am aweary, aweary,
I would that I were dead!'

All day within the dreamy house,
The doors upon their hinges creaked;
The blue fly sung in the pane; the mouse
Behind the mouldering wainscot° shrieked, *board which lines wall*
Or from the crevice peered about.
Old faces glimmered through the doors,
Old footsteps trod the upper floors,
Old voices called her from without.
She only said, 'My life is dreary,
He cometh not,' she said;
She said, 'I am aweary, aweary,
I would that I were dead!'

9 *The cave in which the winds were kept, according to legend.*

The sparrow's chirrup on the roof,
The slow clock ticking, and the sound
Which to the wooing wind aloof
The poplar made, did all confound
Her sense; but most she loathed the hour
When the thick-moted[1] sunbeam lay
Athwart the chambers, and the day
Was sloping toward his western bower.
Then, said she, 'I am very dreary,
He will not come,' she said;
She wept, 'I am aweary, aweary,
Oh God, that I were dead!'

Contextual notes

In an age that saw the first drive towards legal emancipation for women, and the increasing participation of women in public spheres of life, Victorian art veered towards presenting women in enclosed environments. Paintings and poems which showed women in towers, chapels, small rooms, bowers, on balconies, gazing out of windows (and sometimes even tied or chained up), invariably had a nostalgic and even glamorous quality; they evoked a sense of a bygone or magical past. Although this poem describes a woman's misery, the atmosphere it evokes, while melancholy, is definitely not unpleasant. A famous artist, Millais, used this poem as a guide in creating a remarkably beautiful and sensual painting entitled 'Mariana'.

1 *Dense with dust.*

Robert Browning (1812 – 1889)

Browning received an unusual education centred on his father's vast library, and started to write poetry at an early age. On reading Elizabeth Barrett's poems, he began a correspondence with her that led to their secret engagement and subsequent elopement to Italy. After the death of his wife, Browning returned to London and became a well-known figure on the English literary scene. His contemporaries sometimes considered his poetry eccentric; others admired it for its ability to catch the flavour and rhythm of everyday speech. He is best remembered for his dramatic monologues, of which 'My Last Duchess' is an excellent example.*

My Last Duchess

Ferrara

That's my last Duchess painted on the wall,
Looking as if she were alive. I call
That piece a wonder, now: Frà° Pandolf's hands — *friar, brother*
Worked busily a day, and there she stands.
Will't please you sit and look at her? I said
'Frà Pandolf' by design, for never read
Strangers like you that pictured countenance,
The depth and passion of its earnest glance,
But to myself they turned (since none puts by
The curtain I have drawn for you, but I)
And seemed as they would ask me, if they durst,° — *dared*
How such a glance came there; so, not the first
Are you to turn and ask thus. Sir, 't was not
Her husband's presence only, called that spot
Of joy into the Duchess' cheek: perhaps
Frà Pandolf chanced to say 'Her mantle° laps — *cloak*
Over my lady's wrist too much,' or 'Paint
Must never hope to reproduce the faint
Half-flush that dies along her throat:' such stuff
Was courtesy, she thought, and cause enough
For calling up that spot of joy. She had
A heart — how shall I say? — too soon made glad,
Too easily impressed; she liked whate'er
She looked on, and her looks went everywhere.
Sir, 't was all one! My favour at her breast,
The dropping of the daylight in the West,

The bough of cherries some officious° fool *busy*
Broke in the orchard for her, the white mule
She rode with round the terrace — all and each
Would draw from her alike the approving speech,
Or blush, at least. She thanked men, — good! but thanked
Somehow — I know not how — as if she ranked
My gift of a nine-hundred-years-old name
With anybody's gift. Who'd stoop to blame
This sort of trifling? Even had you skill
In speech — (which I have not) — to make your will
Quite clear to such an one, and say, 'Just this
Or that in you disgusts me; here you miss,
Or there exceed the mark' — and if she let
Herself be lessoned so, nor plainly set
Her wits to yours, forsooth, and made excuse,
— E'en then would be some stooping; and I choose
Never to stoop. Oh sir, she smiled, no doubt,
Whene'er I passed her; but who passed without
Much the same smile? This grew; I gave commands;
Then all smiles stopped together. There she stands
As if alive. Will't please you rise? We'll meet
The company below, then. I repeat,
The Count your master's known munificence° *generosity*
Is ample warrant that no just pretence
Of mine for dowry will be disallowed;
Though his fair daughter's self, as I avowed
At starting, is my object. Nay, we'll go
Together down, sir. Notice Neptune,[1] though,
Taming a sea-horse, thought a rarity,
Which Claus of Innsbruck cast in bronze for me!

Contextual notes

The speaker in this poem, the Duke of Ferrara, lived in the sixteenth century. His first wife died very young in mysterious circumstances. Browning here imagines a conversation that might have taken place during the arrangements for his second marriage, to the Count of Tyrol's daughter. Frà Pandolf is an imaginary name for an artist (his title makes it clear that he is a monk or holy man). Claus of Innsbruck is also a invented name.

1 *God of the sea.*

Suggestions for discussion

1. One of the more interesting features about this dramatic monologue is that there is a significant difference, or 'distance' between the poet and the first-person speaker in the poem. How do we know this, and why is this distance created?
2. Given that the only voice we hear is Ferrara's, do you agree that we 'hear' much more than he is telling us? How does he unwittingly reveal himself?
3. What kind of a character sketch would you make of Ferrara? You might feel that he is more than simply a tyrant. Is there an element of fear in his refusal or inability to communicate?
4. The form of the dramatic monologue makes for a much more immediate impact on the reader. Why is this so? In what way are we invited to become 'part' of the poem?

Emily Brontë (1818 – 1848)

Born into the gifted but doomed Brontë family, Emily, together with her siblings, wrote poetry and fantasy from an early age. Together with her sisters Charlotte and Anne, she published a collection of poems under a pseudonym. Both reclusive and fiercely independent, she worked briefly as a governess to support her brother and father, but became ill with longing for her native countryside and spent the rest of her short life at home. She died of tuberculosis brought on by her own self-neglect. She is best remembered for her extraordinary novel, Wuthering Heights.

No Coward Soul Is Mine

No coward soul is mine,
No trembler in the world's storm-troubled sphere:
I see Heaven's glories shine,
And faith shines equal, arming me from fear.

O God within my breast,
Almighty, ever-present Deity!
Life — that in me has rest,
As I — undying Life — have power in thee!

Vain are the thousand creeds° *beliefs, doctrines*
That move men's hearts: unutterably vain;
Worthless as withered weeds
Or idlest froth amid the boundless main,° *sea*

To waken doubt in one
Holding so fast by thine infinity;
So surely anchored on
The steadfast rock of immortality.

With wide-embracing love
Thy spirit animates eternal years,
Pervades and broods above,
Changes, sustains, dissolves, creates and rears.

Though earth and man were gone,
And suns and universes ceased to be,
And thou were left alone,
Every existence would exist in thee.

There is not room for Death,
Nor atom that his might could render void:° *vacant*
Thou — thou art Being and Breath,
And what thou art may never be destroyed.

Walt Whitman (1819 – 1892)

Whitman broke new ground for American poetry, consciously identifying himself with American culture. He was born on the north-eastern coast of the USA, and spent much of his life wandering from job to job, working as a printer, school teacher and journalist. During the American Civil War (the subject of a collection of his poems) he volunteered to nurse the wounded. His poetry was unusual (and considered shocking in his time) for its courageous acknowledgement of his homosexuality, as well as its fascination with the smaller details of daily life.

When I Heard at the Close of the Day[1]

When I heard at the close of the day how my name had been receiv'd with plaudits in the capitol, still it was not a happy night for me that follow'd,
And else when I carous'd,[2] or when my plans were accomplish'd, still I was not happy,
But the day when I rose at dawn from the bed of perfect health, refresh'd, singing, inhaling the ripe breath of autumn,
When I saw the full moon in the west grow pale and disappear in the morning light,
When I wander'd alone over the beach, and undressing bathed, laughing with the cool waters, and saw the sun rise,
And when I thought how my dear friend my lover was on his way coming, O then I was happy,
O then each breath tasted sweeter, and all that day my food nourish'd me more, and the beautiful day pass'd well,
And the next came with equal joy, and with the next at evening came my friend,
And that night while all was still I heard the waters roll slowly continually up the shores,
I heard the hissing rustle of the liquid and sands as directed to me whispering to congratulate me,
For the one I love most lay sleeping by me under the same cover in the cool night,
In the stillness in the autumn moonbeams his face was inclined toward me,
And his arm lay lightly around my breast — and that night I was happy.

1 *This poem is part of a series which Whitman wrote in celebration of what he referred to as 'manly love'.*

2 *See footnote 2, p. 54.*

Matthew Arnold (1822 – 1888)

The son of a distinguished teacher, Arnold himself became an inspector of schools after graduating from Oxford University. His career gave him considerable insight into the educational, social and cultural problems of his age. His poetry is preoccupied with questions arising from these issues, including the loss of a unifying religious belief. He was happily married, and became a professor of poetry at Oxford. Best known in his time for his thoughtful prose, he became one of the most respected critics of his day.

Dover Beach

The sea is calm to-night.
The tide is full, the moon lies fair
Upon the straits;[1] — on the French coast the light
Gleams and is gone; the cliffs of England stand,
Glimmering and vast, out in the tranquil bay.
Come to the window, sweet is the night-air!
Only, from the long line of spray
Where the sea meets the moon-blanch'd° land, *whitened*
Listen! you hear the grating roar
Of pebbles which the waves draw back, and fling,
At their return, up the high strand,
Begin, and cease, and then again begin,
With tremulous cadence slow, and bring
The eternal note of sadness in.

Sophocles[2] long ago
Heard it on the Aegean,[3] and it brought
Into his mind the turbid° ebb and flow *muddy*
Of human misery; we
Find also in the sound a thought,
Hearing it by this distant northern sea.

1 *Headlands on either side of a channel of water.*

2 *Classical Greek author of tragic dramas; much admired by Arnold.*

3 *Part of the Mediterranean Sea between Greece and Turkey.*

The Sea of Faith
Was once, too, at the full, and round earth's shore
Lay like the folds of a bright girdle° furled. *belt*
But now I only hear
Its melancholy, long, withdrawing roar,
Retreating, to the breath
Of the night-wind, down the vast edges drear
And naked shingles° of the world. *pebble beaches*

Ah, love, let us be true
To one another! for the world, which seems
To lie before us like a land of dreams,
So various, so beautiful, so new,
Hath really neither joy, nor love, nor light,
Nor certitude, nor peace, nor help for pain;
And we are here as on a darkling plain
Swept with confused alarms of struggle and flight,
Where ignorant armies clash by night.

Contextual notes

Dover is a port on the south-east coast of England facing France. It is famous for its white chalk cliffs (their colour explains why Arnold describes them as 'glimmering' in this poem.) These cliffs drop sharply to the beach, which is made up of pebbles. (The sound of waves on pebbles is much louder than on sand.)

Anonymous (*c.* 1850)

Translated by Perce Haslam

Kilaben Bay Song

Hail! Dawn is shining glory doing
The sun shining (blazing with warmth)
Night moving
Man stirring
Children restless
Women fire-wood thinking
Birds singing
Animals awakening (sleeping not)
Camp noise grows
Men bush towards moving
Women water gathering
Children they hungry, all shouting
Women water collected
Men spear fish, return
People all eating
Camp quiet again

COMPARISON

This is a traditional Australian aboriginal song or chant. You may wish to compare it with Watson's 'The Rain that is Male' (p. 259). Both are attempts by modern translators to salvage some fragments of the lost or dying cultures of indigenous peoples subjected to genocide or assimilation.

Emily Dickinson (1830 – 1886)

Dickinson was born and lived in the rural town of Amherst in the north eastern USA. Well educated, she wrote startlingly modern poetry from an early age. Although she initially tried to publish, her friends and literary connections were baffled by her poems, almost none of which were published in her lifetime. As she grew older, she became increasingly reclusive, and eventually refused to meet people or leave her room, although she kept up close and often intimate correspondences with a number of close friends and scholars, including various women writers she admired. After her death, there was considerable argument about the fate of her poems, which were eventually published in a heavily edited and censored form. The originals were only made available in the 1950s; since then, Dickinson's distinctive voice has been much admired by critics. Her poetry has inspired several modern poets; see Adrienne Rich's 'I am in Danger — Sir —' *(p. 200)**.*

I Taste a Liquor Never Brewed

I taste a liquor never brewed —
From Tankards scooped in Pearl —
Not all the Vats upon the Rhine[1]
Yield such an Alcohol!

Inebriate of Air — am I —
And Debauchee[2] of Dew —
Reeling — thro endless summer days —
From inns of Molten Blue —

When 'Landlords' turn the drunken Bee
Out of the Foxglove's door —
When Butterflies — renounce their 'drams'° — *drinks, tots*
I shall but drink the more!

Till Seraphs° swing their snowy Hats — *angels*
And Saints — to windows run —
To see the little Tippler
Leaning against the — Sun —

1 *River in Germany, which runs through a region famous for its vineyards and wine.*

2 *Person addicted to sensual indulgence.*

The Bustle in a House

The Bustle in a House
The Morning after Death
Is solemnest of industries
Enacted upon Earth —

The Sweeping up the Heart
And putting Love away
We shall not want to use again
Until Eternity.

Much Madness Is Divinest Sense

Much Madness is divinest Sense —
To a discerning Eye —
Much Sense — the starkest Madness —
'Tis the Majority
In this, as All, prevail —
Assent — and you are sane —
Demur° — you're straightway dangerous — *disagree*
And handled with a Chain —

Wild Nights — Wild Nights

Wild Nights — Wild Nights!
Were I with thee
Wild Nights should be
Our luxury!

Futile — the Winds —
To a Heart in port —
Done with the Compass —
Done with the Chart!

Rowing in Eden —
Ah, the Sea!
Might I but moor — Tonight —
In Thee!

I Felt a Funeral

I felt a Funeral, in my Brain,
And Mourners to and fro
Kept treading — treading — till it seemed
That Sense was breaking through —

And when they all were seated,
A Service, like a Drum —
Kept beating — beating — till I thought
My Mind was going numb —

And then I heard them lift a Box
And creak across my Soul
With those same Boots of Lead, again,
Then Space — began to toll,

As all the Heavens were a Bell,
And Being, but an Ear,
And I, and Silence, some strange Race
Wrecked, solitary, here —

And then a Plank in Reason, broke,
And I dropped down, and down —
And hit a World, at every plunge,
And Finished knowing — then —

Christina Rossetti (1830 – 1894)

Born into a gifted family, Rossetti spent much of her life submerging her passionate personality in religion, charity work, and the care of her family. She was the younger sister of the flamboyant artist and poet Dante Gabriel Rossetti, and their covert rivalry marked much of her life and work. She occupied an ambivalent position on the edges of the Pre-Raphaelite Brotherhood, a new group of artists and writers, headed by her brother, who wished to return to uncorrupted standards of beauty. She had a clear sense of her poetic vocation, and refused marriage twice (ostensibly for religious reasons) in order to focus on her writing. She was much admired by her contemporaries for the subtlety of her work and the originality of her religious poetry (Gerard Manley Hopkins, as well as many other lesser poets, was influenced by her). Rossetti died of breast cancer.

Song

When I am dead, my dearest,
    Sing no sad songs for me;
Plant thou no roses at my head,
    Nor shady cypress tree:
Be the green grass above me
    With showers and dewdrops wet;
And if thou wilt, remember,
    And if thou wilt, forget.

I shall not see the shadows,
    I shall not feel the rain;
I shall not hear the nightingale
    Sing on, as if in pain:
And dreaming through the twilight
    That doth not rise nor set,
Haply I may remember
    And haply may forget.

COMPARISON

This poem has been linked to 'The Unquiet Grave' (p. 10). If you have not already done so, you might like to read the suggestions for comparison and discussion on p. 12.

In an Artist's Studio

One face looks out from all his canvases,
  One selfsame figure sits or walks or leans:
  We found her hidden just behind those screens,
That mirror gave back all her loveliness.
A queen in opal or in ruby dress,
  A nameless girl in freshest summer-greens,
  A saint, an angel — every canvas means
The same one meaning, neither more nor less.
He feeds upon her face by day and night,
  And she with true kind eyes looks back on him,
Fair as the moon and joyful as the light:
  Not wan with waiting, not with sorrow dim;
Not as she is, but was when hope shone bright;
  Not as she is, but as she fills his dream.

Contextual notes

This poem refers to the relationship between the poet's brother, Dante Gabriel Rossetti, and his model-cum-fiancée, Elizabeth Siddal. The unfortunate Siddal was at first obsessively courted by Dante Gabriel, and modelled for many of his paintings. She lived with him while they were engaged, thus jeopardizing her reputation. Meanwhile he fell in love with another woman, and eventually only married Siddal because he believed she was dying. A year after their marriage, she committed suicide. Rossetti never publicly criticized her brother, but this poem stands as an indictment of his cruelty, as well as an unsentimental view of what it meant to be an artist's model. (She herself had posed for numerous pictures.)

Suggestions for discussion

1. In what way does the poet make clear that the woman in the pictures has been robbed of her own identity? Where exactly is she 'found'? (Look at the nouns in lines 3 and 4. Do you agree that these all suggest two-dimensional images? What effect does this have?)
2. What stereotypes is the model turned into? (Read lines 5 to 7.)
3. What link is there between the paintings and the painter's view of his model? What does this suggest about their relationship? Do you think he actually 'sees' her? What does he see?
4. As can be seen from the contextual notes, this poem has a particular history. Can it possibly succeed without this context? What would its message be in a more general sense?

Thomas Hardy (1840 – 1928)

Hardy was born in Dorset, a beautiful rural county in south-western England, which was to be the setting of most of his works. He studied as an architect and worked in London before returning home to write novels. These were successful enough to enable him to become a full-time writer. He married, but the union was an unhappy one. Although he was admired by society, most critics regarded his novels as gloomy and immoral, and a disillusioned Hardy turned to poetry. His eight volumes of poetry focus on the sufferings and ironies of life and love, but they brought him renewed praise and honours.

Drummer Hodge

They throw in drummer Hodge, to rest
    Uncoffined — just as found:
His landmark is a kopje-°crest — *hill*
    That breaks the veldt° around; — *grassy plain*
And foreign constellations west
    Each night above his mound.

Young Hodge the Drummer never knew —
    Fresh from his Wessex[1] home —
The meaning of the broad Karoo,[2]
    The Bush, the dusty loam,° — *soil*
And why uprose to nightly view
    Strange stars amid the gloam.° — *gloom, dusk*

Yet portion of that unknown plain
    Will Hodge forever be;
His homely Northern breast and brain
    Grow to some Southern tree,
And strange-eyed constellations reign
    His stars eternally.

Contextual notes

This poem, written in 1902, refers to the Anglo-Boer War, fought after the establishment of the Orange Free State and the Transvaal as independent Boer (Afrikaner) republics. South Africa was at that stage a British colony, and although the Boers had moved

1 *Name given by Hardy to his home region of south-west England.*

2 *Dry interior plateau of South Africa.*

('trekked') beyond the reach of the established bounds of the colony, the discovery of gold in the Transvaal meant that Britain mounted two full-scale wars on South African territory to recover the 'republics'. After some initial defeats (mainly due to the guerrilla tactics of the heavily outnumbered Boers), the British crushed the rebels. In the process, they burnt down Boer farms and placed Afrikaner women and children in concentration camps, where many of them died. There was considerable international criticism of England's actions during this time.

Hardy (unlike Schreiner — see p. 111) expresses no strong views in this strangely peaceful poem, which was inspired by the death in the war of a young drummer from the poet's home town.

The Voice

Woman much missed, how you call to me, call to me,
Saying that now you are not as you were
When you had changed from one who was all to me,
But as at first, when our day was fair.

Can it be you that I hear? Let me view you, then,
Standing as when I drew near to the town
Where you would wait for me: yes, as I knew you then,
Even to the original air-blue gown!

Or is it only the breeze, in its listlessness
Travelling across the wet mead to me here,
You being ever dissolved to wan wistlessness,° *unconsciousness*
Heard no more again far or near?

Thus I; faltering forward,
Leaves around me falling,
Wind oozing thin through the thorn from norward,° *northwards*
And the woman calling.

Contextual notes

This poem was written after the death of Hardy's first wife. Although they had been unhappy together, he suffered tremendous remorse and grief after losing her, and expressed these feelings in some of his most moving poems.

In Time of 'The Breaking of Nations'

Only a man harrowing° clods *ploughing*
In a slow silent walk
With an old horse that stumbles and nods
Half asleep as they stalk.

Only thin smoke without flame
From the heaps of couch-grass;
Yet this will go onward the same
Though Dynasties pass.

Yonder a maid and her wight° *man*
Come whispering by:
War's annals° will cloud into night *records*
Ere their story die.

Contextual notes

This poem was written during the First World War (1914–1918), sometimes called the Great War for its magnitude and impact on the social structure of Europe. The loss of life alone was staggering. (See Yeats' 'An Irish Airman Foresees His Death' [p. 118], Owen's poems [pp. 144–145], and Brooke's 'The Soldier' [p. 131] for contrasting views of what it meant to fight in this war.) This poem is a response to the growing feeling that things would never be the same after the war. In a strange way, Hardy was both right and wrong in his predictions in this poem. See whether you agree after you have read the poem.

Gerard Manley Hopkins (1844 – 1889)

Hopkins came from a cultured Anglican family and excelled at Oxford University. Here he met the poet Robert Bridges (who was to preserve and eventually publish much of his friend's work) and became caught up in a new intellectual movement towards the Catholic church. Hopkins converted to Catholicism and decided to become a priest, burning much of his poetry as a sign of commitment. While training for the priesthood, he developed unique poetic concepts that combined his delight in the beauty of the natural world with spiritual insight. Encouraged by his superiors, he began writing again. After his ordination he served in a number of industrial parishes, work he found oppressive and exhausting. He was then sent to teach in Ireland, where he became severely depressed and later died. His poetry was first published, and his distinctive genius recognized, 30 years after his death.

The Windhover:[1]

To Christ our Lord

I caught this morning morning's minion,° king- *darling, king's favourite*
dom of daylight's dauphin,[2] dapple-dawn-drawn
Falcon, in his riding
Of the rolling level underneath him steady air, and striding
High there, how he rung upon the rein of a wimpling° wing *rippling*
In his ecstasy! then, off, off forth on swing,
As a skate's heel sweeps smooth on a bow-bend: the hurl and gliding
Rebuffed the big wind. My heart in hiding
Stirred for a bird, — the achieve of, the mastery of the thing!

Brute beauty and valour and act, oh, air, pride, plume, here
Buckle! AND the fire that breaks from thee then, a billion
Times told lovelier, more dangerous, O my chevalier![3]

No wonder of it: shéer plód makes plough down sillion° *furrow*
Shine, and blue-bleak embers, ah my dear,
Fall, gall themselves, and gash gold-vermilion.° *bright red*

1 *Kestrel or falcon; bird of prey known for its ability to hover against the wind.*

2 *Son of (and heir to) the king of France.*

3 *French word for knight or nobleman.*

Contextual notes

This sonnet* is a good introduction to the verbal complexity of Hopkins' poems. This poem is particularly dense; words, associations and images are crammed into a particularly tight and demanding framework (in this case, the sonnet form, with only three rhyming sounds — only one rhyme is used in the whole octave!) This is why Hopkins' poems sometimes have a sense of 'straining at the seams.' The richness of his writing makes critical analysis of his poetry particularly rewarding. Interpreting his poetry is also an extremely personal process; you and your classmates might like to prepare one of his poems individually, and then report your findings back to each other; you might be surprised at the differing interpretations that emerge.

This poem is often given as a good example of the practice of Hopkins' theory of 'inscape'. Here the uniqueness of a natural object at a particular moment of beauty is captured, at the same time as the resulting spiritual insight is celebrated.

Spring and Fall:

to a young child

Márgarét, áre you gríeving
Over Goldengrove unleaving?
Leáves, líke the things of man, you
With your fresh thoughts care for, can you?
Áh! ás the heart grows older
It will come to such sights colder
By and by, nor spare a sigh
Though worlds of wanwood leafmeal lie;
And yet you *will* weep and know why.
Now no matter, child, the name:
Sórrow's spríngs áre the same.
Nor mouth had, no nor mind, expressed
What heart heard of, ghost° guessed: *spirit, soul*
It ís the blight man was born for,
It is Margaret you mourn for.

Contextual notes

A feature of Hopkins' poetry was his gift for putting together or coining new words out of existing ones. The words 'wanwood' and 'leafmeal' (in line 8) are good examples. Various commentators have all come up with slightly different explanations of what they might mean. How would you interpret these words?

You will also notice the abundant use of accents in this poem. This is to mark the unique rhythmic pattern (called sprung rhythm) which Hopkins developed and used in poems such as these. Sprung rhythm involves stressing a series of words so that they resemble normal speech patterns.

No Worst, There Is None

No worst, there is none. Pitched past pitch of grief,
More pangs will, schooled at forepangs, wilder wring.
Comforter, where, where is your comforting?
Mary,[4] mother of us, where is your relief?
My cries heave, herds-long; huddle in a main, a chief-
woe, world-sorrow; on an age-old anvil[5] wince and sing —
Then lull, then leave off. Fury had shrieked 'No ling-
ering! Let me be fell:° force[6] I must be brief.' *savage, fierce*
O the mind, mind has mountains; cliffs of fall
Frightful, sheer, no-man-fathomed. Hold them cheap
May who ne'er hung there. Nor does long our small
Durance° deal with that steep or deep. Here! creep, *endurance*
Wretch, under a comfort serves in a whirlwind: all
Life death does end and each day dies with sleep.

Contextual notes

This poem, one of a series known as the 'terrible' sonnets, was written during a period of what would today be recognized as severe clinical depression, which Hopkins suffered towards the end of his life.

> ### COMPARISON
>
> This poem has already been linked to Herbert's 'The Flower' (p. 38). You might like to look at the suggestions for comparison made there.

4 *Mary, mother of Jesus; a source of religious comfort to Catholic Christians.*

5 *See footnote 5, p. 60.*

6 *Perforce; necessarily.*

Olive Schreiner (1855 – 1920)

Olive Schreiner was born to missionary parents in what was then known as the Cape Colony, and worked as a governess teaching the children of local farmers. She travelled to England, where her novel The Story of an African Farm *was published under a male pseudonym. The success of her book gave her access to progressive circles, and she continued to write passionately on subjects such as women's rights, imperialism, pacifism and racism throughout her life. She returned to South Africa to marry the politician Samuel Cronwright, and although she spent the duration of the First World War in England, she went back to South Africa to die. Unconventional and often confrontational, she never lacked courage in either her writing or her life.*

The Cry of South Africa

Give back my dead!
They who by kop° and fountain *hill*
First saw the light upon my rocky breast!
Give back my dead,
The sons who played upon me
When childhood's dews still rested on their heads.
Give back my dead
Whom thou hast riven° from me *torn*
By arms of men loud called from earth's farthest bound
To wet my bosom with my children's blood!
Give back my dead,
The dead who grew up on me!

Contextual notes

This poem was written in 1900, during the Anglo-Boer War. You will find it helpful to check the contextual notes on p. 105, where you will find another Boer War poem, written by Hardy. How do these two poems differ?

A. E. Housman (1859 – 1936)

Although a brilliant scholar, Housman managed to fail his exams at Oxford and spent the next ten years working as a clerk. He continued his research and academic writing, and recognition of his learned articles led to his appointment as professor of Latin at University College in London. A frustrated homosexual love inspired him to turn to writing poetry, and his first volume of poems, A Shropshire Lad, *was to become extremely popular. He was eventually given a post at Cambridge, and published several more collections of poetry. Serious topics described with simplicity and charm are characteristic of his work.*

To an Athlete Dying Young

The time you won your town the race
We chaired you through the market-place;
Man and boy stood cheering by,
And home we brought you shoulder-high.

Today, the road all runners come,
Shoulder-high we bring you home,
And set you at your threshold down,
Townsman of a stiller town.

Smart lad, to slip betimes away
From fields where glory does not stay
And early though the laurel[1] grows
It withers quicker than the rose.

Eyes the shady night has shut
Cannot see the record cut,
And silence sounds no worse than cheers
After earth has stopped the ears:

Now you will not swell the rout° *crowd*
Of lads that wore their honours out,
Runners whom renown outran
And the name died before the man.

1 *Evergreen shrub; a crown of its leaves signifies victory, or poetic or artistic genius.*

So set, before its echoes fade,
The fleet foot on the sill of shade,
And hold to the low lintel[2] up
The still-defended challenge-cup.

And round that early-laureled head
Will flock to gaze the strengthless dead,
And find unwithered on its curls
The garland briefer than a girl's.

2 *Beam set above a door.*

William Butler Yeats (1865 – 1939)

Ireland's foremost poet, Yeats was born into a gifted family. His father and brother were well-known painters, and he initially followed in their footsteps before deciding on a literary career. Together with Lady Gregory, a writer and cultural nationalist, he began a campaign to revive Irish literature and drama, and founded a national theatre. Yeats was fascinated by traditional Irish legends, as well as the supernatural. He was also an ardent Irish nationalist at a time when the colonial domination of Ireland by England had led to guerrilla warfare by Irish rebels. His passion for a beautiful revolutionary, Maud Gonne, who rejected him, inspired much of his love poetry. He eventually married Georgie Hyde-Lees, who was to influence the mysticism of his later writing. The doomed nationalist uprising of Easter 1916 rekindled Yeats' idealistic hopes for a free Ireland, and in 1922 he was appointed to the Senate of the new Irish Free State. A year later he won the Nobel Prize for Literature. His poetry is significant for encompassing the shift from late Romanticism to the new Modernist principles.*

No Second Troy

Why should I blame her that she filled my days
With misery, or that she would of late
Have taught to ignorant men most violent ways,
Or hurled the little streets upon the great,
Had they but courage equal to desire?
What could have made her peaceful with a mind
That nobleness made simple as a fire,
With beauty like a tightened bow, a kind
That is not natural in an age like this,
Being high and solitary and most stern?
Why, what could she have done, being what she is?
Was there another Troy for her to burn?

Contextual notes

This poem, one of many that Yeats wrote about Maud Gonne, likens her to Helen of Troy, who was reputed to be the most beautiful woman in the world. According to the tales of the Greek writer Homer, Helen's abduction led to the Trojan War and the ultimate destruction of the city and civilization of Troy. (For further details, see the contextual notes to Tennyson's 'Ulysses' on p. 84.)

The Second Coming

Turning and turning in the widening gyre° *spiral*
The falcon cannot hear the falconer;
Things fall apart; the centre cannot hold;
Mere anarchy is loosed upon the world,
The blood-dimmed tide is loosed, and everywhere
The ceremony of innocence is drowned;
The best lack all conviction, while the worst
Are full of passionate intensity.

Surely some revelation is at hand;
Surely the Second Coming is at hand.
The Second Coming! Hardly are those words out
When a vast image out of *Spiritus Mundi*[1]
Troubles my sight: somewhere in sands of the desert
A shape with lion body and the head of a man,[2]
A gaze blank and pitiless as the sun,
Is moving its slow thighs, while all about it
Reel shadows of the indignant desert birds.
The darkness drops again; but now I know
That twenty centuries of stony sleep
Were vexed to nightmare by a rocking cradle,
And what rough beast, its hour come round at last,
Slouches towards Bethlehem[3] to be born?

Contextual notes

The title of this poem borrows from the biblical reference to the second coming of Jesus. This, it was prophesied, would take place after a period of increasing violence and turbulence, and would mark the end of time. However, in this poem Yeats pictures the coming of a frightening and barbaric mythological being, rather than a Christian deity. Written shortly after the First World War, this poem seems to hint at the inevitability of another great war arising out of the brutal settlement of the first.

1 *Literally, 'universal spirit'.*
2 *Reference to the Sphinx, a mythological monster worshipped and feared by the ancient Egyptians and Greeks.*
3 *Birthplace of Jesus.*

Easter 1916

I have met them at close of day
Coming with vivid faces
From counter or desk among grey
Eighteenth-century houses.
I have passed with a nod of the head
Or polite meaningless words,
Or have lingered awhile and said
Polite meaningless words,
And thought before I had done
Of a mocking tale or a gibe° *joke, insult*
To please a companion
Around the fire at the club,
Being certain that they and I
But lived where motley° is worn: *multiple colours*
All changed, changed utterly:
A terrible beauty is born.

That woman's days were spent
In ignorant good-will,
Her nights in argument
Until her voice grew shrill.
What voice more sweet than hers
When, young and beautiful,
She rode to harriers?° *hounds*
This man had kept a school
And rode our wingèd horse;[4]
This other[5] his helper and friend
Was coming into his force;
He might have won fame in the end,
So sensitive his nature seemed,
So daring and sweet his thought.
This other man[6] I had dreamed
A drunken, vainglorious lout.
He had done most bitter wrong
To some who are near my heart,
Yet I number him in the song;
He, too, has resigned his part
In the casual comedy;
He, too, has been changed in his turn,
Transformed utterly:
A terrible beauty is born.

4 *Pádraic Pearse, a teacher and writer; the reference to the winged horse, Pegasus, associated in legend with poetry, suggests the common literary ground shared by Pearse and the poet.*

5 *Thomas MacDonagh, also a poet.*

6 *John MacBride; his marriage to Maud Gonne, whom Yeats loved, was unhappy.*

Hearts with one purpose alone
Through summer and winter seem
Enchanted to a stone
To trouble the living stream.
The horse that comes from the road,
The rider, the birds that range
From cloud to tumbling cloud,
Minute by minute they change;
A shadow of cloud on the stream
Changes minute by minute;
A horse-hoof slides on the brim,
And a horse plashes° within it; *splashes*
The long-legged moor-hens dive,
And hens to moor-cocks call;
Minute by minute they live:
The stone's in the midst of all.

Too long a sacrifice
Can make a stone of the heart.
O when may it suffice?
That is Heaven's part, our part
To murmur name upon name,
As a mother names her child
When sleep at last has come
On limbs that had run wild.
What is it but nightfall?
No, no, not night but death;
Was it needless death after all?
For England may keep faith[7]
For all that is done and said.
We know their dream; enough
To know they dreamed and are dead;
And what if excess of love
Bewildered them till they died?
I write it out in a verse —
MacDonagh and MacBride
And Connolly[8] and Pearse
Now and in time to be
Wherever green is worn,
Are changed, changed utterly:
A terrible beauty is born.

7 *England had promised that once the First World War was over, Ireland would be granted a measure of independence.*

8 *James Connolly, a trade unionist and socialist.*

Contextual notes

Easter 1916 was the date of an attempted coup by Irish nationalists struggling to overthrow English rule. Although the courage of those who participated was remarkable, if arguably foolhardy, the uprising failed, and its leaders (including those named in this poem) were executed. The uprising did not have the full support of the Irish people, but they were nevertheless outraged by the executions, which served to draw together the nation against the English. Those who died were (and still are) regarded as patriotic martyrs, and the wearing of the colour green (referred to in line 78) became a symbol of resistance and remembrance.

This is not the only poem Yeats wrote about his friends involved in the struggle for liberation; you might like to use a library to look up 'On a Political Prisoner', which was inspired by Constance Markievicz (who is described in lines 17–23). Her death sentence for her role in leading the rebellion was commuted to life imprisonment.

An Irish Airman Foresees His Death

I know that I shall meet my fate
Somewhere among the clouds above;
Those that I fight I do not hate,
Those that I guard I do not love;
My country is Kiltartan Cross,[9]
My countrymen Kiltartan's poor,
No likely end could bring them loss
Or leave them happier than before.
Nor law, nor duty bade me fight,
Nor public men, nor cheering crowds,
A lonely impulse of delight
Drove to this tumult in the clouds;
I balanced all, brought all to mind,
The years to come seemed waste of breath,
A waste of breath the years behind
In balance with this life, this death.

9 *A village close to the airman's home in western Ireland.*

Contextual notes

This was written in memory of Major Robert Gregory (the son of Yeats' close friend and colleague, Lady Gregory), who was killed in action during the last year of the First World War. Does this poem sound like a traditional elegy*? In what way is it unusual?

Edwin Arlington Robinson (1869 – 1935)

Robinson grew up in a small town in the north-eastern part of the USA known as New England, and much of his writing is taken up with nostalgic observation of life in this close rural community. He studied at Harvard University, and through the influence of President Franklin Roosevelt, who enjoyed his poetry, he was given a customs post. This gave him financial security and the opportunity to concentrate on writing. His popularity as a poet grew slowly but steadily during his lifetime.

Richard Cory

Whenever Richard Cory went down town,
We people on the pavement looked at him:
He was a gentleman from sole to crown,
Clean favoured, and imperially slim.

And he was always quietly arrayed,
And he was always human when he talked;
But still he fluttered pulses when he said,
'Good-morning', and he glittered when he walked.

And he was rich — yes, richer than a king —
And admirably schooled in every grace:
In fine, we thought that he was everything
To make us wish that we were in his place.

So on we worked, and waited for the light,
And went without the meat, and cursed the bread;
And Richard Cory, one calm summer night,
Went home and put a bullet through his head.

Robert Frost (1874 – 1963)

Frost grew up in New England, the beautiful rural north-eastern corner of the USA, which he was to become famous for describing in his poems. His education included two years at Harvard University, and he made a living teaching, farming, and doing odd jobs. Shortly before the First World War, he spent three years in England, where his poems were published for the first time. He returned home to growing recognition and admiration of his work. Once again he took up teaching, and became one of the best-known modern American poets. Although he is generally admired as a wise observer of the rural scene, some critics have suggested that a more troubled note lies beneath much of his work.

Mending Wall

Something there is that doesn't love a wall,
That sends the frozen-ground-swell under it
And spills the upper boulders in the sun,
And makes gaps even two can pass abreast.
The work of hunters is another thing:
I have come after them and made repair
Where they have left not one stone on a stone,
But they would have the rabbit out of hiding,
To please the yelping dogs. The gaps I mean,
No one has seen them made or heard them made,
But at spring mending-time we find them there.
I let my neighbour know beyond the hill;
And on a day we meet to walk the line
And set the wall between us once again.
We keep the wall between us as we go.
To each the boulders that have fallen to each.
And some are loaves and some so nearly balls
We have to use a spell to make them balance:
'Stay where you are until our backs are turned!'
We wear our fingers rough with handling them.
Oh, just another kind of outdoor game,
One on a side. It comes to little more:
There where it is we do not need the wall:
He is all pine and I am apple orchard.
My apple trees will never get across
And eat the cones under his pines, I tell him.
He only says, 'Good fences make good neighbours.'

Spring is the mischief in me, and I wonder
If I could put a notion in his head:
'*Why* do they make good neighbours? Isn't it
Where there are cows? But here there are no cows.
Before I built a wall I'd ask to know
What I was walling in or walling out,
And to whom I was like to give offense.
Something there is that doesn't love a wall,
That wants it down.' I could say 'Elves' to him,
But it's not elves exactly, and I'd rather
He said it for himself. I see him there,
Bringing a stone grasped firmly by the top
In each hand, like an old-stone savage armed.
He moves in darkness as it seems to me,
Not of woods only and the shade of trees.
He will not go behind his father's saying,
And he likes having thought of it so well
He says again, 'Good fences make good neighbours.'

The Road Not Taken

Two roads diverged in a yellow wood,
And sorry I could not travel both
And be one traveller, long I stood
And looked down one as far as I could
To where it bent in the undergrowth;

Then took the other, as just as fair,
And having perhaps the better claim,
Because it was grassy and wanted wear;
Though as for that, the passing there
Had worn them really about the same,

And both that morning equally lay
In leaves no step had trodden black.
Oh, I kept the first for another day!
Yet knowing how way leads on to way,
I doubted if I should ever come back.

I shall be telling this with a sigh
Somewhere ages and ages hence:
Two roads diverged in a wood, and I —
I took the one less travelled by,
And that has made all the difference.

Suggestions for discussion

Both Frost's poems seem to describe simple, everyday events. Do you agree that both could also stand as extended metaphors* or allegories* for something else? Pick one poem (or study each one in succession), and work out what else the description of mending a wall, or choosing a road, could be about. On what different levels does each poem operate? Compare your interpretations with those of your classmates. How many different messages emerge? Which do you find the most valid, and why?

William Carlos Williams (1883 – 1963)

Williams studied medicine, and became friends with Ezra Pound while at university. After qualifying as a doctor, Williams returned to his home town in the USA. Here he married and spent the rest of his life, working as a paediatrician (a doctor specializing in children's illnesses). His experiences with working-class families influenced much of his writing. Part of a new generation of modern American poets who were moving towards more natural use of language, Williams' poems combine a conversational tone with vivid observation of detail.

The Dance

In Breughel's[1] great picture, The Kermess,[2]
the dancers go round, they go round and
around, the squeal and the blare and the
tweedle of bagpipes, a bugle and fiddles
tipping their bellies (round as the thick-
sided glasses whose wash they impound)° — *take possession of (drink)*
their hips and their bellies off balance
to turn them. Kicking and rolling about
the Fair Grounds, swinging their butts, those
shanks° must be sound to bear up under such — *legs*
rollicking measures, prance as they dance
in Breughel's great picture, The Kermess.

This is Just to Say

I have eaten
the plums
that were in
the icebox

and which
you were probably
saving
for breakfast

1 *Sixteenth-century Flemish painter, who specialized in scenes of peasant life.*

2 *Dutch or Flemish for 'the fair'.*

Forgive me
they were delicious
so sweet
and so cold

Comparison

You might enjoy comparing this poem to Pound's 'In a Station of the Metro' (p. 126). A list of questions about both poems can be found on the following page.

Ezra Pound (1885 – 1972)

Pound was born in the mid-western USA, and became friends with the poets William Carlos Williams and Hilda Doolittle at university. His unconventional behaviour lost him his first teaching post, and he left for Europe, where he established new trends in literary circles. Together with T. S. Eliot and the Irish writer James Joyce, he led the movement towards Modernism in literature. During four years in Paris, he was part of a group of American literary exiles that included the writers Hemingway and Gertrude Stein. Horrified by the aftermath of the First World War, he turned to fascism as the solution to Europe's troubles. During the Second World War he was caught broadcasting right-wing propaganda. He was judged to be insane, and sent to a mental institution instead of standing trial for treason. On his release he returned to Italy, where he lived until his death.*

In a Station of the Metro[1]

The apparition of these faces in the crowd;
Petals on a wet, black bough.

1 *Underground railway system in Paris.*

Comparison

You might find it helpful to compare this poem with another very short poem, Williams' 'This is Just to Say' (p. 124). Here the similarity is not so much one of topic or style, but rather the ability of the poets to evoke a great deal with very few words.

The following questions might help you come to grips with these poems, as well as providing some guidelines for approaching very short poems.

1. What function does the title serve in both poems? How does this differ from (or enlarge on) the usual role of the title in a poem?
2. Both poems concentrate on a very immediate, or fleeting, image or experience. How does the brevity of the poems underline this fleeting quality? Do they succeed in 'preserving the moment'?
3. Both poems have a distinctive shape. What does Williams' poem resemble? For whom is it written, and where do you think it might be found? The shape of Pound's poem, meanwhile, reflects the influence of brief Chinese and Japanese poems in which an image or emotion is described in a set number of words or syllables.
4. In poems this short, every word counts. In Williams' poem, where the words suggest ordinary household communication, it is the way the words are laid out on the page that is significant. What effect does their structuring have? In Pound's poem, however, each word (and each punctuation mark) is carefully chosen for effect. Try critically analysing this poem, considering each word. Does the poet evoke an overall emotion as well as an image?

The River-Merchant's Wife: a Letter

While my hair was still cut straight across my forehead
I played about the front gate, pulling flowers.
You came by on bamboo stilts, playing horse,
You walked about my seat, playing with blue plums.
And we went on living in the village of Chokan:
Two small people, without dislike or suspicion.

At fourteen I married My Lord you.
I never laughed, being bashful.° *shy*
Lowering my head, I looked at the wall.
Called to, a thousand times, I never looked back.

At fifteen I stopped scowling,
I desired my dust to be mingled with yours
Forever and forever and forever.
Why should I climb the look out?

At sixteen you departed,
You went into far Ku-to-yen, by the river of swirling eddies,
And you have been gone five months.
The monkeys make sorrowful noise overhead.

You dragged your feet when you went out.
By the gate now, the moss is grown, the different mosses,
Too deep to clear them away!
The leaves fall early this autumn, in wind.
The paired butterflies are already yellow with August
Over the grass in the West garden;
They hurt me. I grow older.
If you are coming down through the narrows of the river Kiang,
Please let me know beforehand,
And I will come out to meet you
    As far as Cho-fu-Sa.

Contextual notes

This is a free translation of a poem by Li Po (*c.* 700–762), a Chinese poet whose works were much admired by Pound. The place names in this poem all refer to various locations in eighth-century China. You might like to compare this poem to the English translations of works by Li Po's contemporaries (pp. 1–2).

H. D. (Hilda Doolittle) (1886 – 1961)

Doolittle was born in the USA, and became friends with Ezra Pound and William Carlos Williams while studying. She joined Pound in Europe, and with him founded a new movement in modern poetry which focused on the significance of the concrete image. She married the poet Robert Adlington, and worked with him translating the classics and editing a significant literary journal. She also wrote novels, as well as an account of her psychoanalysis by Freud. After her marriage ended, she settled in Switzerland.

Helen[1]

All Greece hates
the still eyes in the white face,
the lustre° as of olives[2] *gloss, sheen*
where she stands,
And the white hands.

All Greece reviles
the wan° face when she smiles, *pale*
hating it deeper still
when it grows wan and white,
remembering past enchantments
and past ills.

Greece sees unmoved,
God's daughter,[3] born of love,
the beauty of cool feet
and slenderest knees,
could love indeed the maid,
only if she were laid,
white ash amid funereal cypresses.[4]

1 *Helen of Troy, whose abduction led to the Trojan War.*

2 *This could be a comparison either to olives themselves, or olive trees, which have silver-coloured leaves.*

3 *Helen was the result of the seduction of Leda (a mortal woman) by Zeus, ruler of the gods in Greek mythology.*

4 *Trees associated with graveyards.*

Comparison

Here we find a completely different vision of Helen of Troy, and the Trojan War, to that found in the poems 'Ulysses' by Tennyson (p. 82) and 'No Second Troy' by Yeats (p. 114). (You will find information on both Helen herself and the Trojan War in the contextual notes to these poems.) Tennyson and Yeats glorify different aspects of the tragic saga; what exactly enthrals each of them? What is H. D.'s response to the legend, and how does her poem contrast with theirs? How do you explain the differences? Do you think the gender of these poets might be a factor?

Rupert Brooke (1887 – 1915)

An attractive and charismatic figure, Brooke was educated at Cambridge University, where he dominated literary circles. His early poetry was well received and he was awarded a fellowship for further study, but he suffered a breakdown soon afterwards, possibly because of the pressures he faced due to his homosexuality. While recovering, he travelled to the USA, Canada, and the Pacific islands. He volunteered to serve in the Navy as soon as the First World War broke out, and the poetry he sent home established him as the most celebrated (if unrealistic) war poet of his times. In 1915 he was sent to the Mediterranean, where he died of blood-poisoning.

The Soldier

If I should die, think only this of me:
    That there's some corner of a foreign field
That is for ever England. There shall be
    In that rich earth a richer dust concealed;
A dust whom England bore, shaped, made aware,
    Gave, once, her flowers to love, her ways to roam,
A body of England's, breathing English air,
    Washed by the rivers, blest by suns of home.

And think, this heart, all evil shed away,
    A pulse in the eternal mind, no less
        Gives somewhere back the thoughts by England given;
Her sights and sounds; dreams happy as her day;
    And laughter, learnt of friends; and gentleness,
        In hearts at peace, under an English heaven.

Contextual notes

This poem is an interesting remnant of a particularly rose-coloured tradition of patriotism, which glorified fighting and dying for one's country. These sentiments were unable to survive the gruesome realities of the First World War; although Europe had a history of bloody wars going back centuries, nothing like the horrors of modern trench warfare had ever been experienced before. This war was also probably the first in which both working-class and aristocratic soldiers suffered equally devastating losses and injuries. Brooke's poem was to be prophetic; his body lies buried on a small Greek island. See Hardy's 'In Time of "The Breaking of Nations"' (p. 107), Yeats' 'An Irish Airman Foresees His Death' (p. 118) and Owen's 'Futility' and 'Dulce et Decorum Est' (pp. 144–145), as well as the contextual notes to these poems, for differing reflections on the First World War.

Comparison

Read this poem carefully, and then turn to Wilfred Owen's 'Dulce et Decorum Est' (p. 145). Consider the following questions (you might find it helpful to read the contextual notes to both poems).

1. Both poets describe a soldier's response to dying in action. Yet the poems differ in their use of language, imagery, tone and central message. Isolate these contrasting elements, establishing how each poet puts together and conveys these components. Your class might like to divide into two groups, one to study each poem, before reporting back.
2. What impact would each poem have on the audience of the time? Why was Brooke's poem so much more popular? Does this suggest any thoughts on the role that poetry might play in a time of crisis?
4. What is the primary emotional intention of each poem? Do you think that both are valid, especially in times of war?
3. Are both poets sincere? How can this be so? Do you agree that Brooke is perhaps a poet of the past, and Owen a poet of the present?

Katherine Mansfield (1888 – 1923)

Mansfield was born in New Zealand, but went to London to study. Her first marriage lasted only a few days, and she became involved with John Middleton Murry, an influential editor and literary figure, whom she later married. They shared a sometimes turbulent friendship and various literary projects with the novelist D. H. Lawrence and his unconventional wife, Frieda. (Lawrence described their relationship in his book Women in Love.*) Mansfield's writing was original and wide-ranging; she was best known for her short stories. She travelled regularly to France and Switzerland in the hopes of shaking off the tuberculosis which was finally to kill her.*

To God the Father

To the little, pitiful God I make my prayer,
The God with the long grey beard
And flowing robe fastened with a hempen° girdle *rope*
Who sits nodding and muttering on the all-too-big throne of Heaven.
What a long, long time, dear God, since you set the stars in their places,
Girded° the earth with the sea, and invented the day and night. *encircled*
And longer the time since you looked through the blue window of Heaven
To see your children at play in a garden . . . .
Now we are all stronger than you and wiser and more arrogant,
In swift procession we pass you by.
'Who is that marionette° nodding and muttering *puppet*
On the all-too-big throne of Heaven?
Come down from your place, Grey Beard,
We have had enough of your play-acting!'
It is centuries since I believed in you,
But to-day my need of you has come back.
I want no rose-coloured future,
No books of learning, no protestations and denials —
I am sick of this ugly scramble,
I am tired of being pulled about —
O God, I want to sit on your knees
On the all-too-big throne of Heaven,
And fall asleep with my hands tangled in your grey beard.

T. S. Eliot (1888 – 1965)

Eliot was born in the USA and studied at Harvard University and Oxford. His friend Ezra Pound encouraged him to settle in England, where he married Vivien Haigh-Wood. Their relationship was an extremely troubled one, and eventually ended in separation. He worked in a bank for several years while gathering a considerable reputation as an editor and critic. Meanwhile his first collections of poetry were establishing him as the sophisticated new voice of a disenchanted age. He became a director at the publishing house Faber and Faber, and guided their publications of poetry along the new lines of Modernism that he and others such as Pound had established. By now he was one of the most influential literary figures in England. He became attracted to the doctrines of High Anglicanism (which marked a shift in his poetry from cynicism to mysticism); he also became increasingly traditional in his politics. He was awarded the Nobel Prize for Literature in 1948.*

Preludes

I

The winter evening settles down
With smell of steaks in passageways.
Six o'clock.
The burnt-out ends of smoky days.
And now a gusty shower wraps
The grimy scraps
Of withered leaves about your feet
And newspapers from vacant lots;
The showers beat
On broken blinds and chimney-pots,
And at the corner of the street
A lonely cab-horse steams and stamps.
And then the lighting of the lamps.

II

The morning comes to consciousness
Of faint stale smells of beer
From the sawdust-trampled street
With all its muddy feet that press
To early coffee-stands.

With the other masquerades° *pretences, play-acting*
That time resumes,
One thinks of all the hands
That are raising dingy shades
In a thousand furnished rooms.

III

You tossed a blanket from the bed,
You lay upon your back, and waited;
You dozed, and watched the night revealing
The thousand sordid images
Of which your soul was constituted;
They flickered against the ceiling.
And when all the world came back
And the light crept up between the shutters
And you heard the sparrows in the gutters,
You had such a vision of the street
As the street hardly understands;
Sitting along the bed's edge, where
You curled the paper from your hair,
Or clasped the yellow soles of feet
In the palms of both soiled hands.

IV

His soul stretched tight across the skies
That fade behind a city block,
Or trampled by insistent feet
At four and five and six o'clock;
And short square fingers stuffing pipes,
And evening newspapers, and eyes
Assured of certain certainties,
The conscience of a blackened street
Impatient to assume the world.

I am moved by fancies that are curled
Around these images, and cling:
The notion of some infinitely gentle
Infinitely suffering thing.

Wipe your hand across your mouth, and laugh;
The worlds revolve like ancient women
Gathering fuel in vacant lots.

Contextual notes

In his poems, Eliot's purpose is to evoke images and emotions by association, rather than description. This practice of using language rather like music — for emotional and aesthetic effect rather than to communicate meaning — was set out by Eliot as a new creative philosophy, and was to become a hallmark of Modernist poetry. In 'Preludes', we are presented with four different cameos or scenes, rather than any narrative progression or philosophical argument.

Journey of the Magi[1]

'A cold coming we had of it,
Just the worst time of the year
For a journey, and such a long journey:
The ways deep and the weather sharp,
The very dead of winter.'
And the camels galled, sore-footed, refractory,° *stubborn, obstinate*
Lying down in the melting snow.
There were times we regretted
The summer palaces on slopes, the terraces,
And the silken girls bringing sherbet.° *sweet Oriental drink*
Then the camel men cursing and grumbling
And running away, and wanting their liquor and women,
And the night-fires going out, and the lack of shelters,
And the cities hostile and the towns unfriendly
And the villages dirty and charging high prices:
A hard time we had of it.
At the end we preferred to travel all night,
Sleeping in snatches,
With the voices singing in our ears, saying
That this was all folly.

Then at dawn we came down to a temperate valley,
Wet, below the snow line, smelling of vegetation;
With a running stream and a water-mill beating the darkness,
And three trees on the low sky,
And an old white horse galloped away in the meadow.
Then we came to a tavern with vine-leaves over the lintel,[2]

1 *According to the Bible, the three wise men from the east who travelled to pay homage to the baby Jesus.*

2 *Beam set above a door.*

Six hands at an open door dicing for pieces of silver,
And feet kicking the empty wine-skins.
But there was no information, and so we continued
And arrived at evening, not a moment too soon
Finding the place; it was (you may say) satisfactory.

All this was a long time ago, I remember,
And I would do it again, but set down
This set down
This: were we led all that way for
Birth or Death? There was a Birth, certainly,
We had evidence and no doubt. I had seen birth and death,
But had thought they were different; this Birth was
Hard and bitter agony for us, like Death, our death.
We returned to our places, these Kingdoms,
But no longer at ease here, in the old dispensation,
With an alien people clutching their gods.
I should be glad of another death.

Contextual notes

Eliot wrote this poem, about a life-changing experience, in the same year in which he converted to the Anglican church and finally took on British citizenship — both choices which meant permanent changes in his life. The first five lines are adapted from a seventeenth-century sermon, and the second stanza is packed with allusions to the New Testament. The 'three trees' in line 24 refer to the three crosses which feature in the crucifixion story; the 'vine-leaves' and the 'lintel' in line 26 suggest the parables Jesus told in which he metaphorically described himself as a vine and a door; the 'dicing' in line 27 possibly alludes to the soldiers gambling for Jesus' clothes at the foot of the cross; the 'pieces of silver' in the same line refer to the 30 pieces of silver which Judas, one of Jesus' disciples, was paid as a reward for betraying his master; and the 'wine-skins' in line 28 suggest another parable, which features the image of new wine in old wine-skins.

Marina

What seas what shores what grey rocks and what islands
What water lapping the bow[3]
And scent of pine and the woodthrush° singing through the fog *bird*
What images return
O my daughter.

Those who sharpen the tooth of the dog, meaning
Death
Those who glitter with the glory of the hummingbird, meaning
Death
Those who sit in the sty of contentment, meaning
Death
Those who suffer the ecstasy of the animals, meaning
Death

Are become unsubstantial, reduced by a wind,
A breath of pine, and the woodsong fog
By grace dissolved in place

What is this face, less clear and clearer
The pulse in the arm, less strong and stronger —
Given or lent? more distant than stars and nearer than the eye

Whispers and small laughter between leaves and hurrying feet
Under sleep, where all the waters meet.

Bowsprit[4] cracked with ice and paint cracked with heat.
I made this, I have forgotten
And remember.
The rigging weak and the canvas rotten[5]
Between one June and another September.
Made this unknowing, half unconscious, unknown, my own.
The garboard strake[6] leaks, the seams need caulking.[7]
This form, this face, this life
Living to live in a world of time beyond me; let me
Resign my life for this life, my speech for that unspoken,
The awakened, lips parted, the hope, the new ships.

3 *Front part of a boat or ship.*
4 *Spar of wood extending from the front of a sailing boat.*
5 *Rigging refers to the ropes which support masts; canvas refers to the sails.*
6 *Planks closest to the base or bottom of a boat.*
7 *Seams are the gaps between planks; caulking refers to sealing these.*

What seas what shores what islands towards my timbers
And woodthrush calling through the fog
My daughter.

Contextual notes

This poem was inspired by Shakespeare's play *Pericles*, in which the central character, who believes he has lost his family, is guided towards them by visions. This is a modern version of the recognition scene, in which the hero is joyously reunited with his daughter, whom he discovers after sailing to a foreign country. The boating terminology used by the poet underlines the metaphor of voyaging.

Claude McKay (1890 – 1948)

Born in Jamaica in the Caribbean, Claude McKay went to the USA as a young man. A writer skilled in various fields, he wrote both poetry and novels. His poems reflect his perceptions of life in Jamaica and New York, and his novels deal unflinchingly with the experiences of black communities in the Caribbean, the USA and Europe. He also produced a respected sociological work on life in Harlem (a black residential area in New York City).

If We Must Die

If we must die, let it not be like hogs
Hunted and penned in an inglorious spot,
While round us bark the mad and hungry dogs,
Making their mock at our accursèd lot.
If we must die, O let us nobly die,
So that our precious blood may not be shed
In vain; then even the monsters we defy
Shall be constrained° to honour us though dead! *forced*
O kinsmen! we must meet the common foe!
Though far outnumbered let us show us brave,
And for their thousand blows deal one deathblow!
What though before us lies the open grave?
Like men we'll face the murderous, cowardly pack,
Pressed to the wall, dying, but fighting back!

Contextual notes

This poem was written as a response to race riots which took place in Harlem in 1919. Later, it was to become a poem of encouragement in times of war. In its use of the sonnet form, it borrows directly from the poetry of preceding ages. Do you agree that it sounds more like a nineteenth-century (or earlier) poem than a twentieth-century one? What features does it share with the sonnets by Wordsworth (p. 65) or Milton (p. 42), for example?

Edna St. Vincent Millay (1892 – 1950)

Millay was born in the USA and educated at Vassar College, a prestigious university for women. She soon established a reputation as an audacious and witty poet, and was the leader of a new generation of writers who were sophisticated and daring both in their writing and their lifestyles.

I, Being Born a Woman and Distressed

I, being born a woman and distressed
By all the needs and notions of my kind,
Am urged by your propinquity° to find — *closeness*
Your person fair, and feel a certain zest° — *enthusiasm*
To bear your body's weight upon my breast:
So subtly is the fume° of life designed, — *essence*
To clarify the pulse and cloud the mind,
And leave me once again undone, possessed.
Think not for this, however, the poor treason
Of my stout° blood against my staggering brain, — *strong*
I shall remember you with love, or season
My scorn with pity, — let me make it plain:
I find this frenzy insufficient reason
For conversation when we meet again.

Suggestions for discussion

1. At first glance, this poem looks like a formal sonnet.* However, we soon discover that it is wickedly funny and mocking in its intention. What basic message is the poet trying to spell out, and to whom? Why is its presentation here humorous?
2. If you agree that contrast forms the main ingredient of the humour, identify how this operates. What tone is used? And what level of language? Given the message of the poem, do you think this is appropriate, or deliberately inappropriate? How does the use of language and syntax compare with the topic (or argument) of the poem?
3. How does the poet use the formal structure of the sonnet to emphasize her argument?
4. Traditionally, the sonnet was often used as a form of love poetry. (See, for example, the sonnets of Sidney [p. 20], Spenser [p. 17] and Shakespeare [p. 25]). Do you agree that this sonnet, however, is almost an anti-love poem? In what ways does it subvert the tradition?

Archibald MacLeish (1892 – 1982)

Born in the mid-western USA, MacLeish was educated at Harvard University. He joined the circle of American artists in Paris in the 1920s, where he was much influenced by Ezra Pound. Another significant influence was T. S. Eliot. A notable poet and playwright, MacLeish became increasingly absorbed by politics. On his return to the USA, he held a series of important governmental positions, including that of Assistant Secretary of State. He was later appointed to a professor's post at Harvard.

Ars Poetica[1]

A poem should be palpable° and mute — *tangible, real*
As a globed fruit,

Dumb
As old medallions to the thumb,

Silent as the sleeve-worn stone
Of casement° ledges where the moss has grown — — *window*

A poem should be wordless
As the flight of birds.

A poem should be motionless in time
As the moon climbs,

Leaving, as the moon releases
Twig by twig the night-entangled trees,

Leaving, as the moon behind the winter leaves,
Memory by memory the mind —

A poem should be motionless in time
As the moon climbs.

1 *This title (which means 'the art of poetry') is taken from a work on the subject of poetry by the classical Latin poet, Horace.*

A poem should be equal to:
Not true.

For all the history of grief
An empty doorway and a maple leaf.

For love
The leaning grasses and two lights above the sea —

A poem should not mean
But be.

Wilfred Owen (1893 – 1918)

Owen came from a humble background and began writing poetry at an early age. Unable to afford university fees, he studied at a technical college, and did community work in an impoverished parish. Two years before the First World War broke out, he went to France to teach English. After the war began he returned to England to join the army. His first-hand experience of the horrific conditions and casualties involved in the fighting in Europe were to have a dramatic influence on his poetry. He was injured and sent to hospital in Scotland to recover. Here he met the poet Siegfried Sassoon, who encouraged his writing. He returned to battle and was awarded the Military Cross for bravery, only to be killed a week before the war ended. At first his brutally realistic and bitter war poems were ignored by the public; however, he slowly came to be recognized as one of the finest poets of the First World War.

You might like to compare his poems with Rupert Brooke's 'The Soldier'. Suggestions for discussion can be found on p. 132.

Futility

Move him into the sun —
Gently its touch awoke him once,
At home, whispering of fields unsown.
Always it woke him, even in France,
Until this morning and this snow.
If anything might rouse him now
The kind old sun will know.

Think how it wakes the seeds —
Woke, once, the clays of a cold star.
Are limbs, so dear-achieved, are sides,
Full-nerved — still warm — too hard to stir?
Was it for this the clay grew tall?
— O what made fatuous° sunbeams toil *pointlessly foolish*
To break earth's sleep at all?

Dulce et Decorum Est

Bent double, like old beggars under sacks,
Knock-kneed, coughing like hags, we cursed through sludge,
Till on the haunting flares we turned our backs
And towards our distant rest began to trudge.
Men marched asleep. Many had lost their boots
But limped on, blood-shod. All went lame; all blind;
Drunk with fatigue; deaf even to the hoots
Of tired, outstripped Five-Nines[1] that dropped behind.

Gas! GAS! Quick, boys! — An ecstasy of fumbling,
Fitting the clumsy helmets just in time;
But someone still was yelling out and stumbling
And flound'ring like a man in fire or lime[2] . . .
Dim through the misty panes and thick green light,
As under a green sea, I saw him drowning.

In all my dreams, before my helpless sight,
He plunges at me, guttering, choking, drowning.

If in some smothering dreams you too could pace
Behind the wagon that we flung him in,
And watch the white eyes writhing in his face,
His hanging face, like a devil's sick of sin;
If you could hear, at every jolt, the blood
Come gargling from the froth-corrupted lungs,
Obscene as cancer, bitter as the cud
Of vile, incurable sores on innocent tongues, —
My friend, you would not tell with such high zest
To children ardent for some desperate glory,
The old Lie: Dulce et decorum est
Pro patria mori.[3]

Contextual notes

One of the features of the First World War was the use of chemical weapons for the first time. The most notorious was 'mustard' gas, which killed its victims by corroding their lungs. Soldiers used gas-masks (the 'helmets' in line 10) to protect themselves. This poem graphically describes the effects of such a gas attack.

1 *Chemical gas bombs.*

2 *Corrosive, sticky chemical sometimes used to trap birds.*

3 *Ironic quotation from the Latin poet Horace: 'Sweet and fitting it is to die for one's country'.*

Elizabeth Cloete

No information is available about Cloete, other than that she was a South African who wrote this poem in 1931.

The Spartan Woman

A spartan° woman is Africa, *tough, austere*
Under the sun's relentless rays she lies,
With stern fingers pointing steadily upwards,
Her broad breast bare to the sky,
She watches with an immovable face,
Those who seek to nestle on her heart,
But it is hard, and the heat of her breath is scorching.
Vainly they strive to rest in her treacherous arms.
They cling to the hem of her garments praying for life,
Yet not a quiver betrays her thought.
Yet how they love her!
Once having seen her, once having known her,
They see, they love, they know no other.
Their last cry is always to be buried on her breast.
None but the bravest, none but the best
Shall earn her favour,
From them she will withhold nothing.
And maybe there shall arise a mighty race,
That maybe shall move with iron tread,
Towards the hills of God.

Mao Tse-Tung (1893 – 1976)

Mao Tse-Tung (also spelt Zedong) came from a peasant background, and was attracted to communism as a young man. He helped to form the Chinese Communist Party, and acted as its leader for 50 years. His followers fought a prolonged civil war for control of the country, eventually overcoming both the occupying Japanese and the Chinese Nationalists who were fighting for power. The Chinese People's Republic, with Mao as its president, was established in 1949, and embarked on a programme of accelerated economic and industrial development. Mao remained effectively in control of the country until his death in 1976. Despite evidence of various abuses of power, he attained almost mythical status among his followers. In China, his teachings and poems were so extensively distributed as to make him probably the most widely read poet of the twentieth century.

Lou Mountain Pass

February 1935

West wind fierce,
immense sky, wild geese honking,
frosty morning moon.
Frosty morning moon.
Horse hooves clanging,
bugles sobbing.

Tough pass,
long trail, like iron.
Yet with strong steps
we climbed that peak.
Climbed that peak:
green mountains like oceans,
setting sun like blood.

Contextual notes

During the civil war, Mao led his followers on the gruelling 'Long March', a 9 700 km trek across some of China's wildest terrain. It took over a year, and bonded those who survived into a close and determined military unit. Mao wrote this poem to celebrate a battle during the Long March, the taking of a particularly daunting mountain pass from the Nationalist forces.

E. E. Cummings (1894 – 1962)

The son of a clergyman, Cummings studied at Harvard University and joined a volunteer ambulance unit in France during the First World War. He was talented both as a painter and a writer, and his first book, an account of his experiences in a French detention camp, generated much excitement. He introduced striking visual and typographical innovations in his poetry, and his unorthodox use of punctuation and lower-case letters has had a lasting impact on twentieth-century poetry. His work ranges from sharp satire to romantic and moving lyrics.

anyone lived in a pretty how town

anyone lived in a pretty how town
(with up so floating many bells down)
spring summer autumn winter
he sang his didn't he danced his did.

Women and men(both little and small)
cared for anyone not at all
they sowed their isn't they reaped their same
sun moon stars rain

children guessed(but only a few
and down they forgot as up they grew
autumn winter spring summer)
that noone loved him more by more

when by now and tree by leaf
she laughed his joy she cried his grief
bird by snow and stir by still
anyone's any was all to her

someones married their everyones
laughed their cryings and did their dance
(sleep wake hope and then)they
said their nevers they slept their dream

stars rain sun moon
(and only the snow can begin to explain
how children are apt to forget to remember
with up so floating many bells down)

one day anyone died i guess
(and noone stooped to kiss his face)
busy folk buried them side by side
little by little and was by was

all by all and deep by deep
and more by more they dream their sleep
noone and anyone earth by april
wish by spirit and if by yes.

Women and men(both dong and ding)
summer autumn winter spring
reaped their sowing and went their came
sun moon stars rain

'next to of course god america i

'next to of course god america i
love you land of the pilgrims' and so forth oh
say can you see by the dawn's early my
country 'tis of centuries come and go
and are no more what of it we should worry
in every language even deafanddumb
thy sons acclaim your glorious name by gorry
by jingo by gee by gosh by gum
why talk of beauty what could be more beau-
tiful than these heroic happy dead
who rushed like lions to the roaring slaughter
they did not stop to think they died instead
then shall the voice of liberty be mute?'

He spoke. And drank rapidly a glass of water

Contextual notes

This sonnet* is a particularly witty satire on American patriotism. The 'pilgrims' in line 2 are a reference to the first European settlers, who fled to North America during the seventeenth century to escape religious persecution; the phrase 'oh/ say can you see by the dawn's early' (lines 2 and 3) is an absurdly shortened version of the first line of the American national anthem (it should read 'dawn's early light'); 'by gorry/by jingo by gee by gosh by gum' (lines 7 and 8) are examples of American slang of the time. Note how two very different voices are contained in this sonnet; you will find it useful to work through the poem 'separating' these voices.

Bertolt Brecht (1898 – 1956)

A German by nationality, Brecht was sympathetic to issues of class and capital, and aligned himself with local communist groups. His radical and outspoken writings were banned by the Nazis, and after the establishment of Hitler's totalitarian regime in Germany during the 1930s, he emigrated to the USA. Here he worked translating and producing his plays. After the Second World War, he returned to East Berlin where he founded a company of actors, the Berliner Ensemble, as a vehicle for his work and theories of acting. He married the actress Helene Weigel, and she continued to direct the company after his death. Today he is recognized as a leading modern German poet and playwright.

Questions from a Worker who Reads

Translated by Michael Hamburger

Who built Thebes of the seven gates?
In the books you will find the names of kings.
Did the kings haul up the lumps of rock?
And Babylon, many times demolished,
Who raised it up so many times? In what houses
Of gold-glittering Lima did the builders live?
Where, the evening that the Wall of China was finished
Did the masons go? Great Rome
Is full of triumphal arches. Who erected them? Over whom
Did the Caesars triumph? Had Byzantium, much praised in song,
Only palaces for its inhabitants? Even in fabled Atlantis
The night the ocean engulfed it
The drowning still bawled° for their slaves. *yelled, shouted*

The young Alexander conquered India.
Was he alone?
Caesar beat the Gauls.
Did he not have even a cook with him?
Philip of Spain wept when his armada
Went down. Was he the only one to weep?
Frederick the Second won the Seven Years' War. Who
Else won it?

Every page a victory.
Who cooked the feast for the victors?

Every ten years a great man.
Who paid the bill?

So many reports.
So many questions.

Contextual notes

To footnote every allusion in this poem would be difficult and unwieldy, so brief explanations are provided here. Thebes (lines 1–3) was the burial place of kings, and a temple site in ancient Egypt. Babylon (lines 4–5) was a great capital of the ancient Middle East; successive empires destroyed and rebuilt it. Lima (line 6) is the capital of the South American country Peru; it was once the stronghold of the ancient and wealthy Inca civilization. The Great Wall of China (line 7) was a long, fortified defence built to repel invaders (see also footnote 2, p. 1). Rome (lines 8–10) was the centre of the Roman empire; its rulers were known as Caesars. Many of them ordered monuments or arches to be built to mark the conquest of other lands or peoples. Byzantium (lines 10–11) was the eastern capital of the Roman Empire, later named Constantinople. Today it is the capital of Turkey, and is called Istanbul. Atlantis (lines 11–13) was a mythical island civilization which was supposedly engulfed by the sea. Alexander, also known as Alexander the Great (line 14), was a brilliant young general of the ancient world, who conquered an empire which stretched from Greece to India. The Gauls (line 16) were the inhabitants of France who were defeated by Julius Caesar, probably the greatest of the Roman rulers. Philip of Spain (line 18) was the king of Spain during the sixteenth century; he sent a fleet of ships known as the Armada to attack England, but it was defeated. Frederick the Second (line 20) was an eighteenth-century German king, and a key figure in a major war in central Europe which lasted seven years.

Hart Crane (1899 – 1932)

Crane's short life was not a tranquil one. He did not finish high school, but nevertheless his two volumes of poetry marked him as a talented and powerful writer, albeit with a bleak vision of life. His work resembles Whitman's in its fascination with American experiences and values. An alcoholic, he had a succession of unhappy love affairs with both men and women. On a voyage home after a period of travel and study in Mexico, he committed suicide by jumping over the side of the ship.

My Grandmother's Love Letters

There are no stars to-night
But those of memory.
Yet how much room for memory there is
In the loose girdle° of soft rain. *belt*

There is even room enough
For the letters of my mother's mother,
Elizabeth,
That have been pressed so long
Into a corner of the roof
That they are brown and soft,
And liable to melt as snow.

Over the greatness of such space
Steps must be gentle.
It is all hung by an invisible white hair.
It trembles as birch limbs webbing the air.

And I ask myself:

'Are your fingers long enough to play
Old keys that are but echoes:
Is the silence strong enough
To carry back the music to its source
And back to you again
As though to her?'

Yet I would lead my grandmother by the hand
Through much of what she would not understand;
And so I stumble. And the rain continues on the roof
With such a sound of gently pitying laughter.

Malvina Reynolds (1900 – 1978)

Reynolds was an American singer, guitarist and song-writer who followed in the protest folk tradition established by musicians such as Woodie Guthrie and Pete Seeger. Their aim was to express political criticism in a way that was both powerful and accessible, in the form of ballads, chants and easily remembered songs. Reynolds' songs are often apparently simple and understated, but make telling points nevertheless.

What Have They Done to the Rain?

Just a little rain falling all around,
The grass lifts its head to the heavenly sound,
Just a little rain, just a little rain,
What have they done to the rain?

Just a little breeze out of the sky,
The leaves nod their heads as the breeze blows by,
Just a little breeze with some smoke in its eye,
What have they done to the rain?

Just a little boy standing in the rain,
The gentle rain that falls for years,
And the grass is gone, the boy disappears,
And rain keeps falling like helpless tears,
And what have they done to the rain?

Contextual notes

This song was written at the height of the 'Cold War' between the USA and its allies and what was then the communist Eastern bloc, headed by the USSR. It refers to the threat of radioactive 'fallout' (minute particles of deadly waste matter from either a nuclear bomb explosion or a nuclear power station, which would be spread through the atmosphere by wind and rain) that preoccupied most of the northern hemisphere for decades. There was tremendous concern about the sickness, death and long-term poisoning that such fallout would bring for decades after the initial explosion or leak.

Roy Campbell (1901 – 1957)

*Born in Natal, Campbell studied at Oxford University for a year and lived briefly in Britain, where he successfully published his first volume of poetry, establishing himself as an energetic and inventive writer. On his return to South Africa, he founded a satirical literary journal (*Voorslag, *which means 'whiplash') together with the poet William Plomer. He left again, and lived in France and Spain before settling in Portugal. A prolific writer and translator, he regularly published poetry as well as two autobiographies. His personality was as colourful and flamboyant as his writing (his jobs included a brief stint as a bull-fighter), and his support of fascism earned him considerable criticism. However, he fought on the side of the British during the Second World War. He died in a car crash in Portugal.*

The Zulu Girl

When in the sun the hot red acres smoulder,
Down where the sweating gang its labour plies,
A girl flings down her hoe, and from her shoulder
Unslings her child tormented by the flies.

She takes him to a ring of shadow pooled
By thorn-trees: purpled with the blood of ticks,
While her sharp nails, in slow caresses ruled,
Prowl through his hair with sharp electric clicks.

His sleepy mouth plugged by the heavy nipple,
Tugs like a puppy, grunting as he feeds:
Through his frail nerves her own deep languors ripple
Like a broad river sighing through its reeds.

Yet in that drowsy stream his flesh imbibes° *drinks*
An old unquenched unsmotherable heat —
The curbed ferocity of beaten tribes,
The sullen dignity of their defeat.

Her body looms above him like a hill
Within whose shade a village lies at rest,
Or the first cloud so terrible and still
That bears the coming harvest in its breast.

Suggestions for discussion

1. This poem is particularly interesting because it combines a far-sighted warning with stereotypical (and perhaps even patronizing) views of its topic. Do you agree, and if so, can you locate these elements?
2. Look very closely at the presentation of both the Zulu mother and her baby. What positive and negative attributes are suggested by the language the poet uses to describe them?
3. This poem conveys an atmosphere that is both tranquil and threatening. What words are used to sustain both moods? Look especially closely at the last stanza. What is the final message of the poem?
4. In the presentation of the Zulu mother, we find a return to the Romantic tradition of likening the female body to natural phenomena. (Wordsworth's 'Three Years She Grew' [p. 63] is a good example of this practice.) How exactly does Campbell do this here, and what effect does it have?

Sterling Brown (1901 –)

Brown was one of the first recognized Afro-American poets. He was educated at Williams and Harvard universities, and was a teacher before becoming professor of English at Howard University, a post he held for over 50 years. His writings focused on the struggles of black Americans of African descent (then known as Negroes) during the period between the two world wars. As well as poetry, he wrote critical works on the presentation and significance of blacks in American literature. His poems borrow from traditions of story-telling and songs. Together with Langston Hughes, he dispelled the sentimental and patronizing myth of the happy, childlike rural Negro, giving powerful and authentic testimony to the sufferings and triumphs of Afro-Americans.

Children's Children

When they hear
These songs, born of the travail° of their sires, *labour, suffering*
Diamonds of song, deep buried beneath the weight
Of dark and heavy years;
They laugh.

When they hear
Saccharine[1] melodies of loving and its fevers,
Soft-flowing lies of love everlasting;
Conjuring divinity out of gross flesh itch;
They sigh
And look goggle-eyed
At one another.

They have forgotten, they have never known,
Long days beneath the torrid Dixie[2] sun
In miasma'd° riceswamps; *foul air*
The chopping of dried grass, on the third go round
In strangling cotton;[3]
Wintry nights in mud-daubed makeshift huts,
With these songs, sole comfort.

1 *Chemical used as an artificial sweetener.*

2 *The southern states of the USA, which relied heavily on slave labour until civil war between the northern and southern states in the 1860s ended slavery.*

3 *Cotton was the chief crop of the southern states; harvesting it was back-breaking work.*

They have forgotten
What had to be endured —

That they, babbling young ones,
With their paled faces, coppered lips,
And sleek hair cajoled° to Caucasian[4] straightness, *coaxed*
Might drown the quiet voice of beauty
With sensuous stridency;

And might, on hearing these memoirs of their sires,
Giggle,
And nudge each other's satin clad
Sleek sides ....

Contextual notes

This poem is addressed to the grandchildren of black Americans who were slaves before being liberated after the American Civil War. The poet argues that the young descendants of slaves have lost touch with their history and heritage of suffering.

4 *Racial type of white European origin.*

Langston Hughes (1902 – 1967)

One of the first major black poets in the USA, Hughes was born in the southern part of America and travelled in Europe and Africa before returning home to study and write. A leader of the Harlem Renaissance (a flowering of talent and cultural creativity in Harlem, a black suburb of New York City), he became known as the 'poet laureate of Harlem'. Together with Sterling Brown, he was an influential figure in advancing 'Negritude', a cultural movement which promoted black achievement. He was an innovator of 'jazz' poetry, which was drawn from the speech and music of black Americans, and worked with musicians to perfect this genre. A meticulous writer, he continually reworked his poems, while also writing novels, children's books and newspaper articles.*

Mother to Son

Well, son, I'll tell you.
Life for me ain't been no crystal stair.
It's had tacks in it,
And splinters,
And boards torn up,
And bare places with no carpet on the floor . . .
Bare.
But all the time
I'se been a-climbin' on,
And reachin' landin's
And turnin' corners,
And sometimes goin' in the dark
Where there ain't been no light.
So, boy, don't you turn back.
Don't you set down on the steps
'Cause you'll find it kinder hard.
Don't you fall now . . .
For I'se still goin' honey,
I'se still climbin',
And life for me ain't been no crystal stair.

The Negro[1] Speaks of Rivers

I've known rivers:
I've known rivers ancient as the world and older than the flow
of human blood in human veins.

My soul has grown deep like the rivers.

I bathed in the Euphrates[2] when dawns were young.
I built my hut near the Congo[3] and it lulled me to sleep.
I looked upon the Nile[4] and raised the pyramids above it.
I heard the singing of the Mississippi[5] when Abe Lincoln[6] went
down to New Orleans,[7] and I've seen its muddy bosom turn
all golden in the sunset.

I've known rivers:
Ancient, dusky rivers.

My soul has grown deep like the rivers.

Contextual notes

This was one of Hughes' first poems, begun while he was still at school; it attracted public attention and supplied the first boost to his career as a writer.

1 *Until the 1960s, the official and accepted term for Americans of African descent. Since then, it has been discredited and is no longer used.*

2 *Middle Eastern river, sometimes described as 'the cradle of civilization'.*

3 *Great central African river; now known as the Zaire River.*

4 *Longest river in Africa; the sophisticated ancient Egyptian civilization (which built the pyramids) was completely dependent on it.*

5 *Greatest North American river; it flows through the southern states of the USA.*

6 *Abraham Lincoln, president of the USA during the 1860s. His insistence on emancipating slaves and banning slavery led to the American Civil War.*

7 *Southern city on the mouth of the Mississippi River, known for its beautiful architecture and vibrant black cultural life.*

Stevie Smith (1902 – 1971)

Smith, born Florence Margaret, was nicknamed after a racing jockey because she was so short. She lived in London throughout her life, and published three novels and two volumes of poetry before her eccentric style became popular. Her poetry, often illustrated with her own comic drawings, was mischievous and witty, even when handling darker themes. She worked as a radio broadcaster, and had a distinctive voice; many of her admirers remember her reading her poems aloud over the air.

Not Waving but Drowning

Nobody heard him, the dead man,
But still he lay moaning:
I was much further out than you thought
And not waving but drowning.

Poor chap, he always loved larking° *joking, teasing*
And now he's dead
It must have been too cold for him his heart gave way,
They said.

Oh, no no no, it was too cold always
(Still the dead one lay moaning)
I was much too far out all my life
And not waving but drowning.

William Plomer (1903 – 1973)

Plomer was born in the Transvaal to British parents, and was educated in both South Africa and Britain. During his twenties he managed a store in Zululand, and wrote the novel Turbott Wolfe, *which earned him recognition. Together with the poet Roy Campbell (and later the writer Laurens van der Post) he put together a satirical literary magazine,* Voorslag *(which means 'whiplash'). This was followed by a period of teaching in Japan, before he settled in England. Here he moved in stimulating literary and critical circles. He became friends with the famous novelist Virginia Woolf and her husband, and worked for the distinguished publisher Jonathan Cape. His poems often returned to the topic of South Africa and its tensions. As well as poetry and fiction, he also wrote librettos (opera scripts) for the composer Benjamin Britten.*

A Transvaal Morning

A sudden waking when a saffron° glare *bright yellow*
Suffused the room, and sharper than a quince° *sour fruit*
Two bird-notes penetrated there
Piercing the cloistral[1] deep veranda twice.

The stranger started up to face
The sulphur[2] sky of Africa, an infinite
False peace, the trees in that dry place
Like painted bones, their stillness like a threat.

Shoulders of quartz[3] protruded from the hill
Like sculpture half unearthed; red dust,
Impalpable as cinnamon softly sifted, filled
With heaped-up silence rift and rut.

Again those two keen bird-notes! And the pert
Utterer, a moss-green thrush, was there
In the veranda-cave, alert,
About to flit into the breathless air.

1 *Secluded, as in a monastery or convent.*
2 *Greenish-yellow chemical.*
3 *Geometrically shaped stone.*

The strangeness plucked the stranger like a string.
'They say this constant sun outstares the mind,
Here in this region of the fang, the sting,
And dulls the eye to what is most defined.

'A wild bird's eye on the *qui vive*[4]
Perhaps make vagueness clear and staleness new;
If undeceived one might not then deceive;
Let me', he thought, 'attain the bird's-eye view.'

4 *Literally, 'who lives'; here it means 'alert'.*

W. H. Auden (1907 – 1973)

The son of a learned doctor, Auden went to Oxford University to study science. However, he became part of a group of creative young poets, and recognition of his own poetic skills inspired him to change careers. After university he travelled widely, witnessing the civil wars in both China and Spain. A radical socialist as a young man, he was to become more conservative in later years. His first poems were accepted for publication by T. S. Eliot, and he was recognized as a brilliant new contributor to modern poetry. A homosexual, he married Erika Mann, daughter of the famous writer Thomas Mann, so that she could flee persecution in Nazi Germany. In 1939 he left for the USA, where he eventually took up American citizenship, a decision which cost him some popularity. Nevertheless, he was appointed professor of poetry at Oxford, where he spent the rest of his life. His poetry remains astonishing for its range and its ability to transform conventional forms.

Roman Wall Blues

Over the heather[1] the wet wind blows
I've lice in my tunic and a cold in my nose.

The rain comes pattering out of the sky,
I'm a Wall soldier, I don't know why.

The mist creeps over the hard grey stone,
My girl's in Tungria;[2] I sleep alone.

Aulus goes hanging around her place,
I don't like his manners, I don't like his face.

Piso's a Christian, he worships a fish;[3]
There'd be no kissing if he had his wish.

She gave me a ring but I diced it away;
I want my girl and I want my pay.

When I'm a veteran with only one eye
I shall do nothing but look at the sky.

1 *Small grey-green bushes with purple flowers typically found in the north of England and Scotland.*

2 *Province in Italy.*

3 *A fish was one of the figures used by the early Christians to symbolize Jesus as the risen Christ.*

Contextual notes

In early times, Britain was one of the Roman Empire's occupied territories, and Roman soldiers were sent there to enforce the authority of the conqueror. However, the occupying militia had difficulty with fierce local tribes, who attacked from the north. Thus the Roman Wall (also known as Hadrian's Wall, named after the Emperor at the time) was built as a defence across the northern part of England. (See Introductory Notes, p. xx.)

Lullaby

Lay your sleeping head, my love,
Human on my faithless arm;
Time and fevers burn away
Individual beauty from
Thoughtful children, and the grave
Proves the child ephemeral:° *transitory*
But in my arms till break of day
Let the living creature lie,
Mortal, guilty, but to me
The entirely beautiful.

Soul and body have no bounds:
To lovers as they lie upon
Her tolerant enchanted slope
In their ordinary swoon,
Grave the vision Venus[4] sends
Of supernatural sympathy,
Universal love and hope;
While an abstract insight wakes
Among the glaciers and the rocks
The hermit's carnal° ecstasy. *fleshly*

4 *Classical goddess of love.*

In Memory of W. B. Yeats

I

He disappeared in the dead of winter:
The brooks were frozen, the airports almost deserted,
And snow disfigured the public statues;
The mercury[5] sank in the mouth of the dying day.
What instruments we have agree
The day of his death was a dark cold day.

Far from his illness
The wolves ran on through the evergreen forests,
The peasant river was untempted by the fashionable quays;
By mourning tongues
The death of the poet was kept from his poems.

But for him it was his last afternoon as himself,
An afternoon of nurses and rumours;
The provinces of his body revolted,
The squares of his mind were empty,
Silence invaded the suburbs,
The current of his feeling failed; he became his admirers.

Now he is scattered among a hundred cities
And wholly given over to unfamiliar affections,
To find his happiness in another kind of wood
And be punished under a foreign code of conscience.
The words of a dead man
Are modified in the guts of the living.

But in the importance and noise of to-morrow
When the brokers are roaring like beasts on the floor of the Bourse,[6]
And the poor have the sufferings to which they are fairly accustomed,
And each in the cell of himself is almost convinced of his freedom,
A few thousand will think of this day
As one thinks of a day when one did something slightly unusual.
What instruments we have agree
The day of his death was a dark cold day.

5 *Liquid metal sensitive to heat and cold, used in thermometers.*

6 *The French stock exchange.*

II

You were silly like us; your gift survived it all:
The parish of rich women,[7] physical decay,
Yourself. Mad Ireland hurt you into poetry.
Now Ireland has her madness and her weather still,
For poetry makes nothing happen: it survives
In the valley of its making where executives
Would never want to tamper, flows on south
From ranches of isolation and the busy griefs,
Raw towns that we believe and die in; it survives,
A way of happening, a mouth.

III

Earth, receive an honoured guest:
William Yeats is laid to rest.
Let the Irish vessel lie
Emptied of its poetry.

In the nightmare of the dark
All the dogs of Europe bark,
And the living nations wait,
Each sequestered° in its hate; *locked up, isolated*

Intellectual disgrace
Stares from every human face,
And the seas of pity lie
Locked and frozen in each eye.

Follow, poet, follow right
To the bottom of the night,
With your unconstraining voice
Still persuade us to rejoice;

With the farming of a verse
Make a vineyard of the curse,
Sing of human unsuccess
In a rapture of distress;

In the deserts of the heart
Let the healing fountain start,
In the prison of his days
Teach the free man how to praise.

7 *Reference to Yeats' patrons and supporters, among them Lady Gregory (see pp. 114, 119).*

Contextual notes

The great Irish poet Yeats (see p. 114) died in France at a time when fascism was rife in Europe and a major world war was about to break out; this is referred to in the second stanza of the third section of this poem.

Theodore Roethke (1908 – 1963)

Born in the USA, Roethke was the son of a greenhouse gardener. He was deeply affected by his father's death, which occurred when he was a teenager, and attributed his later breakdowns to this bereavement. His poetry won him most of the major American literary awards, and he taught at several American universities, including the University of Washington in the north-western USA. Here, he was one of the first modern poets to be appointed poet-in-residence at an American university. He constantly encouraged young writers, and was to have a considerable influence on a later generation of poets.

Elegy for Jane

(My student, thrown by a horse)

I remember the neckcurls, limp and damp as tendrils;
And her quick look, a sidelong pickerel[1] smile;
And how, once startled into talk, the light syllables leaped for her,
And she balanced in the delight of her thought,
A wren, happy, tail into the wind,
Her song trembling the twigs and small branches.
The shade sang with her;
The leaves, their whispers turned to kissing;
And the mould sang in the bleached valleys under the rose.

Oh, when she was sad, she cast herself down into such a pure depth,
Even a father could not find her:
Scraping her cheek against straw;
Stirring the clearest water.

My sparrow, you are not here,
Waiting like a fern, making a spiny shadow.
The sides of wet stones cannot console me,
Nor the moss, wound with the last light.

If only I could nudge you from this sleep,
My maimed darling, my skittery° pigeon. *restless*
Over this damp grave I speak the words of my love:
I, with no rights in this matter,
Neither father nor lover.

1 *A pickerel is a young pike (a type of fish); it is debatable whether the poet is suggesting that his student has a fish-shaped smile, or underlining her youth and potential for growth.*

Modikwe Dikobe (1913 –)

*Dikobe was born in the Transvaal and raised in Sophiatown, a black township which came to be known for its cultural diversity. He had limited access to schooling, and gained much of his education by correspondence. He held a variety of humble jobs, including selling newspapers. His first novel (*The Marabi Dance*), together with his poetry, identified him as a writer passionately concerned with black oppression under apartheid.*

Khoikhoi-Son-Of-Man

I thought I was soul and skin
Pedigree muntu[1]
Until yesterday I heard the truth
Grandfather was a Khoisan.[2]

A slave of a trekboer
Fleeing from the Cape laws
Freeing slaves.[3]

At night
He was tied to an oxwagon wheel
Groaning
Day by day leading sixteen span° *pairs of oxen*
Fleeing from the Cape.

Night by night
Somewhere there was a cock-crow
A barking dog
A smell of damp fuel
Then he realized that beyond that ridge
Could be a village
Of people like him.

1 *Slang term for an African; now considered degrading.*
2 *Hunter-gatherer tribe (initially called Bushmen) indigenous to the Cape; now largely exterminated.*
3 *The 'trekboers' were farmers of Dutch descent who left the Cape and travelled ('trekked') on wagons drawn by oxen into the interior of the country. One of the reasons they left was to escape new laws which made slavery illegal, and which would have freed their slaves.*

He unfastened himself,
Trotted out of the camp,
Vanished into the night.

At dawn he was at a village
Begging to be taken into the tribe
 'A tribesman, hunter, chief's servant and messenger.'

Swift as an antelope° was he *buck*
Outstripping runners
Chased by dogs.
 'Ka modimo',[4] they swore.
 'He is a man of the cloud.
 Ompone ke tswa kae?'[5]
A legendary tale: where have you seen me?
 'I have seen you from the cloud.'
Khoikhoi-Son-of-Man.

I knew since yesterday
that he was my grandfather
Khoikhoi-Son-of-Man.

4 *'By God' or 'I swear on oath' (Tswana).*

5 *These words are translated in the next line.*

Jack Cope (1913 – 1992)

Cope grew up in Natal, where he tried farming before turning to journalism as a career. He worked in London for several years before returning to South Africa to become a full-time writer. He wrote novels and short stories as well as poems, and edited the influential literary journal Contrast. *One of his aims was to make South African writing accessible to a wider audience. He returned to England some time before his death.*

The Flying Fish[1]

(For Ingrid)

The level ocean lies immeasurably blind
swept through green deeps to glutinous° weed. *sticky*

But the flying fish, how they leap away
in water-flashes to the enamelled° sun! *coated with glossy metal*
They break along the foam-lipped chorus
of sea swells. Mysterious
the sounds they loosen, arrows
singing on the air and lost:
mysterious the glass-winged birds
of the long blind sea.

On the storm-swung streams they ride
over free oceans over the locked ice
the groans of midnight fires
and moons returning on the tide.
Light as great winged travellers
of the endless South
urgent as birth
from gloomed fishweed and the dead underwave
the flying fish sing to light.

1 *Flying fish are small tropical fish with wing-like fins which they use to leap from the sea into the air.*

Contextual notes

This poem is an elegy for the Afrikaans poet, Ingrid Jonker, who committed suicide at a young age by drowning. (See p. 212 for notes on Jonker herself and an example of her poetry.)

COMPARISON

After reading this poem, turn to Sally Bryer's 'Ingrid Jonker' (p. 239). Both poems are written to honour the same poet, and use similar metaphors. Yet they are also quite different.

1. What central imagery do both poets use, and why did they choose these images? (Jonker's method of suicide will give you a clue.)
2. What are the chief differences in the way that the two poets approach their topics? Look, for example, at the use of pronouns in Bryer's poem, and the way the dead woman is physically conjured up. Apart from the subtitle, is Cope's poem specifically addressed to anyone? Does any human figure actually appear in it?
3. One of these poems, while written as an elegy, also functions as a straightforward lyrical poem. Which one is it? How then do we know that the poet has Jonker's life and death in mind?
4. Which poem do you prefer? Which is more personal? Which one offers the greater hope? (Remember that there are no 'right' or 'wrong' answers to these questions!)

Dylan Thomas (1914 – 1953)

Born in Wales, Thomas was the son of a teacher, and began writing as a teenager. Initially a journalist, he gained popularity as a broadcaster and poet. He was a meticulous writer who laboured at his poems, which became famous for their vivid natural imagery and intensely lyrical style. A colourful and tragic figure, he was an alcoholic, a fact which was unfortunately glamourized as part of his larger-than-life persona. He was a popular public reader, and began a series of lecture tours to the USA. On his fourth tour, he died of alcohol poisoning after a prolonged drinking spree.

And Death Shall Have No Dominion

And death shall have no dominion.° *kingdom, power*
Dead men naked they shall be one
With the man in the wind and the west moon;
When their bones are picked clean and the clean bones gone,
They shall have stars at elbow and foot;
Though they go mad they shall be sane,
Though they sink through the sea they shall rise again;
Though lovers be lost love shall not;
And death shall have no dominion.

And death shall have no dominion.
Under the windings of the sea
They lying long shall not die windily;
Twisting on racks when sinews give way,
Strapped to a wheel, yet they shall not break;
Faith in their hands shall snap in two,
And the unicorn[1] evils run them through;
Split all ends up they shan't crack;
And death shall have no dominion.

And death shall have no dominion.
No more may gulls cry at their ears
Or waves break loud on the seashores;
Where blew a flower may a flower no more
Lift its head to the blows of the rain;
Though they be mad and dead as nails,
Heads of the characters hammer through daisies;
Break in the sun till the sun breaks down,
And death shall have no dominion.

1 *Mythical horse-like animal, with a long horn on the forehead.*

In My Craft or Sullen Art

In my craft or sullen art
Exercised in the still night
When only the moon rages
And the lovers lie abed
With all their griefs in their arms,
I labour by singing light
Not for ambition or bread
Or the strut and trade of charms
On the ivory stages
But for the common wages
Of their most secret heart.

Not for the proud man apart
From the raging moon I write
On these spindrift° pages *sea-spray*
Nor for the towering dead
With their nightingales and psalms
But for the lovers, their arms
Round the griefs of the ages,
Who pay no praise or wages
Nor heed my craft or art.

Suggestions for discussion

1. How does the poet see his 'art', according to the first stanza? What words suggest that the business of creating poetry is hard work?
2. Thomas was famous for 'transferring' words which describe a specific mood to ordinary nouns; see, for example, 'the moon rages' (line 3) and 'singing light' (line 6). What do these mean? Is the poet describing the moon and the light, or something else? Can you find other examples of this kind of pairing in this poem?
3. Closely examine the structure of the poem. Look at the words which begin each line; with one exception, how many syllables does each one have? What word or words are repeated? What effect is created as a result? Also look at the rhyme scheme. How many rhyme-end sounds are there in the whole poem, and how are these laid out? How does the poet's careful use of rhyme underline the theme of the poem?
4. Why does the poet refer to his pages as 'spindrift' (line 14)? What does this suggest about the nature of poetry?
5. A central irony* is suggested throughout this poem. What is it? (See the last two lines.)

Anthony Delius (1916 – 1989)

Born in Simonstown in the Cape, Delius was educated at Rhodes University. He was a respected journalist (at one stage he was the leader writer for the liberal newspaper The Cape Times*), as well as a poet, satirist and travel writer. Later he moved to London and worked there in broadcasting. His poetry and fiction won him a number of prizes.*

Deaf-and-dumb School

On the black tarmac playground dark
Nuns, a white statue of the Virgin[1] watch
Bare feet of the muted children jerk
And scuffle over endless silence. Such

Is their element. Though I have heard
Them flute like evening swallows in the sky
The sounds were sad, irrelevant, absurd
And could not pierce the silences of play,

Nor break the glass that frames their world.
A soundless quality of painting grips
A small boy leaning from a bench enthralled
In thoughts that dance on other finger-tips.

One with the cry and stiffness of a crane
Dances before a dumb-struck clientele,
Beyond, some cheerless footballers bemoan
A speechless player's bungled goal.

And all around communication glimmers
From hand to eye, and each attentive face
Turns to a dream of mimicry and mummers,° *play-actors*
Like songless planets signalling through space.

1 *The Virgin Mary, mother of Jesus.*

Sound there is, but silence underlies
The fire-flies of gesture. One cannot catch
Exactly what the muffled outcry says,
Or what it is the nuns and children watch.

Silence like a window shows the room
Of minds that make their signs and mouth their cries,
But what leans out to touch you from the dream
Only the white statue and the darkness realise.

Gwendolyn Brooks (1917 –)

Brooks grew up in Chicago in the USA. Her distinctive poetic voice earned her a place as one of the first major black American women poets. She has been appointed 'poet laureate' of Illinois, the American state in which she lives. She has received 51 honorary degrees, as well as numerous fellowships and awards, including the Pulitzer Prize, probably the USA's most prestigious literary award.

We Real Cool

The Pool Players.
Seven at the Golden Shovel.[1]

We real cool. We
Left school. We

Lurk late. We
Strike straight. We

Sing sin. We
Thin gin. We

Jazz June. We
Die soon.

1 *A typical local club.*

Guy Butler (1918 –)

Butler was brought up on a farm in the Eastern Cape, an experience lovingly described in the first volume of his autobiography. During the Second World War he served in North Africa and Italy, and then studied at Oxford. Until his retirement, he was Professor of English at Rhodes University, Grahamstown. A respected South African poet and educationalist, he has always been fascinated by the tension between the influence of Europe and the experience of Africa in the works of many local poets.

Near Hout Bay

Stopping the car, our childhood friends, now hosts,
suggested we stroll to the fabulous view.
Blinding sun, and heat beating up from a path
gritty with pinkish granite crystals,
curtains of pines permitting
expected glimpses of throbbing cerulean° sky — *blue*
and steep striated° rockface plunging — *grooved*
through broken mirrors, torn lace, beautiful lawns of sea.

There had been much talk in the car, far less on the climb:
talk which, try as we would to make it heal or hide,
only exposed the gaps, unbandaged sentence by sentence
the gashes and wounds of time, great spaces and falls
between us all. Each thread of phrase drifted from lips
like a spider's web from a cave in a thousand-foot cliff,
out, out into distance, finding nothing to cling to —
the next land Buenos Aires.[1]

We gave up the effort. They tried a bit longer,
stopped in mid-sentence as we all stopped moving
in the space and the heat
before the sufficiently epic view.

Silence took charge, a blessed burial of words.
Each forgot his failure, longing, boredom, fury
in that subsidence of even a pretence at speech.

1 *Port on the Atlantic coast of South America.*

We stood a long time, still, just listening:
ten thousand sun-struck cicadas[2] ecstatically screaming;
near and far hundreds of doves in relays
imperturbably repeating themselves to each other;
pine wood sighing into the wind from a thousand shimmering needles;
wind already burdened with the grumbling,
perpetual, unpitied,
crumbling of the surf.

Returning, the talk returned
but attempted nothing whatever.
What can be healed or hidden?
We accepted separation
as the ear those ignorant sounds
that filled that primitive silence
with sadness and with praise:
cicadas; doves; wind; surf.

2 *Insects that make a high, rhythmic chirping sound.*

Ruth Miller (1919 – 1969)

Miller was born in the Cape. She was first a typist, then a teacher in Johannesburg. She wrote short stories, radio plays and poetry; her first collection of poems won her the Ingrid Jonker Memorial Prize, and displayed a rare sensitivity to South African landscapes and wildlife. Miller died of cancer. A complete edition of her writings was recently published by the poet Lionel Abrahams.

Honey

The helicopter bee fines down
His motor to a midget drone.
The creamfurred throat engulfs him. Soon
His legs grow pantaloons° of gold. *leggings*

His thousand brothers sing and thrust
Their piston legs, their pinion° gauze, *wing*
Blind to the plundering soft raid
On catacombs° of murmuring halls. *tunnels, tombs*

Now cool long jars gleam with the taste
Of amber hours suavely° stolen *smoothly*
From summer swooning in the heat;
Till smooth and pale, and pale and golden,
There slides like bliss upon the tongue
A bawd's° red kiss, a drudge's song. *prostitute*

Blue-mantled Mary

Blue-mantled Mary[1]
Bloody in the byre° *cow-shed*
Brought forth. The hawthorn[2] was as white
As milk, the berries all on fire.

1 *Mother of Jesus.*

2 *Thorny shrub with red berries.*

Nine months waiting.
Nine months waiting.

Now I remember
The months ago annunciation —
First feathery thrust of the angel
Nine months ago, this December.
The tall touch of the stranger
On my breast, on my skin,
His insupportable maculate° breath *defiled*
Breathing as I did, out and in,
Out and in
Waiting for the time of birth.

Untouched by man, blue-mantled Mary ran
Ran on her pencilled feet into the light
Of the cathedral window, serene as snow.
How was she then to know
What would be done? Whose Will it was she knew.

And I remember
Unhallowed, un-Mary'd, this seed must grow
Slowly toward its day — though each day is holy —
Toward the windowless
Breathless lusty breath
Of a full-term Death.

Contextual notes

This poem is based on the New Testament story of the Annunciation. This was the occasion on which an angel appeared to Mary, and told her that regardless of her virginity, she was to conceive and give birth to the new 'Messiah', or saviour of humanity.

Lawrence Ferlinghetti (1919 –)

The American poet Ferlinghetti was one of the first representatives of the 'Beat Generation', a style of poetic writing and song-writing that sprang up in the 1950s. The object was to escape from middle-class conventional values, and write poetry which reflected mysticism, youth culture, radical political and social stances, and which had an improvized or informal style.

Constantly Risking Absurdity

Constantly risking absurdity
and death
whenever he performs
above the heads
of his audience
the poet like an acrobat
climbs on rhyme
to a high wire of his own making
and balancing on eyebeams
above a sea of faces
paces his way
to the other side of day
performing entrechats° *balletic leaps*
and sleight-of-foot tricks
and other high theatrics
and all without mistaking
any thing
for what it may not be

For he's the super realist
who must perforce perceive
taut truth
before the taking of each stance or step
in his supposed advance
toward that still higher perch
where Beauty stands and waits
with gravity
to start her death-defying leap
And he
a little charleychaplin man
who may or may not catch
her fair eternal form
spreadeagled in the empty air
of existence

Es'kia (Ezekiel) Mphahlele (1919 –)

Mphahlele was born in the Transvaal. He became literary editor of Drum, *the influential magazine of black culture in the 1950s. His writing was banned in South Africa, and he spent 20 years in exile, first living in Nigeria, and then teaching in France and the USA. His literary achievements, both as a novelist and a poet, are impressive, and have gained him international recognition. On his return to South Africa, he was placed under a banning order, but was nevertheless granted the post of professor of African literature at the University of the Witwatersrand, a position he still holds.*

A Poem

What is there that we can do or say
will sustain them
in those islands
where the sun was made for janitors?

What is there that we can say or do
will tear the years
from out the hands
of those who man the island galleys,

will bring them home and dry and mend them
bring them back
to celebrate
with us the song and dance and toil of living?

What is it that we must do or say
for children scattered
far from home
by hawks let loose to stay the judgement day?

The weeds run riot where our house is fallen
ourselves we roam
the wilderness.
'Go tell them there across the seas go tell him,'

so they say, 'his mother's dead six years,
he dare not come
he dare not write
the stars themselves have eyes and ears these days.'

You who fell before the cannon or
the sabred° tooth *sword-like*
or lie on hallowed
ground: oh tell us what to say or do.

So many routes have led to exile since
your day our Elders
we've been here
and back in many cycles oh so many:

no terrain different drummers borrowed
dreams, and there
behind us now
the hounds have diamond fangs and paws of steel.

No time for dirge° or burial without corpses: *mourning song*
teach us, Elders,
how to wait
and feel the centre, tame the time like masters,
sing the blues
so pain will bleed and let the islands in,
for exile is a ghetto° of the mind. *slum*

Contextual notes

Written when apartheid was at its height, this poem refers to the fate of imprisonment or exile which faced most activists. The first three stanzas refer to Robben Island, a small island just off the coast of Cape Town, for years a notorious maximum-security prison for those convicted of political offences.

David Wright (1920 – 1994)

Deaf from childhood, Wright left South Africa for Britain as a teenager, and was educated first at a school for the deaf and then at Oxford University. He pursued a distinguished career as a writer and academic, which included writing poetry, literary criticism, anthologizing, and translating Old and Middle English. He repeatedly visited South Africa, and maintained a strong interest in South African literature.

From On the Margin

An anniversary approaches:[1] of the birth of god
In a stable, son of a virgin and a carpenter,
But really issued from loins of omnipotent° glory: *all-powerful*
A babe, ejected from the thighs, greased in mucus and blood,

Weeping with its first breath, suffering the cold air, high king
Of the galaxies, and powerless as a fieldmouse.
Over him breathe the oxen; shepherds who have seen a star
Honour the obscure event; and, they say, three travelling

Magi,[2] or charlatans.° This is the messenger of hope; *imposters, cheats*
The military have been instructed to deal with him.
A wholesale killing, their invariable strategy,
While abolishing a generation, fails of effect.

We are asked to believe all this (it's only to start with).
What a jumble of the impossible and casual,
Of commonplace mixed with violence; ordinary muddle;
The props and characters scruffy; at best unheroic.

Yet accordant with the disposition of things holy
As we understand them; whose epiphanies° are banal,° *revelations / commonplace, boring*
Not very aesthetic; gnomic,[3] unremarkable;
And very much like what we have to put up with daily.

1 *The festival of Christmas.*
2 *Wise men from the east.*
3 *Brief moralizing statement or generalization.*

Contextual notes

This poem presents a version of the story of the birth of Jesus as told in the New Testament. This event took place in a stable, to which three wise men (who had been warned of a significant event by the appearance of a guiding star) travelled to pay homage. The ruler of the territory meanwhile heard of the birth of a powerful new king, and ordered the occupying Roman forces to murder all boys under the age of two years. The baby Jesus, however, escaped the massacre. (These are the events referred to in the third stanza.)

Comparison

You might like to compare this poem to Eliot's 'Journey of the Magi' (p. 136), a very different work on the same topic.

1. What elements do the poems share? Both contain notes of practical realism, even cynicism; can you identify these? Why do the respective poets introduce these details?
2. What are the chief differences in tone between the two poems? It will help if you identify who is speaking in each poem. Whose is the more detached voice?
3. How does the poet's own voice emerge or operate in the Eliot poem? Judging from these poems, what perspectives would you say the authors have on the religious events they describe?
4. Towards the end of each poem, there is a shift in tone that results in a rather surprising conclusion. What is the final message of each poem, and how do they differ?

Tatamkulu Afrika (1921 –)

A reclusive figure with a fascinating life history, Afrika writes under the above pseudonym to maintain his privacy. A staunch convert to Islam, he found a home in the Cape Muslim community after spending much of his life wandering around the world. Although he has written fiction since an early age, he began writing and publishing poetry only in the late 1980s, and is already recognized as one of South Africa's leading new poets. His poetry is marked by a compassionate and acute observation of the shabbier side of urban life; he is also a strikingly original political poet.

The Handshake

(For Nelson Mandela)

The day before,
I saw the low sun fell
my shadow inwards from the door.
Longer than the floor,
head, shoulders, kinked
up onto the opposite wall,
it could have been yours,
you suddenly such
a very tall man,
and I knew
I dared not sing your praises though
I am a spinner of words that readily strings
baubles° of glass and sounding brass, *trinkets, cheap decorations*
and have a way
with the most of men.
So there were no pattings of drums,
clashings of calabash,[1]
rattlings of teeth or shells,
as you stood, garlanded, in the great hall.
But I thought you smiled a little
at the ordinariness of my poems:
or did you mock
the shaking of my hands?
I could not tell.

1 *Container made from hollowed-out fruit or vegetable.*

The light, bright
as an interrogation's, beat
down from the far,
imperial roof and I could have touched
you, had I stretched
an arm, but we were trapped,
insectile, in the shared
yet isolating amber[2] of the air,
the white quiff of your hair
stilled as a flame
in a stopped cinema reel,
lean, aware
guards about you, poised,
patient, stepped
with you from a TV frame,
and I could not tell.
Kingliness clung
to you, less
in classic Roman folds[3]
than a tribal blanket's fall:
yet you were no tribal man,
skin's almost olive stayed
midway, your wide, encompassing smile
neither chief's nor tsar's.[4]
Only your immobility,
slow tongue, quiet tap
of your papers on the podium,
showed you knew
you were the icon,[5] must
take us with you in a dream
less cliché than a hunger of the soul.
At the end, you turned,
took my hand,
tricked me into thinking we were alone,
thanked me with the grave
courtesy of the old.
But I hardly heard:
as old ears opened now
to only the language of the eyes.
A little shy,
yours met mine,
like any other old man's, shared
the loneliness of the long road.

2 *Gold-coloured fossilized plant sap; insects were sometimes trapped in it.*

3 *Reference to the togas (garments) worn by rulers of the Roman Empire.*

4 *Russian emperor.*

5 *Holy image or symbol.*

I did not have to ask you why
you sometimes walk
the silent places in the last of night,
remembering your dear dead,
refurbishing your dream.
We could have been friends:
but you have so many hands to shake,
how will you remember mine,
holding to yours like a drowning man's?
And though your feet stayed flesh,
you are the truer icon for that,
must fill so wide a space you would never hear
me bonga-ing[6] in my skins in the wind.

6 *Sound made by African drums.*

Philip Larkin (1922 – 1985)

Born in England and educated at Oxford University, Larkin spent most of his life as a university librarian in the north of England, deliberately avoiding the literary scene of London. His writing is remarkable for its transformation of ordinary topics and practical language into thought-provoking poetry. A great fan of jazz music, he was a columnist on the subject for the newspaper The Daily Telegraph.

Talking in Bed

Talking in bed ought to be easiest,
Lying together there goes back so far,
An emblem° of two people being honest. *sign, symbol*

Yet more and more time passes silently.
Outside, the wind's incomplete unrest
Builds and disperses clouds about the sky.

And dark towns heap up on the horizon.
None of this cares for us. Nothing shows why
At this unique distance from isolation

It becomes still more difficult to find
Words at once true and kind,
Or not untrue and not unkind.

Agostinho Neto (1922 – 1979)

An Angolan nationalist who fought to liberate his country, Neto was also a poet who was deeply concerned with the issues facing colonial and post-colonial Africa. During Portugal's rule over Angola, he was repeatedly imprisoned for revolutionary activities.

The Grieved Lands

The grieved lands of Africa
in the tearful woes of ancient and modern slave
in the degrading sweat of impure dance
of other seas
grieved

The grieved lands of Africa
in the infamous sensation of the stunning perfume of the flower
crushed in the forest
by the wickedness of iron and fire
the grieved lands

The grieved lands of Africa
in the dream soon undone in jinglings of gaolers' keys
and in the stifled laughter and victorious voice of laments
and in the unconscious brilliance of hidden sensations
of the grieved lands of Africa

Alive
in themselves and with us alive

They bubble up in dreams
decked with dances by baobabs[1] over balances
by the antelope° *buck*
in the perpetual alliance of everything that lives

They shout out the sound of life
shout it
even the corpses thrown up by the Atlantic
in putrid° offering of incoherence and death *rotten*
and in the clearness of rivers

1 *African trees bearing edible fruit.*

They live
the grieved lands of Africa
in the harmonious sound of consciences
contained in the honest blood of men
in the strong desire of men
in the sincerity of men
in the pure and simple rightness of the stars' existence

They live
the grieved lands of Africa
because we are living
and are imperishable particles
of the grieved lands of Africa.

Denise Levertov (1923 –)

Levertov was born in England to a Russian-Jewish family. Her father converted to Christianity and became a priest, but remained determined to draw the two religions together. During the 1930s, the Levertov home was a refuge for Jews escaping from Nazi Germany. Levertov was educated privately at home; during the Second World War she worked as a nurse, and afterwards married an American soldier, also a writer. She returned with him to the USA, and has remained there, teaching at various universities and writing and editing poetry. She was a noted anti-war activist during the American war in Vietnam during the 1960s and 70s. Her work is significant for the power of its imagery and close observation of daily human events.

What Were They Like?

(1) Did the people of Viet Nam
use lanterns of stone?
(2) Did they hold ceremonies
to reverence the opening of buds?
(3) Were they inclined to quiet laughter?
(4) Did they use bone and ivory,
jade[1] and silver, for ornament?
(5) Had they an epic poem?
(6) Did they distinguish between speech and singing?

1 *Green semi-precious stone, often used in Oriental carving and sculpture.*

(1) Sir, their light hearts turned to stone.
It is not remembered whether in gardens
stone lanterns illumined pleasant ways.
(2) Perhaps they gathered once to delight in blossom,
but after the children were killed
there were no more buds.
(3) Sir, laughter is bitter to the burned mouth.
(4) A dream ago, perhaps. Ornament is for joy.
All the bones were charred.
(5) It is not remembered. Remember,
most were peasants; their life
was in rice and bamboo.
When peaceful clouds were reflected in the paddies
and the water buffalo stepped surely along terraces,
maybe fathers told their sons old tales.
When bombs smashed those mirrors
there was time only to scream.
(6) There is an echo yet
of their speech which was like a song.
It was reported their singing resembled
the flight of moths in moonlight.
Who can say? It is silent now.

Contextual notes

This poem deals with the shattering effect of war on the Vietnamese people. During the 1960s and 70s, the USA sent conscripted troops to Vietnam to fight against the guerrillas who were striving to unite North and South Vietnam under socialist rule. This intervention in what amounted to a civil war was enormously costly, especially in terms of lives lost, caused acute suffering to the Vietnamese people, and was eventually ineffectual. Many Americans protested bitterly against their country's involvement in a foreign nation's struggle.

Dennis Brutus (1924 –)

Brutus was born in Zimbabwe, then known as Rhodesia, and educated at the universities of Fort Hare and the Witwatersrand. He was a teacher before being imprisoned for political activism. On his release, during the mid-1960s, he went into exile. A past president of the South African Non-Racial Olympic Committee (SANROC), his writings were until recently banned in South Africa. He remains a prolific writer, and his many collections of poetry demonstrate his passion for his home country. He is currently lecturing in the USA, where he has held several prestigious university posts.

Letter to Camden

Burial place of Walt Whitman

You old greybeard poet
who sang of a free world
where men loved men freely
and all enjoyed earth's bounty
still I salute you
and wish to send words of praise

but if words cannot make something happen
cannot ring out to crack
this obdurate° and heartless firmament° *hard, stubborn / sky*
let me be dumb
let my lips be silent
let my mouth be stopped
with grime and dust
here where I see decay
where blood runs in the streets
earth shudders in agony
and men gagged by blood clots, plead for pity
let me be courageous
to cry out for a just world
cry 'Justice,' 'Justice,' 'Justice'
or let me fall silent.

What will it take
to make the heartless unhumans of the world
listen to our cries?
I will go on my knees

like a dog,
a starved chained dog
howling at the moon
and cry 'Justice,' 'Justice,' 'Justice'
until my corpse falls
worn-out and rigid and silent.

Contextual notes

This poem is written to honour the American poet Walt Whitman (see p. 96 for notes on Whitman, and an example of his poetry). Brutus sees a link between his own desire to cry out for justice, and Whitman's honest and courageous call for an end to social condemnation of homosexuality.

Sydney Clouts (1926 – 1982)

Clouts grew up in Cape Town, and was educated at the universities of Cape Town and Rhodes. In 1961 he moved to London, and worked there as a librarian. His first volume of poetry marked him as a brilliant new talent; however, he did not publish again during his lifetime. After his death, a further collection of his poems was published.

Poetry is Death Cast Out

Poetry is death cast out
though it gives one chance to retaliate.
Death takes it but the poem moves
a little further beyond death's gate,

and I know the proof of this. Once walking
amongst bushes and lizard stones I found
a little further than I had thought
to go, a stream with a singing sound.

Maya Angelou (1928 –)

Angelou was born and brought up in the southern USA, and the flavour of her black working-class roots marks her writing. She was sexually abused as a child by a family friend, an experience which left her mute (unable to speak) for years. One of the first black American writers to identify herself with feminist concerns, she is best known for her autobiographical books. She is currently teaching at an American university.

Still I Rise

You may write me down in history
With your bitter, twisted lies,
You may trod me in the very dirt
But still, like dust, I'll rise.

Does my sassiness° upset you? *cheeky wit*
Why are you beset with gloom?
'Cause I walk like I've got oil wells
Pumping in my living room.

Just like moons and like suns,
With the certainty of tides,
Just like hopes springing high,
Still I'll rise.

Did you want to see me broken?
Bowed head and lowered eyes?
Shoulders falling down like teardrops,
Weakened by my soulful cries.

Does my haughtiness offend you?
Don't you take it awful hard
'Cause I laugh like I've got gold mines
Diggin' in my own back yard.

You may shoot me with your words,
You may cut me with your eyes,
You may kill me with your hatefulness,
But still, like air, I'll rise.

Does my sexiness upset you?
Does it come as a surprise
That I dance like I've got diamonds
At the meeting of my thighs?

Out of the huts of history's shame
I rise
Up from a past that's rooted in pain
I rise
I'm a black ocean, leaping and wide,
Welling and swelling I bear in the tide.

Leaving behind nights of terror and fear
I rise
Into a daybreak that's wondrously clear
I rise
Bringing the gifts that my ancestors gave,
I am the dream and the hope of the slave.
I rise
I rise
I rise.

Thomas Kinsella (1928 –)

Kinsella was raised and educated in Dublin, the capital of Ireland. He spent the first half of his life as a civil servant, reaching a high rank in the Department of Finance, and was instrumental in setting up several new Irish publishing concerns. He then took up a series of teaching positions in the USA, and now moves between Dublin and America. As well as poetry, he has undertaken translations from Irish into English. His work borrows from both Irish and wider sources; the poetry of Auden is a strong influence. He is a particular master of the monologue in poetry.*

Sacrifice

Crowded steps, a sea of white faces
streaked with toil.

The scrutiny is over, in sunlight,
terrible black and white.

There is the mark . . . In those streaks . . .
Their hands are on her.
Her friends gather.
The multitudes sigh and bless
and persuade her heavily forward to her tears
in doomed excitement
down the cup of light
and onto her back on the washed bricks
with breasts held apart
and midriff fluttering in the sun.

The souls gather unseen, like wisps of hunger,
hovering above the table, not interfering,
as it is done in a shivering flash.
The vivid pale solid of the breast
dissolves in a crimson flood.
The heart flops in its sty.

*

Never mind the hurt. I've never felt
so terribly alive, so ready, so gripped
by love — gloved fingers slippery
next the heart!
                                        Is it very difficult?

The blinding pain — when love goes direct
and wrenches at the heart-strings! But the pangs
quickly pass their maximum, and then
such a fount of tenderness!

Are you stuck?
Let me arch back.

I love how you keep muttering
'You know now . . .' — and your concern . . .
but you must finish it.
I lose my mind gladly, thinking:
the heart — in another's clutches!

We are each other's knowledge. It is peace that counts,
and knowledge brings peace, even thrust crackling
into the skull and bursting with tongues of fire.
Peace. Love dying down, as love ascends.

I love your tender triumph, straightening up,
lifting your reddened sleeves. The stain spreads downward
through your great flushed pinions.° *wings*
You are a real angel.
My heart is in your hands: mind it well.

Helen Segal (1929 – 1988)

Segal was born in Johannesburg, and educated at the universities of the Witwatersrand and South Africa. She worked both as a typist and a teacher. Her poetry is characterized by short, irregular lines.

The Sea is all Male

The sea is all male
that is why some women
walk in it
till they drown in ecstasy.
No earthly man
could hold them
handle
rule them;
the secret depths
salt-song
reckless order of the sea
tosses aside imagination
because it is.

They seek heroic consummation;
brains and bones
blood and brawn
have baffled.

On the floor of the sea
ploughing the heavy waters
they strain to the limit
beyond their limit
crash, are crushed,
jet to surface for a breath;
have found a land-locked lover
foaming blind words
in deafened ears;
whirled in cruel embrace
that peaks their world-wise shell
breaking brittle bonds
they are.

On the surface
Spent and placid

weedy hair
combing waves

Adrienne Rich (1929 –)

One of America's leading feminist poets and critics, Rich belongs to a generation which first married and had children, then moved on to more politically radical and women-centred lifestyles. While teaching at university, she became involved in protesting against the American war in Vietnam during the 1960s and 70s.

In the 1970s she was awarded a major prize for literature, which she personally rejected, but claimed on behalf of the black lesbian poet Audre Lorde and 'in the name of all women'. Her poetry is sometimes angry, sometimes tender, and explores new ways of using language to tell women's stories.

'I am in Danger — Sir —'

'Half-cracked'° to Higginson, living, *half-mad*
afterward famous in garbled versions,
your hoard of dazzling scraps a battlefield,
now your old snood° *hairnet*

mothballed at Harvard
and you in your variorum monument
equivocal° to the end — *double meaning*
who are you?

Gardening the day-lily,
wiping the wine-glass stems,
your thought pulsed on behind
a forehead battered paper-thin,

you, woman, masculine
in single-mindedness,
for whom the word was more
than a symptom —

a condition of being.
Till the air buzzing with spoiled language
sang in your ears
of Perjury° *lies told under oath*

and in your half-cracked way you chose
silence for entertainment,
chose to have it out at last
on your own premises.

Contextual notes

This poem refers to the nineteenth-century American poet Emily Dickinson. (For details of Dickinson's life and a selection of her poems, see p. 100). Higginson (line 1) was a friend with literary contacts to whom Dickinson wrote for advice on her poems. His response was not encouraging, and she gave up trying to publish her work. Harvard University holds much Dickinson memorabilia (lines 4–5); the 'variorum monument' (line 6) refers to the publication of Dickinson's poems (which finally took place during the 1950s), together with editorial comments. The last stanza refers to Dickinson's decision to withdraw from human contact and society during the last years of her life.

Comparison

You might enjoy placing Rich's poem against those of Dickinson, to see how Rich borrows from the earlier poet. What obvious feature of Rich's poem immediately suggests Dickinson's poetry? How else does Rich suggest her debt to Dickinson?

Ted Hughes (1930 –)

Much of Hughes' poetry reflects his encounters with nature while growing up in rural Yorkshire (in the north-east of England). He focuses not only on the beauty but on the violence of the natural world, a distinctive and sometimes brutal approach, which can make reading his poetry an uneasy experience. While studying at Cambridge, he met the gifted young poet Sylvia Plath and they married in 1956. Although they had two children, the marriage was not a success. Also an author of children's books and plays, Hughes was appointed Poet Laureate in 1984.

The Thought-Fox

I imagine this midnight moment's forest:
Something else is alive
Beside the clock's loneliness
And this blank page where my fingers move.

Through the window I see no star:
Something more near
Though deeper within darkness
Is entering the loneliness:

Cold, delicately as the dark snow,
A fox's nose touches twig, leaf;
Two eyes serve a movement, that now
And again now, and now, and now

Sets neat prints into the snow
Between trees, and warily a lame
Shadow lags by stump and in hollow
Of a body that is bold to come

Across clearings, an eye,
A widening deepening greenness,
Brilliantly, concentratedly,
Coming about its own business

Till, with sudden sharp hot stink of fox
It enters the dark hole of the head.
The window is starless still; the clock ticks,
The page is printed.

Suggestions for discussion

1. Identify the central metaphor* on which this poem is based, and trace its development. (The title will help you.) Why do you think the poet has chosen a fox returning to its lair to symbolize the dawning of an idea?
2. What does this metaphor suggest about the creative process, as viewed by this poet? According to this poem, how does he experience composing or writing?
3. Although the fox in this poem is a symbolic or metaphorical one, it is described in vividly realistic terms. How does the close observation of the animal and its movements in stanzas three to six correspond with the coming of inspiration? In the last stanza, what role does the poet play?

Tractor

The tractor stands frozen — an agony
To think of. All night
Snow packed its open entrails. Now a head-pincering gale,
A spill of molten ice, smoking snow,
Pours into its steel.
At white heat of numbness it stands
In the aimed hosing of ground-level fieriness.

It defies flesh and won't start.
Hands are like wounds already
Inside armour gloves, and feet are unbelievable
As if the toe-nails were all just torn off.
I stare at it in hatred. Beyond it
The copse° hisses — capitulates miserably *clump of trees*
In the fleeing, failing light. Starlings,
A dirtier sleetier snow, blow smokily, unendingly, over
Towards plantations Eastward.
All the time the tractor is sinking
Through the degrees, deepening
Into its hell of ice.

The starting lever
Cracks its action, like a snapping knuckle.
The battery is alive — but like a lamb
Trying to nudge its solid-frozen mother —
While the seat claims my buttock-bones, bites
With the space-cold of earth, which it has joined
In one solid lump.

I squirt commercial sure-fire
Down the black throat — it just coughs.
It ridicules me — a trap of iron stupidity
I've stepped into. I drive the battery
As if I were hammering and hammering
The frozen arrangement to pieces with a hammer
And it jabbers laughing pain-crying mockingly
Into happy life.

And stands
Shuddering itself full of heat, seeming to enlarge slowly
Like a demon demonstrating
A more-than-usually-complete materialisation —
Suddenly it jerks from its solidarity
With the concrete, and lurches towards a stanchion[1]
Bursting with superhuman well-being and abandon
Shouting Where Where?

Worse iron is waiting. Power-lift kneels
Levers awake imprisoned deadweight,
Shackle-pins bedded in cast-iron cow-shit.
The blind and vibrating condemned obedience
Of iron to the cruelty of iron,
Wheels screeched out of their night-locks —

Fingers
Among the tormented
Tonnage and burning of iron

Eyes
Weeping in the wind of chloroform[2]

And the tractor, streaming with sweat,
Raging and trembling and rejoicing.

1 *Post, device used to shut cattle up in stalls.*

2 *Strong-smelling anaesthetic gas.*

Essop Patel (1930 –)

Patel is an attorney who lives in Johannesburg. His first volume of poetry established him as a compelling and committed political poet. Together with Tim Couzens he edited The Return of the Amasi Bird: Black South African Poetry, *an anthology which was to expose to a wide audience the wealth of black poetry in South Africa.*

In the Shadow of Signal Hill

in the howling wind
by the murky waters
of the sea
children of colour
gather shells
and hold them to their ears
and listen to the lamentations of slaves
in the dungeon of death

in the howling wind
by the murky waters
of the sea
sons of langa
gather at the ruins of district six
and sharpen the spears of the night
and the heroes from the island urge
go towards the fiery dawn . . . .

Contextual notes

Signal Hill is a strikingly shaped hill or small peak overlooking the harbour of Cape Town. It has been used as a lookout post since the early days of the Cape colony. From it, the viewer can see Robben Island (during the apartheid years, a notorious prison for those convicted of political crimes: see also the notes to Mphahlele's 'A Poem', p. 183); the bare scar where the suburb of District Six stood before its occupants were evicted and its buildings demolished under the Group Areas Act (apartheid legislation which restricted racial groups to certain residential areas); and Langa, a black township on the fringes of Cape Town.

Sylvia Plath (1932 – 1963)

Plath was born in the north-eastern USA. Her father, a German immigrant and biology professor, died after a long and traumatic illness when she was eight, an experience which featured in her later writing. She met the poet Ted Hughes while on a scholarship to Cambridge, married him and had two children. However, their marriage broke down. Plath had a history of clinical depression, and shortly after the publication of her first novel, she committed suicide. Although some of her poetry is relentlessly gloomy, it is always strikingly original, and capable of extreme tenderness and compassion.

You're

Clownlike, happiest on your hands,
Feet to the stars, and moon-skulled,
Gilled like a fish. A common-sense
Thumbs-down on the dodo's[1] mode.
Wrapped up in yourself like a spool,
Trawling your dark as owls do.
Mute as a turnip from the Fourth
Of July[2] to All Fools' Day,[3]
O high-riser, my little loaf.

Vague as fog and looked for like mail.
Farther off than Australia.
Bent-backed Atlas,[4] our travelled prawn.
Snug as a bud and at home
Like a sprat° in a pickle jug. *small fish*
A creel° of eels, all ripples. *fishing basket*
Jumpy as a Mexican bean.
Right, like a well-done sum.
A clean slate, with your own face on.

1 *Flightless bird, now extinct.*
2 *Day of Independence in the USA.*
3 *April Fool's Day, 1 April.*
4 *Mythical figure who, according to legend, carried the world on his back.*

Pheasant[5]

You said you would kill it this morning.
Do not kill it. It startles me still,
The jut of that odd, dark head, pacing

Through the uncut grass on the elm's hill.
It is something to own a pheasant,
Or just to be visited at all.

I am not mystical: it isn't
As if I thought it had a spirit.
It is simply in its element.

That gives it a kingliness, a right.
The print of its big foot last winter,
The tail-track, on the snow in our court —

The wonder of it, in that pallor,
Through crosshatch of sparrow and starling.
Is it its rareness, then? It is rare.

But a dozen would be worth having,
A hundred, on that hill — green and red,
Crossing and recrossing: a fine thing!

It is such a good shape, so vivid.
It's a little cornucopia.[6]
It unclaps, brown as a leaf, and loud,

Settles in the elm, and is easy.
It was sunning in the narcissi.[7]
I trespass stupidly. Let be, let be.

5 *Large bird (about the size of a guinea fowl) with green and red feathers; usually hunted and eaten.*

6 *Horn filled with natural produce; a symbol of abundance.*

7 *White spring flowers.*

Douglas Livingstone (1932 – 1996)

Livingstone was born in Malaya, and came to South Africa as a boy. He trained as a marine bacteriologist, and was in charge of research in this field at the Centre for Scientific and Industrial Research in Durban until his death. His poetry vividly describes the characters and wildlife of South Africa, and is often witty and satirical. He was also a critic and the author of several radio plays. A winner of many awards, he is considered one of South Africa's leading poets.

Dust

The bundle in the gutter had its skull
cracked open by a kierie.° *stick*
The blunt end of a sharpened bicycle
spoke grew a solitary
silver war-plume from the nape of his neck.
I turned him gently. He'd thinned to a wreck.

It was my friend Mketwa. He was dead.
Young Mac the Knife, I'd called him,
without much originality. Red
oozed where they'd overhauled him.
An illegal five-inch switchblade,° his 'best' *knife*
possession, was stuck sideways in his chest.

He had been tough; moved gracefully, with ease.
We'd bricked, built walls, carted sand;
pitting strength against cement-bags, we'd seize
and humpf, steadied by a hand.
I paid the regulation wage plus fifty
per cent, his room, his board. He wasn't thrifty.

We were extending the old house I'd bought.
Those baked-lung middays we'd swill
the dust with cans of ice-cold beer. I thought
he must be unkillable,
except by white men. Each night the beerhall
took him: stoned wide, he would not stall or fall.

I don't think he learnt anything tangible
from me. From him, I learnt much:
his mother, cattle, kraal;° the terrible — *enclosure, tribal home*
cheat that repaired his watch; such
and such pleased a woman; passes;[1] bus queues;
whereabouts to buy stolen nails and screws.

His wife in Kwa Mashu, a concubine
in Chesterville,[2] a mistress
in town: all pregnant. He'd bought turpentine[3]
but they wouldn't drink it. This
was the trouble with women. Letters came
we couldn't read. He found another dame.

He left — more money, walls half-done, him tight —
to join Ital-Constructions.
Perhaps it had been white men: I am white.
Now, I phoned the ambulance
and sat with him. It came for Mac the Knife;
bore his corpse away; not out of my life.

1 *Until recently, all black South Africans had to carry passes permitting them to work and travel in white areas.*

2 *Durban townships.*

3 *Oil or solvent used to thin paint; drinking it supposedly induced abortion.*

Sipho Sepamla (1932 –)

Born in the Transvaal, Sepamla trained as a teacher, and worked in Johannesburg as a personnel officer. He has been instrumental in encouraging and training black writers, and is currently the director of the Federated Union of Black Arts (FUBA). Together with Serote and Mtshali, he was one of the giants of the black poetry movement of the 1970s, sometimes called 'the new black poetry' or 'Soweto poetry'. This described the lives of black South Africans with uncompromising realism, and was deeply critical of apartheid. Sepamla's poetry is unique for the way it blends English with township dialects and vernacular languages.

Hurry Up to It!

By all means
Get married,
That's been the idea
These past ten years

And so,
You must hurry,
Hurry up for your sake and mine
For age can move ahead of wishes.

You say
You love her
Love her face:
Eyes brighter than house lights
Nostrils wider than windows
Limbs firmer than men's hearts.

But son,
Make certain she's a desirable person;
For love is:
Knowing the girl's homeland,
Knowing her papers are right,
Knowing she has permission to marry,
And above all
Love is:
Knowing if you can make children;
For remember, son,

You will be required
To buzz thoughts of manhood
In a men's hostel;
She will be expected
To nurse the ache
Of an ill-used womb
In a women's hostel.

Hurry up
You need to register
For a certified permit
To have sex—
In good time!

Contextual notes

This poem satirizes the various apartheid laws which regulated the movements of black South Africans. Where one could live depended on the status of one's pass or 'papers' (line 19), which stated where Africans were permitted to go or stay; this often depended on what 'homeland' (line 18) one was assigned. (Homelands were supposedly self-governing rural territories set aside under the apartheid government. These divided the black population into various tribal groupings.) The last two stanzas refer to the migrant labour system, which allowed men to travel to and live in the cities, where they provided labour for the mines. Here they lived in single-sex hostels, as their wives and families were forbidden to join them.

The Loneliness Beyond

Like raindrops pattering
They come singly and in pairs
Then as a torrent the rush of feet
Shuffles onto platforms
Dragging the last strains of energy.

I've seen hearts palpitating
Behind a single maskless face
Tired from the hurrying of the city
Spirits maimed by commands.

I've heard the clicks of tongues
Laughter rising above the grouse° of mouths *grumbling*
That never rest
From grinding complaints.

Like sheep herded into a kraal° *enclosure*
They crowd numbered coaches
Hopeful of a safe landing.

I've watched the multitudes rub shoulders
And I've wondered what they do
With the loneliness beyond;

I've seen throngs of people
Disappear into little holes of resting
And I've pondered what might be happening
With the loneliness beyond.

Ingrid Jonker (1933 – 1965)

One of South Africa's leading young Afrikaans poets, Jonker was born in the Cape and spent her short life in Cape Town. She was outspoken in her condemnation of apartheid, and her writing was also unusual in its intimate portrayal of often painful emotions. Deeply disheartened by her private and political circumstances, she committed suicide by walking into the sea and drowning. Local scholars and poets continue to translate and be inspired by her poems.

The Child who was Shot Dead by Soldiers at Nyanga

The child is not dead
the child lifts his fists against his mother
who shouts Afrika! shouts the breath
of freedom and the veld° *grasslands*
in the locations of the cordoned° heart *fenced-in*

The child lifts his fists against his father
in the march of the generations
who shout Afrika! shout the breath
of righteousness and blood
in the streets of his embattled pride

The child is not dead
not at Langa nor at Nyanga
not at Orlando nor at Sharpeville
nor at the police station at Philippi
where he lies with a bullet through his brain.

The child is the dark shadow of the soldiers
on guard with rifles saracens[1] and batons
the child is present at all assemblies and law-givings
the child peers though the windows of houses and into the hearts of mothers
this child who just wanted to play in the sun at Nyanga is everywhere
the child grown to a man treks through all Africa
the child grown into a giant journeys through the whole world

Without a pass

Contextual notes

This poem was written in response to the notorious killings at Sharpeville in 1960. Police opened fire on an unarmed crowd of blacks who were protesting against the degrading pass laws which restricted their movements and freedom. Riots and further deaths followed throughout the country, including the various townships and places listed in this poem.

President Nelson Mandela chose this poem to introduce his first parliamentary address immediately after the first non-racial and democratic elections in South Africa in 1994.

1 *Name given to armoured cars.*

Audre Lorde (1934 – 1993)

Lorde was an outspoken black American poet who fearlessly used her writing to proclaim her identity as a feminist and a lesbian. She was active in the black power movements of the late 1960s, and taught at various universities in the USA. In the last years of her life she retired to the Caribbean, where she died after a long and courageous battle against cancer.

Coal

I
is the total black, being spoken
from the earth's inside.
There are many kinds of open
how a diamond comes into a knot of flame
how sound comes into a word, coloured
by who pays what for speaking.

Some words are open like a diamond
on glass windows
singing out within the passing crash of sun
Then there are words like stapled wagers
in a perforated book — buy and sign and tear apart —
and come whatever wills all chances
the stub remains
an ill-pulled tooth with a ragged edge.
Some words live in my throat
breeding like adders. Others know sun
seeking like gypsies over my tongue
to explode through my lips
like young sparrows bursting from shell.
Some words
bedevil me.

Love is a word, another kind of open.
As the diamond comes into a knot of flame
I am Black because I come from the earth's inside
now take my word for jewel in the open light.

Wole Soyinka (1934 –)

Doubtlessly Nigeria's foremost writer, Soyinka was educated both at home and in England. A political prisoner during the 1960s, he has held a number of prestigious teaching posts at universities in Nigeria, Africa, Britain and the USA, and was the founding director of a number of Nigerian theatres. A dramatist, poet, critic and novelist of great stature, he has been awarded the Nobel Prize for Literature.

Capital

It cannot be
That germ which earth has nurtured
Man tended — once I watched a waterfall
Of germ, a grain-spray plentitude
Belched from chutes of wide-mouthed
Glad satiation; I swear the grains
Were singing —

It cannot be
That policy, deliberation
Turns these embers of my life
To ashes, and in polluted seas
Lays sad beds of yeast to raise
Dough
On the world market.

Kofi Awoonor (1935 –)

Awoonor was educated in his home country (Ghana), London and the USA. He was detained on suspicion of terrorism during the 1970s. Considered Ghana's leading poet, he has held a number of prestigious academic and diplomatic posts (he is currently ambassador to Cuba), and has edited various literary journals. His works include plays, critical works and a novel as well as poetry, which specializes in 'lyric lament'.

The Weaver Bird

The weaver bird built in our house
And laid its eggs on our only tree
We did not want to send it away
We watched the building of the nest
And supervised the egg-laying.
And the weaver returned in the guise of the owner
Preaching salvation to us that owned the house
They say it came from the west
Where the storms at sea had felled the gulls
And the fishers dried their nets by lantern light
Its sermon is the divination of ourselves
And our new horizons limit at its nest
But we cannot join the prayers and answers of the communicants.[1]
We look for new homes every day,
For new altars we strive to rebuild
The old shrines defiled by the weaver's excrement.

Contextual notes

This poem is a metaphorical lament on the impact of Western missionaries on African traditional culture.

1 *Those who participate in the Christian ritual of holy communion.*

Don Mattera (1935 –)

Mattera grew up in Sophiatown, and now lives in Johannesburg. His colourful past has included spells as a footballer and gang leader. He founded a union for black journalists, and was banned for his part in the black consciousness movement of the 1970s. (Serote's poem 'For Don M. — Banned' was written for Mattera during this period; see p. 237.) Mattera is best known for his poetry, but has also written short stories, plays and an autobiography. He has received both literary and human rights awards.

Remember

Remember to call at my grave
When freedom finally
Walks the land
So that I may rise
To tread familiar paths
To see broken chains
Fallen prejudice
Forgotten injury
Pardoned pains.

And when my eyes have filled their sight
Do not run away for fright
If I crumble to dust again

It will only be the bliss
Of a long-awaited dream
That bids me rest
When freedom finally walks the land . . .

Contextual notes

This poem was written during the apartheid years, and the speaker envisages freedom in South Africa only in the distant future, long after his death. Fortunately Mattera is still alive, and one hopes that he is pleased that the prophecy in this poem has come to fulfilment sooner than expected!

Valente Malangatana

No dates could be found for this Mozambican poet.

Woman

In the cool waters of the river
we shall have fish that are huge
which shall give the sign of
the end of the world perhaps
because they will make an end of woman
woman who adorns the fields
woman who is the fruit of man.

The flying fish makes an end of searching
because woman is the gold of man
when she sings she ever seems
like the fado[1]-singer's well-tuned guitar
when she dies, I shall cut off
her hair to deliver me from sin.

Woman's hair shall be the blanket
over my coffin when another Artist
calls me to Heaven to paint me
woman's breasts shall be my pillow
woman's eye shall open up for me the way to heaven
woman's belly shall give birth to me up there
and woman's glance shall watch me
as I go up to Heaven.

1 *Portuguese song or lament.*

Geoffrey Haresnape (1939 –)

Born in Natal, Haresnape is currently head of the English Department at the University of Cape Town. His critical works include a collection of pioneering writings and a study of the novels of the South African writer Pauline Smith. He has always maintained a keen interest in South African poetry, and took over from Jack Cope as the editor of the literary magazine Contrast. *He has published two collections of poems to date:* Drive of the Tide *(1976) and* New-born Images *(1991). His poems and his first novel have won a variety of prizes.*

Pruning a Mulberry in Autumn

Climbing a propped-up ladder, I'm daunted
by the tree's springing and spreading. Its top-
most, tapering poles are bare: but the sap
still flows along its horizontal limbs
to feed the scale-like leaves — some red, some green.

I call to my sons: 'Can I please have some help here?'
They emerge from the garage armed like knights.
Bush-saws and the fat-beaked secateurs° *garden clippers*
will be good weapons for their purposes.
Each toppling branch will own their sway.

Back on the ground, I watch the brothers climb,
assess the weights of wood, prepare to fell.
Two persevering princes on a quest,
they break the hydra's[1] hegemonic° hold *ruling, dominant*
upon this corner of our garden plot.

Absorbed in battle, they use up the day.
Only I remember the delicate seedling
I planted here to feed their silkworms.
This tree was once at risk to mandibles° *jaws, mouth-parts*
of dragons long since tombed in silken cells.

1 *Legendary serpent or monster, with many heads; these had the power to grow back after being cut off.*

In and Around the Yacht Basin — Simon's Town[1]

Beyond
the rigging[2] tangle
are

rhyzomes
of Club Mykonos[3]
apartments

Cape
Dutch[4] gable
fungi

floral
filigrees[5]
of English iron.

The
scrubby hills
protest

that Europe's garden
wasn't always
planted here.

* * *

old cling strings giant
tyres like of
necklacing
mussels the pier.

* * *

1 *Naval base and residential area on the Cape Peninsula.*
2 *Ropes which support masts.*
3 *Luxury resort on the Cape west coast.*
4 *Eighteenth-century farm architecture, famous for its simple beauty.*
5 *Ornamental patterning in wire and metal.*

Masts I
(red hard-
yell- ly
ow dare
blue) to
are breathe
pick- when
up lift-
sticks ing
criss- each
crossed im-
or press-
slant- ion:
ed one
when slip
the would
o- jar
cean the
breathes whole.

* * *

A brash South Easter[6]
barges in
upon the game,
displacing
all.

Suggestions for discussion

1. This poem is a delightful experiment in form and shape. Why has the poet laid out the words on the page this way? How do the differing patterns contribute to meaning?
2. Read the second section carefully; you will need to do some reorganizing to make sense out of the word order. Why does the poet 'scatter' the words like this? Do you get the impression of a 'picture' of the scene being visually presented?
3. Parts of the poem seem to play with words and patterns to create different moods and mental pictures; yet part of it has a serious message. Can you identify this?

6 *Wind which blows during summer in the Cape.*

Seamus Heaney (1939 –)

Born into a Catholic family in rural Northern Ireland, Heaney was a student and later a lecturer at Queen's University in Belfast. He holds a significant place in the tradition of Irish poetry, and his work is deeply rooted in the history of his country, which includes for him the tragic violence of modern-day Northern Ireland. He was awarded the Nobel Prize for Literature in 1995. Currently he lives in Dublin.

Follower

My father worked with a horse-plough,
His shoulders globed like a full sail strung
Between the shafts and the furrow.
The horses strained at his clicking tongue.

An expert. He would set the wing
And fit the bright steel-pointed sock.
The sod rolled over without breaking.
At the headrig,° with a single pluck *harness*

Of reins, the sweating team turned round
And back into the land. His eye
Narrowed and angled at the ground,
Mapping the furrow exactly.

I stumbled in his hob-nailed[1] wake,
Fell sometimes on the polished sod;
Sometimes he rode me on his back
Dipping and rising to his plod.

I wanted to grow up and plough,
To close one eye, stiffen my arm.
All I ever did was follow
In his broad shadow round the farm.

I was a nuisance, tripping, falling,
Yapping always. But today
It is my father who keeps stumbling
Behind me, and will not go away.

1 *Reference to 'hob-nailed' boots (boots wth metal studs in the sole).*

Wopko Jensma (1939 –)

Raised in South Africa, Jensma is of Dutch descent. An artist as well as a poet, his collections of poetry feature his own woodcuts. Although he is white, his unorthodox and angry poetry, distinctive for its lack of punctuation, has always been identified with black protest poetry, and his second volume of poems was banned. He was institutionalized and lived in a Salvation Army shelter in later years. He went missing several years ago and it is not known whether he is still alive.

From Not Him

he forbids us to dance
he always leads the church service
he has a stable job
he is always on time for work
he never gets drunk
he has respect for most people
everybody respects him
we love our daddy
but sometimes I notice
when a kwela[1] blasts from the radio
he wiggles his toes

1 *Lively black township music, featuring the penny-whistle.*

Henry Pote (1939 –)

Pote is a Zimbabwean poet who studied in Zimbabwe and Lesotho. Formerly a teacher, he is now active in local government.

To a White Child

Your mother and father, eccentrics
And venturesome, made us friends.
You, innocent, guileless,° saw no tricks *without deceit*
And always accepted my presence
With nonchalance and little wonder.
Something about my grins won you over,
You would constantly wait and hover
Till opportunity turned to tell your secret naïve
About your doll, your prowess, and how you strive
And need my aid to reconstruct a broken toy.
Will your trust vanish when you grow older?
Will you think you alone can order?
It cannot be: you're already too wise
To somersault and move anti-clockwise.

Mbuyiseni Oswald Mtshali (1940 –)

Mtshali was born in the Orange Free State but moved to Johannesburg, where the publication of his first volume of poetry, Sounds of a Cowhide Drum, *was a huge success. Probably the first collection of poems to describe daily life in black townships under apartheid, it sold more copies than any other book of poetry in South Africa. Mtshali, who has studied in the USA and taught in Soweto, was one of the first exponents of the 'new black poetry' of the black consciousness movement of the 1970s. His work was banned for several years.*

Men in Chains

The train stopped
at a country station.

Through sleep curtained eyes
I peered through the frosty window,
and saw six men:

men shorn
of all human honour
like sheep after shearing,
bleating at the blistering wind,
'Go away! Cold wind! Go away!
Can't you see we are naked?'

They hobbled into the train
on bare feet,
wrists handcuffed,
ankles manacled
with steel rings like cattle at the abbatoirs
shying away from the trapdoor.

One man with a head
shaven clean as a potato
whispered to the rising sun,
a red eye wiped by a tattered
handkerchief of clouds,
'Oh ! Dear Sun!
Won't you warm my heart
with hope?'
The train went on its way to nowhere.

Suggestions for discussion

1. A close examination of this poem will be useful in identifying different kinds of imagery. Remember that similes* are usually indicated by the use of the words 'as' and 'like', whereas metaphors* are more directly stated. What similes and metaphors can you identify here?
2. We find two central similes that are used to describe the men in chains. What do they have in common? Why does the poet use this kind of imagery? Is his intention to patronize the prisoners, or is he using these images for a different reason? What is the accumulative impact?
3. How does the poet describe the sun in the fifth stanza? (Think of the qualities we normally associate with the sun; does the imagery here seem surprising?) How does this add to the overall tone of the poem?
4. What effect does the last line have?

An Abandoned Bundle

The morning mist
and chimney smoke
of White City Jabavu[1]
flowed thick yellow
as pus oozing
from a gigantic sore.

It smothered our little houses
like fish caught in a net.

Scavenging dogs
draped in red bandanas° of blood *scarves, strips of material*
fought fiercely
for a squirming bundle.

I threw a brick;
they bared fangs
flicked velvet tongues of scarlet
and scurried away,

1 *Black township.*

leaving a mutilated corpse —
an infant dumped on a rubbish heap —
'Oh! Baby in the Manger[2]
sleep well
on human dung.'

Its mother
had melted into the rays of the rising sun,
her face glittering with innocence
her heart as pure as untrampled dew.

2 *Allusion to the infant Jesus, who was born in a stable with a manger as a crib.*

Arthur Nortje (1942 – 1970)

Nortje studied at the University of the Western Cape, and was a teacher before winning a scholarship to Oxford University. He then taught in Canada before returning to Oxford. It would seem from his poetry, which reflects an extreme sense of personal and cultural dislocation, that he regarded his time overseas as a period of exile. He died tragically young as a result of a drug overdose.

In Exile

Open skies flare wide enough
to make me vaguely anxious.
Nimbus° wisps *storm-cloud*
trace patterns of the past.

Wind sweeps between the towers
through tunnels, old and new.
My heart is
hollowed with the boots passing through.

Garments gather and play about
my limbs: they tremble to a return
gust. Leaves and transient° *passing*
streetscape conjure up that southern

blue sky and wind-beautiful
day, creating paradise.
Otherwise:
the soul decays in exile.

But wrong pigment has no scope,
so clot the blue channel of memory.
On a sand slope
I build a picture of the sea.

The grains that slide away
are wind-breathed, are stirred by finger.
Benign, a cloud
obscures the sun, this hunger.

Comparison

You might find it interesting to compare and contrast this poem with Stephen Watson's poem of the same title on p. 260. What features do they have in common, and what differences can you find?

Eva Bezwoda (1942 – 1976)

Bezwoda grew up in South Africa and studied at Natal University. Together with the poet Lionel Abrahams and her husband, Robert Royston, she began a publishing venture which introduced the works of black poets to the public. Bezwoda was a psychologist, and her poetry reflects her concern for inner suffering. She died in London, probably as a result of suicide, after a long period of depressive illness.

A Woman's Hands

A woman's hands always hold something:
A handbag, a vase, a child, a ring, an idea.
My hands are tired of holding
They simply want to fold themselves.
On a crowded bus, I watched a nun's empty hands
Till I reminded myself that she clutched God.
My hands are tired of holding.
I'd gladly let them go, and watch a pair of hands
Run ownerless through the world,
Scattering cooking pots and flowers and rings.

Jeni Couzyn (1942 –)

Couzyn was born in Johannesburg and has lived in London since the mid-1960s. She was a founder member of the Poet's Conference and the Poet's Union, and has taught at the University of Victoria in Canada. Her poetry includes chants and spells for women.

The Red Hen's Last Will and Testament to the Last Cock on Earth

Mr Cockatoo I'm through.
You
can take your splendid
reasoning and quick
precision and elegant
vision somewhere
else.
You can take your
fine red comb and fast
feathered sex and high
concepts somewhere
else.
Your race can take its
good influence and careful
words and strong wings and
bright eyes some other
place.
You may be the
last manifestation but
you're not worth it.
Now
that there's artificial
insemination[1] since the
evolution of the cock

as a different species
you may as well wither
too.
Hens need something
else. You make us feel
abandoned. You make us

1 *Impregnation by medical means.*

feel like a place cocks
Pop into. We stay in the
place alone.
We await your
visitation. You pop in and
pop out. When we wake up
in the morning it is
silent.
All the hens in the
farmyard feel exactly as
I do about you. We have
decided to quit.
You all
can take off on your
massive Coxes High Powered
Jet Propelled
wings.
We hens will stay here
laying our eggs in the
warm straw, dreaming of
foxes.

Mutiswayo Shandu

No dates are available for this South African poet.

Bye Bye, Overcoat

The day before yesterday Mr Straun
gives me this overcoat. Today I catch
this train to my Stepmother's, wearing it.
It is a splendid coat, fawn°, almost new *pale brown*
— just this small gap in the seam of one sleeve.

It is past midday, the train not crowded
with mostly shoppers and halfday meisies.° *girls*
Still, I am standing, straphanging, swaying
but I prefer it: such a cool garment
of such swaggering cut should not be creased.

Comes payday: a good hat — maybe a fine
snapbrim fedora, perhaps from PATEL'S[1]
is quite definitely indicated.
Stepmama has a Singer[2] at her place . . .
The air around me goes into deepfreeze.

Turning, I see at the far end: Main Ou[3]
has joined us, accompanied by a pair
of toughlooking tsotsis.[4] Over dozens
of heads his eyes meet mine. He is staring
at my new overcoat. Tixo![5] Such luck!

They start working the silent, sullen folks,
towards me: peering in wallets, purses,
emptying handbags; some men have to stand
to have their back-pockets patted. Main Ou
does not work or hang on. His legs are braced.

He hardly moves with the train's rock and roll.
He taps a bicyclespoke with a stained
wood handle, coolly, on his left thumbnail.
His two thugs work quietly and quickly:
it is nearly all money and trinkets . . .

But one man has already lost his fine
leather jacket. Bruce Lee,[6] where are you now!
There are dozens of us, just three of them.
As usual, each of us is alone
against the predator, the oppressor . . .

For once, even the SAP[7] would do!
When I reach Stepmama's distinctive house
I am too sad to speak, and she sees it.
She serves me tea, strokes my defeated neck.
Her Singer stays, unused, under her bed.

1 *Name of a shop selling men's clothing.*
2 *Type of sewing machine.*
3 *Slang term for the gang leader, literally 'most important man' or 'big guy'.*
4 *Township slang for young men, usually criminals or gangsters.*
5 *Xhosa oath meaning Lord or God.*
6 *Star of series of martial arts films, in which he played a hero who defeated criminals with his superior fighting skills.*
7 *The South African Police.*

Nikki Giovanni (1943 –)

Giovanni was at the forefront of the second generation of Afro-American poets whose work reflected the political concerns and pride of black Americans in the 1960s and 70s. She has taught at various universities in the USA.

A Poem for Carol

(MAY SHE ALWAYS WEAR RED RIBBONS)

when I was very little
though it's still true today
there were no sidewalks in lincoln heights[1]
and the home we had on jackson street
was right next to a bus stop and a sewer
which didn't really ever become offensive
but one day from the sewer a little kitten
with one eye gone
came crawling out
though she never really came into our yard but just
sort of hung by to watch the folk
my sister who was always softhearted but able
to act effectively started taking milk
out to her while our father would would only say
don't bring *him* home and everyday
after school i would rush home to see if she was still
there and if gary had fed her but i could never
bring myself to go near her
she was so loving
and so hurt and so singularly beautiful and I knew
i had nothing to give that would
replace her one gone eye

and if I had named her which i didn't I'm sure
i would have called her carol

1 *Black suburb in an American city.*

Wally Mongane Serote (1944 –)

Serote was born in Sophiatown, and received schooling in the townships of Alexandra and Soweto. His activism led to a period of detention, and after studying art at Columbia University in the USA, he lived in exile in Botswana. His return in recent years marked the beginning of a period in which a number of exiled South African artists and musicians came home. He has won a number of noteworthy awards, and is probably the most significant poet to have emerged from the politically radical 'new black poetry' movement of the 1970s.

Alexandra[1]

Were it possible to say,
Mother, I have seen more beautiful mothers,
A most loving mother,
And tell her there I will go,
Alexandra, I would have long gone from you.

But we have only one mother, none can replace,
Just as we have no choice to be born,
We can't choose mothers;
We fall out of them like we fall out of life to death.

And Alexandra,
My beginning was knotted to you,
Just like you knot my destiny.
You throb in my inside silences
You are silent in my heart-beat that's loud to me.
Alexandra often I've cried.
When I was thirsty my tongue tasted dust,
Dust burdening your nipples.
I cry Alexandra when I am thirsty.
Your breasts ooze the dirty waters of your dongas,[2]
Waters diluted with the blood of my brothers, your children,
Who once chose dongas for death-beds.
Do you love me Alexandra, or what are you doing to me?

1 *Black township outside Johannesburg.*
2 *Ravines caused by soil erosion; associated with drought and poverty.*

You frighten me, Mama,
You wear expressions like you would be nasty to me,
You frighten me, Mama,
When I lie on your breast to rest, something tells me,
You are bloody cruel.
Alexandra, hell
What have you done to me?
I have seen people but I feel like I'm not one,
Alexandra what are you doing to me?
I feel I have sunk to such meekness!
I lie flat while others walk on me to far places.
I have gone from you, many times,
I come back.
Alexandra, I love you;
I know
When all these worlds became funny to me,
I silently waded back to you
And amid the rubble I lay,
Simple and black.

City Johannesburg[3]

This way I salute you:
My hand pulses to my back trousers pocket
Or into my inner jacket pocket
For my pass, my life,
Jo'burg City.
My hand like a starved snake tears my pockets
For my thin, ever lean wallet,
While my stomach groans a friendly smile to hunger,
Jo'burg City.
My stomach also devours coppers and papers
Don't you know?
Jo'burg City, I salute you;
When I run out, or roar in a bus to you,
I leave behind me, my love,
My comic houses and people, my dongas[4] and my ever whirling dust,
My death,
That's so related to me as a wink to the eye.

3 *City at the heart of the urban sprawl centred on the mining industries in the Transvaal. Historically, it has relied on black labour while remaining a white residential area.*

4 *See footnote 2, p. 234.*

Jo'burg City
I travel on your black and white and robotted roads,
Through your thick iron breath that you inhale,
At six in the morning and exhale from five noon.
Jo'burg City
That is the time when I come to you,
When your neon[5] flowers flaunt from your electrical wind,
That is the time when I leave you,
When your neon flowers flaunt their way through the falling darkness
On your cement trees.
And as I go back, to my love,
My dongas, my dust, my people, my death,
Where death lurks in the dark like a blade in the flesh,
I can feel your roots, anchoring your might, my feebleness
In my flesh, in my mind, in my blood,
And everything about you says it,
That, that is all you need of me.
Jo'burg City, Johannesburg,
Listen when I tell you,
There is no fun, nothing, in it.
When you leave the women and men with such frozen expressions,
Expressions that have tears like furrows of soil erosion,
Jo'burg City, you are dry like death,
Jo'burg City, Johannesburg, Jo'burg City.

Comparison

The above two poems by Serote have already been compared with Blake's 'London'. You might wish to turn to p. 59, and work through the questions set out there.

5 *Luminous gas used in lighting and coloured signs.*

For Don M. — Banned

it is a dry white season
dark leaves don't last, their brief lives dry out
and with a broken heart they dive down gently headed for the earth
not even bleeding.
it is a dry white season brother,
only the trees know the pain as they still stand erect
dry like steel, their branches dry like wire,
indeed, it is a dry white season
but seasons come to pass.

Contextual notes

Under the apartheid government, a banning order meant exile to a remote rural location, restrictions on movement, no contact with colleagues or fellow activists, and an embargo on any speeches, publication or political activity. Serote wrote this brief but powerful poem for Don Mattera, a friend and fellow poet who was banned during the 1970s. (See p. 217 for further information on Mattera, and a example of his writing.)

Suggestions for discussion

1. This short poem is deceptively simple. Much of the language and imagery operates on two different levels. Work through the poem identifying these 'double' words and images. Do you agree that the poem is a mini-allegory*? If so, what lesson does it teach?
2. What tone or mood is conveyed by this poem? Examine how the poet evokes this.
3. The first line is repeated three times in the poem, and slightly altered each time. What effect do these small changes have on the tone and development of the poem?
4. This poem also speaks to two very different audiences. It carries a very personal message of comfort for Don Mattera; but who else does it address?

That's Not My Wish

My wishes are the flames
On my life, the wax
That slowly melts
As they burn.

My candlestick is my blackness
That is like a cordless phone
Waiting to live. Oh! the priceless gift
That gets the white refusal: WAIT!

It has been my wish,
My daily eternal wish,
Not to pivot the see-saw of night and day,
But my tears, TEARS! are frozen to be this pivot.

My zithering[6] melting life
Shall drip and shape the candlestick
A burnt liquified gold.
I hope to maintain its gem.

To talk for myself,
I hate to hate,
But how often has it been
I could not hate enough.

6 *A zither is a stringed musical instrument; zithering possibly refers to musical lamentation.*

Sally Bryer (1947 –)

Bryer was the daughter of professional and artistic parents, and was brought up and educated in Johannesburg. She pursued further studies in art in Italy. She published relatively few poems before producing her first collection. She now lives in Canada.

Ingrid Jonker

(Afrikaans poet, drowned herself aged 33)

You walked straight into the water
like a hungry bird, your curly head
intent as a heron.[1]
You walked into the waves
like Persephone[2] herself,
your eyes dried seeds, your body a husk of light.
Your punishment was finding yourself
in a foreign element. You spoke
through interpreters. Your lips and fingers
betrayed you, turned away
from the darkness behind your eyes,
tried to sell themselves.
Your child dies, and lives on.
Your screams become seasonal.

We travel in packs. Hunting and hunted
We carry nets and each of us captures
a relic of pain, stark as bone.
Those of us who never saw a likeness
learn to tell the seasons of madness
from the sea. In every fragment of glass and shell
I pass, your dark eyes encounter me.

1 *Bird that fishes in rivers or dams.*

2 *Figure in Greek legend who was kidnapped by the king of the underworld (the realm of the dead). Her return to the earth heralded the coming of spring, but while underground, she ate six seeds of a pomegranate (fruit), thus condemning herself to spend winter there each year.*

Charles Mungoshi (1947 –)

Mungoshi is part of a generation of Zimbabwean poets who consciously sought to express their sense of identity and nationalism during the struggle for liberation in that country during the 1970s. He has worked as an editor, publisher and academic. Internationally recognized as a writer, his work includes novels and short stories as well as poems.

A Letter to a Son

Now the pumpkin is ripe.
We are only a few days from
the year's first mealie cob.
The cows are giving us lots of milk.
Taken in the round it isn't a bad year at all —
if it weren't for your father.
Your father's back is back again
and all the work has fallen on my shoulders.
Your little brothers and sisters are doing
fine at the day-school. Only Rindai
is becoming a problem. You will remember
we wrote you — did you get our letter? —
you didn't answer — you see, since your
father's back started we haven't been able
to raise enough to send your sister Rindai
to secondary school. She spends most of the time
crying by the well. It's mainly because of her
that I am writing this letter.
I had thought you would be with us last Christmas
then I thought maybe you were too busy
and you would make it at Easter —
it was then your father nearly left us, son.
Then I thought I would come to you some time
before the cold season settled in — you know how
I simply hate that time of year —
but then your father went down again
and this time worse than any other time before.
We were beginning to think he would never see
another sowing season. I asked your sister Rindai
to write you but your father would have none of it
— you know how stubborn he can get when
he has to lie in bed all day or gets
one of those queer notions of his that
everybody is deserting him!

Now, Tambu, don't think I am asking for money —
although we had to borrow a little from
those who have it to get your father to hospital
and you know how he hates having to borrow!
That is all I wanted to tell you.
I do hope that you will be with us this July.
It's so long ago since we last heard from you —
I hope this letter finds you still at the old address.
It is the only address we know.

YOUR MOTHER

Richard Ntiru

No dates could be found for this Ugandan poet.

The Gourd[1] of Friendship

Where is the curiosity we've lost in discovery?
Where is the discovery we've lost in knowledge?
Where is the knowledge we've lost in communication?
Where is the communication we've lost in mass media?
Where is the message we've lost in the medium?
And where the community we've lost in all these?
It is easy to go to the moon:
There, there are no people.
It is easier to count the stars:
They will not complain.

But the road to your neighbour's heart —
Who has surveyed it?
The formula to your brother's head —
Who has devised it?
The gourd that doesn't spill friendship —
In whose garden has it ever grown?
You never know despair
Until you've lost hope;
You never know your aspiration
Until you've seen others' disillusionment.
Peace resides in the hearts of men
Not in conference tables and delegates' signatures
True friendship never dies —
It grows stronger the more it is tested.

1 *Container made from hollowed-out fruit.*

Solly Kaplinski (1948 –)

Kaplinski, as the child of Jews who survived the Holocaust (the extermination of six million Jews by the Nazis before and during the Second World War), has sought to reflect his heritage in his collection of poems, Lost and Found: a Second Generation Response to the Holocaust. *He was educated both in Cape Town and in Jerusalem in Israel, and is currently head of Herzlia High School in Cape Town.*

Story-telling in the Singular

They say
it's all myth-making
After all
martyrs make for good heroes
and
nation building depends on mythology.

Heart-rending stories
tear-jerking tragedy
we all know
is the very stuff
of loyal adherents
and
rooted followers
and
passionate converts to the cause

O.K.
so let's pretend it wasn't
six million
say it was just
one murder
only
one gas chamber[1]
just
one Adolf[2]

1 *Most concentration camps had special rooms in which inmates (mostly Jews) were gassed to death.*

2 *Adolf Hitler, the German leader who formulated Nazism.*

I won't call you a liar and a cheat
if you say
it was
only one.

How then do you expect me to respond?

It's still one too many.

Contextual notes

This poem refers to the phenomenon called 'Holocaust revisionism', a pseudo-scholarly trend which has arisen in some parts of the world. This seeks to deny that the Holocaust ever happened, or argues that the deaths and sufferings of European Jews under Nazism are grossly exaggerated. In its extreme form, it preaches the values of Nazism as a misunderstood form of social and political control.

Shabbir Banoobhai (1949 –)

Banoobhai lives in Durban and works as an accountant. His poems are striking for their lyrical simplicity and expression of political, personal and spiritual passion.

last poem for the year:

the early morning was lit with hope
the day raced across the skies
like a child with candy in the wind
running blindly to where the child-world ends
waits to die
waits to be reborn
to a new world
but not until god has spilt the night
over an incandescent° day *luminous, alight*

if you are beautiful
like an evening
an evening that falls
gently as the dew
or if you throb
every word quivering
like the drums of the evening year
eager for the birth
of the morning one
then
last poem for the year
die quickly
beautifully throbbing
strongly quivering
so that
the first poem of the morning year
may be caught spellbound
mysteriously
like the rays of the sun
within the drops of the evening dew

god, please …

do not let them turn me into a shop
to be opened at six in the morning
and closed at six in the evening

regulated in the thoughts i may
and may not display
advised on who i may
and may not welcome
in the sovereign° territory of my being *possessing independence*

remember that i've tried
to keep my books of account
as you've asked me to
crediting the right
and criticising the wrong
diligently, faithfully
honestly
because i know no other way

call back these self-appointed auditors
of my soul
who have declared me insolvent
and have condemned me
to a work-house
where i shall be fed
impoverished thoughts
for the best years of my life

god, please . . .

Jeremy Cronin (1949 –)

Cronin was a philosophy student at the University of Cape Town when he was charged under the Terrorism Act during the apartheid regime. He subsequently spent seven years as a political prisoner. On his release, he returned to Cape Town and published a collection of poems about his prison experiences, which attracted immediate recognition.

Faraway City, there

Faraway city, there
with salt in its stones,
under its windswept doek°, *head-scarf*

There in our Cape Town where
they're smashing down homes
of the hungry, labouring people
— will you wait for me, my love?

In that most beautiful,
desolate city of my heart
where if staying on were passive
life wouldn't be what it is.

Not least for those rebuilding
yet again their demolished homes
with bits of plastic, port jackson° saplings, *species of tree*
anything to hand — unshakeably

Defiant, frightened, broken,
and unbreakable are the people of our city.

— Will you wait for me, my love?

Contextual notes

While Cronin was in prison, his wife died unexpectedly. This is one of the poems he wrote as a response; it is partly a love poem, partly an elegy,* and partly a political statement.

Ingrid de Kok (1951 –)

De Kok was raised and educated in South Africa. She has spent part of her life living and studying in Canada, and often grapples in her writing with the difficulties of shifting between the two cultures. At present, she works in the Adult Education Department at the University of Cape Town. Her poems have been published both at home and abroad. She occasionally writes under her married name of Fiske.

Small Passing

For a woman whose baby died stillborn, and who was told by a man to stop mourning, 'because the trials and horrors suffered daily by black women in this country are more significant than the loss of one white child.'

1

In this country you may not
suffer the death of your stillborn,
remember the last push into shadow and silence,
the useless wires and cords on your stomach,
the nurse's face, the walls, the afterbirth in a basin.
Do not touch your breasts
still full of purpose.
Do not circle the house,
pack, unpack the small clothes.
Do not lie awake at night hearing
the doctor say 'It was just as well'
and 'You can have another.'
In this country you may not
mourn small passings.

See: the newspaper boy in the rain
will sleep tonight in a doorway.
The woman in the busline
may next month be on a train
to a place not her own.
The baby in the backyard now
will be sent to a tired aunt,

grow chubby, then lean,
return a stranger.
Mandela's daughter tried to find her father
through the glass. She thought they'd let her touch him.[1]

And this woman's hands are so heavy when she dusts
the photographs of other children
they fall to the floor and break.
Clumsy woman, she moves so slowly
as if in a funeral rite.

On the pavements the nannies meet.
These are legal gatherings.
They talk about everything, about home,
while the children play among them,
their skins like litmus,[2] their bonnets clean.

2

Small wrist in the grave.
Baby no one carried live
between houses, among trees.
Child shot running,
stones in his pocket,
boy's swollen stomach
full of hungry air.
Girls carrying babies
not much smaller than themselves.
Erosion. Soil washed down to the sea.

3

I think these mothers dream
headstones of the unborn.
Their mourning rises like a wall
no vine will cling to.

1 *During President Mandela's years as a political prisoner, visits by family members had to be conducted from behind a glass panel. No physical contact was allowed.*

2 *Chemical substance which changes colour to pinkish-red under acid conditions.*

They will not tell you your suffering is white.
They will not say it is just as well.
They will not compete for the ashes of infants.
I think they may say to you:

Come with us to the place of mothers.
We will stroke your flat empty belly,
let you weep with us in the dark
and arm you with one of our babies
to carry home on your back.

> **COMPARISON**
>
> This poem has already been compared with Jonson's 'On My First Son' and 'On my First Daughter' (see pp. 34–35). You might like to turn to the suggestions for comparative discussion which appear on p. 35.

Mending

In and out, behind, across.
The formal gesture binds the cloth.
The stitchery's a surgeon's rhyme,
a Chinese stamp, a pantomine

of print. Then spoor°. Then trail of red. *footprints, trail*
Scabs rise, stigmata° from the thread. *scars*
A cotton chronicle congealed.
A histogram° of welts and weals. *graph*

The woman plies her ancient art.
Her needle sutures[1] as it darts,
scoring, scripting, scarring, stitching,
the invisible mending of the heart.

1 *Stitches put in by a doctor to close a wound.*

Antonio Jacinto

No dates could be found for this Angolan poet.

Letter from a Contract Worker

I wanted to write you a letter
my love,
a letter that would tell
of this desire
to see you
of this fear
of losing you
of this more than benevolence that I feel
of this indefinable ill that pursues me
of this yearning to which I live in total surrender . . .

I wanted to write you a letter
my love,
a letter of intimate secrets,
a letter of memories of you,
of you
of your lips red as henna° *reddish dye*
of your hair black as mud
of your eyes sweet as honey
of your breasts hard as wild orange
of your lynx° gait *wild cat*
and of your caresses
such that I can find no better here . . .

I wanted to write you a letter
my love,
that would recall the days in our haunts
our nights lost in the long grass
that would recall the shade falling on us from the plum
trees
the moon filtering through the endless palm trees
that would recall the madness
of our passion
and the bitterness
of our separation . . .

I wanted to write you a letter
my love,
that you would not read without sighing
that you would hide from papa Bombo
that you would withhold from mama Kieza
that you would reread without the coldness
of forgetting
a letter to which in all Kilombo
no other would stand comparison . . .

I wanted to write you a letter
my love
a letter that would be brought to you by the passing wind
a letter that the cashews and coffee trees
the hyenas and buffaloes
the alligators and grayling° *fish*
could understand
so that if the wind should lose it on the way
the beasts and plants
with pity for our sharp suffering
from song to song
lament to lament
gabble to gabble
would bring you pure and hot
the burning words
the sorrowful words of the letter
I wanted to write to you my love . . .

I wanted to write you a letter . . .

But oh my love, I cannot understand
why it is, why it is, why it is, my dear
that you cannot read
and I — Oh the hopelessness! — cannot write!

Rushdy Siers (1952 –)

Siers was born in District Six in Cape Town, an area from which his family was evicted under apartheid legislation. He has a history of activism in political and cultural circles. At present, he works at the Centre for Development Studies at the University of the Western Cape. His writing includes poetry and short stories.

Sets of Two and their Silence

Today children our lesson will be about sets ....
Kanalla[1] *cheacher nie vandagie* — *Please teacher not today.*

Does every body know what a set is?
Yaa, a snytjie brood en a snytjie brood maak a sanwich. — *Yes, a slice of bread and a slice of bread make a sandwich*

Good, please pay attention and don't look so sleepy!
Ek slaap tot ek dai klokkie hoor — kostyd! — *I'm sleeping until I hear the bell — time to eat!*

Many things and any number of things can make a set ....
Ek wonne wat gan op 'ie brood wies? — *I wonder what will be on the bread?*

For example, a tea set and a cutlery set ....
Nou moet jy nogal van kosgoed praat. — *Now you have to talk about food utensils.*

Can anyone give me an example of a set? quickly ....
Set and ready to go, as ek dai klokkie hoor. — *Set and ready to go, when I hear that bell.*

Class what is wrong?
Niks verkeet 'ie net honger. — *Nothing's wrong, just hungry.*

Can nobody give me an example of a set?
Cheacher lat ek net slaap tot netnou. — *Teacher let me sleep for a while.*

1 *'Please'; a colloquial greeting in the Cape Muslim community, which translates literally as 'please in the name of God'.*

Children you must pay attention!
Ya a snytjie brood en a snytjie brood maak a sanwich. *Yes a slice of bread and a slice of bread make a sandwich.*

And why this silence?
Jy's fokken doef as jy nie my maag kan hoor nie! *You're fucking deaf if you can't hear my stomach!*

Contextual notes

This poem combines conventional use of the English language with use of one of the dialects found within the Cape Malay community. This particular dialect combines Afrikaans and English, and flavours both with distinctive borrowings from the local community. Note how flat and tame the English translation on the right-hand side of the page seems when compared with the original. What does this suggest about the value of dialect?

John Agard

No dates could be found for this writer from the Caribbean.

Poetry Jump-Up[1]

Tell me if ah seeing right
Take a look down de street

Words dancin
words dancin
till dey sweat
words like fishes
jumpin out a net
words wild and free
joining de poetry revelry
words back to back
words belly to belly

Come on everybody
come and join de poetry band
dis is poetry carnival
dis is poetry bacchanal[2]
when inspiration call
take yu pen in yu hand
if you dont have a pen
take yu pencil in yu hand
if you dont have a pencil
what the hell
so long de feeling start to swell
just shout de poem out

Words jumpin off de page
tell me if Ah seeing right
words like birds
jumpin out a cage
take a look down de street
words shakin dey waist
words shakin dey bum

1 *In Caribbean dialect, a party.*
2 *Drunken and joyous festival; named after Bacchus, the Greek god of wine.*

words wit black skin
words wit white skin
words wit brown skin
word wit no skin at all
words huggin up words
an saying I want to be a poem today
rhyme or no rhyme
I is a poem today
I mean to have a good time

Words feelin hot hot hot
big words feelin hot hot hot
lil words feelin hot hot hot
even sad words cant help
tappin dey toe
to de riddum of de poetry band

Dis is poetry carnival
dis is poetry bacchanal
so come on everybody
join de celebration
all yu need is plenty perspiration
an a little inspiration
plenty perspiration
an a little inspiration

Contextual notes

Like Siers' poem on p. 253, this is written in a particular dialect or variation of English. Here the influence is predominantly Caribbean or West Indian. The spelling is largely phonetic, so it is especially important to read this poem aloud.

Damian Ruth (1954 –)

Ruth has worked as an academic development officer at the University of the Western Cape and as a lecturer at the University of the North. His poems have appeared in many literary magazines.

Sunday Morning Breakfast

Wake up slowly stretch and snuggle
my body against warm sheets.
I could lie longer, but breakfast
tugs my feet
from under the sheets and pads me down the passage.

A gentle stumble round the bathroom,
then the fridge, and
a long cool draught of orange juice.
Drinking happy colours, first thing in the morning.

Getting dressed, any old sloppily how
and strolling out into the street.
The lighter touch of Sunday things;
crowded cars headed out of town,
friends calling from doorways,
people buying papers slowly,
looking at the headlines before they move away
Time for a word to the paperseller,
'It's a nice day, isn't it?'
'Yes, it is, isn't it?'

If there's one morning a week to believe
it might be a wonderful world
it must be Sunday.

Buying the milk and maybe some mid-morning treat,
and wandering, open to any delay, a
window display or bill sticker.

Back to the kitchen table,
to a great languid° soothing ceremony. *slow, lazy*
Drink more colour while the hot plate's warming,
settle down with the cereal and paper,
listen to the bacon and eggs jump about in the pan.

Sunday breakfast is painting plates and bowls;
the off-white speckled muesli,° *breakfast cereal*
the dark brown nuts and fruit.
A plate with rich brown toast,
two yellow suns,
circles of paling red tomatoes with whitening pips,
and crusty ochre° bacon. *reddish-brown*

The smells and colours dancing
between stove and table,
and the last lap of toast,
smearing melting butter,
laying swathes of jam,
washed down with huge mugs of tea,
and a headline here and there,
and getting the paper stuck
on a ring left by a mug.

The aimless talk, vague plans for the day
interrupted by a headline that starts a long digression.
The chores done easy the day is free, coming in,
the breakfast fades and we push slowly into lazy Sunday
slowly kissing nibbling eating playing
with the promise of the day.

Stephen Watson (1954 –)

Watson has spent most of his life, apart from brief periods in Britain and Australia, in Cape Town. He lectures in the English Department at the University of Cape Town, and is the author of several volumes of poetry (including a translation of /Xam legends), as well as a collection of critical essays.

The Rain that is Male

The rain that is male is an angry rain.
It brings with it lightning loud like our fear.
It brings water storming, making smoke out of dust.

And we, we beat our navels with our rigid fists.
We, we press a hand, flat to the navel.
We snap our fingers at the angry, male rain.

And we stand outside in the force of the water,
we stand out in the open, close to its thunder,
we snap our fingers and chant while it falls:

'Rain, be gone quickly! Fall but be gone!
Rain, turn away! Turn back from this place!
Rain, take your anger, be gone from our place!'

For we want the other, the rain that is female,
the one that falls softly, soaking into the ground,
the one we can welcome, feeding the plains —

So bushes sprout green, springbok° come galloping. *indigenous buck*

Contextual notes

This poem is drawn from the records of a nineteenth-century linguist from the Cape and his sister-in law, who together transcribed legends passed on to them by members of an almost extinct tribe of indigenous people, the /Xam. They have since been completely eradicated or assimilated, and their language has died out. Watson's poem is thus a translation of a translation, and is an example of the attempts by modern writers and anthropologists to recover the cultures of indigenous peoples who have been exterminated. (See also 'Kilaben Bay Song' on p. 99.)

In Exile

for Douglas Reid Skinner

To be rooted is perhaps the most important and least recognized need of the human soul — Simone Weil

Waiting for a tram, his gaze incurious, vague, as jaded
as the fog long rising off the Main, as the cold gone brown,
polluted in whatever sky there is, in what's left of day
even now, years later, years after he had to leave, to flee,
dusk comes like a coma, his stare still hangs, abandoned,
as useless as his hands. The cobbled streets stretch away,
numb and bloodless as shin-bones. The stunted light lies
still and dead, diluted, never mellowing. In the early dark,
cold with lights, under the factory sky of Frankfurt am Main,[1]
the waters of the river, muffled, frigid in this German wind,
the misted hulks of barges, hold no echo, are faceless still,
the flagstones, leaden, fouled, are nothing but tombstones.

Again, the ash-trees turn to charcoal before his eyes.
He hears the echoes that damp footsteps hollow out on stone,
he looks upon the dead wood, the wooden faces, at buildings
that have blurred, are vague, indefinite as some threat,
and still can't hear, can't see — he can't feel a thing.
Nine years later, nothing, hardly anything has changed:
even now, as that torpor in the evening cold takes hold,
as something wads his hands, and fogs his eyes, both ears,
he's still standing there — the tram has left without him —
he's straining, is like a man possessed, going blind
for what he still sees, for what he can remember seeing.

And it's always one place only, always that same place
where a road swings high, climbing around a mountain-side.
It's the highway of his childhood, of many years before
that he's travelling now in memory, once more looking out
at hills, far-off, linear, naked, miles north across a bay.
Again, there's sunlight in blonde grass, there's that scent
of pine in dust, a heat that carries him still further back
to those folded slopes, unfolding, peppery with rough scrub,
to that very bend where the road swings left to right
and through the slanted pine-trunks, from its final crest,
backed by a mountain-wall, opening out along an oval bay,

1 *Major manufacturing city in Germany; Main is the name of the river on which it is built.*

an entire city lies revealed, frozen in silence, far below —
Cape Town stands there, suddenly, revealed for what it is:
a city of the southern hemisphere, more full of sky than streets.

Even now, years later, when at night the longing comes
nothing matters any more — not his memory of the people,
the vile, pretentious rich, corrupted poor, those politics
that beggar all description, that all but beggared him —
nothing matters now but his desire, but this mad longing
to know that there is still a place, that it still exists,
that you can come on that same road round Devil's Peak[2]
and there will be, as there was before, almost any evening,
that softness in the summer dark, the same warmth rising,
breathing from an earth long out of reach of its sunset.
All the rest's irrelevant; nothing matters now, or ever,
but to know that he can come, return to that road's crest
when the harbour's lighting up, the lights are shining
thinly through the pine-tops, in wind that's amber-toned,
and there will be the same view, clear across the city:
from the trees thinned out against the mass of Signal Hill,[3]
against that day's after-glow, down to a mountainy skyline
going far down the south peninsula, where the early stars —
the first he ever saw — will be out along the mountains.

He has to know there is a place — if only just one place —
where the water is not flat with cold, the silted colour
of cement; where the stones are not just made of stone
but are full of stories, memories. There has to be
that place where with a hand upon a stone you can touch
the time that went before, the years that will outlast you.
There has to be a place. He's tired of watching, waiting,
while years pass quickly, blankly, become ever more unreal.
Tonight he's tired of talking, smiling, and knowing he's not
really talking, not smiling — it's just his lips, his teeth.
These rush-hour people passing by, all with somewhere to go
the buses that come shuddering past, these trams squealing
to a halt, that always jolt him back to this same street —
here, he can't find peace — the calm — to rest his nerves.

And shivers.... That tram of his left almost an hour ago.
It's left him in a nearly ended year, with one more view
of leaves, long dead already, drowning in a wayside gutter.
He's still standing there, still transfixed as night falls,

2 *Distinctive peak in the Table Mountain range which encircles central Cape Town.*

3 *See the contextual notes on p. 205.*

as that other, loved city fades away, floats ten years off,
and he comes back to these dead things, to the dead years,
to a smell of air pollution freezing, falling below zero.
He's still lost in it, in his estranging gape, one of many,
a man without a wife, a child, arms wrapped round himself,
a man who has been left behind. And now he's growing smaller
is no larger than his pipe's glow as the river fog moves in,
flows over the embankment, blanking out what he once saw,
blotting out a figure, thin and frosted, dwindling quickly,
an exile, solo, incognito, in transit through another night.

COMPARISON

You might want to turn back to Arthur Nortje's poem, also titled 'In Exile' (p. 228) and compare it with Watson's piece.

Fhazel Johennesse (1956 –)

Johennesse was born and lives in Johannesburg. He has worked on various creative projects with other South African poets, and has published a respected collection of poetry.

A Young Man's Thoughts Before June the 16th

tomorrow i travel on a road
that winds to the top of the hill
i take with me only the sweet
memories of my youth
my heart aches for my mother
for friday nights with friends
around a table with a broad belch of beer
i ask only for a sad song
sung by a woman with downturned eyes
and strummed by an old man with
a broken brow
o sing my sad song sing for me
for my sunset is drenched with red

Contextual notes

June 16 marks the anniversary of the 1976 uprising begun by schoolchildren in Soweto to protest against the compulsory use of Afrikaans, perceived as the language of the oppressor, in black classrooms. Over 1 000 people, many of them young, lost their lives.

Chris van Wyk (1957 –)

Van Wyk was born in Johannesburg, where he currently lives. He has worked for various South African publishers and is currently a freelance writer working on materials for adult literacy programmes. His writing includes children's literature, poems and short stories. His poetry combines elements of the personal and the political in fresh ways.

On Learning Sotho[1]

(For Isaac Sephoka)

I was a young Sotho boy then
a baby wetting a layette° of words *babies' clothing*
and all of you laughed boisterously
when I swore at myself
not knowing the difference then
between 'nna' and 'wena'.° *you / me*
And I'd impress all the ladies
with 'dumela ausi!'° *greetings sister*
or 'moratiwa!'° when I was randy. *hallo lovely*

The words crawled at first
no matter how they tried to walk
among the grown, bombastic° men. *eloquent*
Oh I was a child again
joyfully sucking on the tits
of a language new to me
though it had always been
dangling invitingly from Agnes who makes the tea
or Mrs Mabuja who sweeps the office.

Thank you for your patience brother
and your English to guide my Sotho.
I'm growing now
and one day I will be as big as you
and Joseph and Walter and Lucky.
Then I will also laugh when you do
or cry
and understand why.

1 *Vernacular language spoken by the Sotho people.*

Memory

Derek is dangling on the kitchen chair
while I'm shuffling about in a flutter of flour.
Mummy is making vetkoek[1] on the primus.[2]
Derek is too small to peer over the table,
that's why Mummy has perched him on the chair.
His dummy twitters so he's a bird.

I'm not that small; I was four in July.
I'm tall enough to see what's going on;
I'm a giraffe and the blotches of shadow
on the ceiling and the walls
from the flames of the primus and candle
are the patches on my back.

Daddy's coming home soon
from the factory where they're turning him into
a cupboard that creaks,
but the vetkoek are sizzling and growing
like bloated gold coins,
we're rich!

This is the first vivid memory of childhood.
Why have I never written it all down before?
Maybe because the pan falls with a clatter
and the oil swims towards the twittering bird.
Mummy flattens her forearm on the table
stopping the seething flood.

As she does so she pleads with the bird to fly away,
but quietly so as not to ruffle his feathers.
But my brother clambers off the chair
as if he has all the time in the world.
Sensing danger, the twittering gives way to a wail
and the giraffe's patches flare on the restive walls.

Ma gives a savage scream that echoes across the decades
and cauterizes° my childhood like a long scar. *burns*

1 *Cakes made of dough and fried in oil.* 2 *Portable gas stove.*

Gcina Mhlophe (1958 –)

One of South Africa's most innovative and talented actresses and directors, Mhlophe also writes plays and poetry. She has worked to advance the art of story-telling, and tours the country to bring her performances to as many levels of society as possible.

Say No

Say No, Black Woman
Say No
When they call your jobless son
a Tsotsi[1]
Say No

Say No, Black Woman
Say No
When they call
Your husband at the age of 60
a boy
Say No

Say No, Black Woman
Say No
When they rape your daughter
in detention and call her
a whore
Say No

Say No, Black Woman
Say No
When they call your white sister
a madam
Say No

Say No, Black Woman
Say No
When they call your white brother
a Baas
Say No

1 *See footnote 4, p. 232.*

Say No, Black Woman
Say No
When they call a trade unionist
a terrorist
Say No

Say No, Black Woman
Say No
When they give you a back seat
in the liberation wagon
Say No
Yes Black Woman
a Big NO

Erika Gouws (1961 –)

Gouws works as a translator and freelance editor. She lives in Cape Town, and writes the music and lyrics for her own bilingual songs.

Kaap van Goeie Hoop

In the mother city's arms
small children sleep
wrapped up in day-old news
best long forgotten

in the city's inner heart
desolate vagrants hide
sheltered in cold doorways
that lead nowhere

maar innie geilheid van Constantia
leef ons decadently swierig
en in Houtbaai se paleise
bly Afrikaners nog plesierig

but in the comfort of Constantia
we live in decadent luxury
and in the palaces of Hout Bay
Afrikaners are still having fun

under harbour city's lights
lonely women wait
painted in neon[1] colours
to mask the pain

in dark city streets
angry gangsters prowl
armed with flashing blades
to fight the fear

maar innie stil van Vredehoek
vergeet ons van die vrees
en in Oranjezicht se rosy glow
kannie Kaap nog Hollands wees[2]

but in the quietness of Vredehoek
we forget the fear
and in the rosy glow of Oranjezicht
the Cape can still be Dutch

1 *See footnote 5, p. 236.*

2 *Colloquial Afrikaans saying, implying that the status quo is maintained.*

so vergeet ons van die werklikheid
want ignorance is bliss
en dit is mos die fairest Cape
wie kan nou daarmee twis

so we forget the reality
because ignorance is bliss
and this is the fairest Cape after all
who can argue with that

of is dit dalk tog eintlik nog
die Kaap van Goeie Hoop

or perhaps is it still
the Cape of Good Hope

Contextual notes

The title of this song refers to the name early European navigators gave to the Cape, and which means 'the Cape of Good Hope'. Constantia, Hout Bay, Vredehoek and Oranjezicht are all upmarket white suburbs of Cape Town.

Dean Brogden (1965 –)

Brogden has lived in Cape Town all his life. He works in a bank, and has been writing poetry for several years. His writing is characterized by short lines and a lack of punctuation, which focus attention on the words used.

april 1993

we murder our heroes
in driveways
point a loaded gun
at the back of their head
assassinate our dreams dead
to the word
you and i speak
here down another beer
to the twenty four hour
armed response
our heart
in the hands of the blue
sign another driveway
death to me death to you

Contextual notes

This poem was written in the wake of the assassination of the ANC leader Chris Hani, which took place in the driveway of his own home in April 1993, and sparked a wave of mourning and protest throughout the country. The reference to 'another driveway' alludes to the death of anti-apartheid activist David Webster, also shot down in his driveway.

Lisa Combrinck (1967 –)

Combrinck was born in Cape Town, and started writing poetry at an early age. She is a postgraduate student at the University of Cape Town, where she is researching South African short stories. She has been involved in cultural and teaching activities for the Congress of South African Writers (COSAW).

To the Reader

Why should a woman not write erotic love poems?
It is true that most of my poems are about the struggle:
shaping words into the stones we throw at the oppressor,
shaping words into the slogans we shout;
shaping words into salve°-covered swabs to heal our wounds, *soothing ointment*
shaping words into spears with which to forge ahead.

But these cold stones, these slogans of struggle,
these wounds, these spears cannot be free
until they come to terms with femininity
and feel the freedom of love.

No one is in love with the struggle.
We fight for the rights of people
to have land and love. We lose our lives
to liberate those we love.

In this struggle, let us leave some space
for people to love, love's bleeding lips, a blushing face.

And allow this woman the right unconditionally
to write lines and lines of erotic love poetry.

Lisa Combrinck (1967–)

Lisa Combrinck was born in Cape Town [illegible] writing poetry at an early age. She is a postgraduate student at the University of Cape Town, where she is researching [illegible]. She has been [illegible] for the Congress of South African Writers (COSAW).

To the Reader

Why should a woman write erotic love poetry
In a time that most women are [illegible] the struggle?
Shaping words into stones of [illegible] at the
oppressor
Shaping words into the slogans we shout
Shaping words into [illegible]
woman
Shaping words into spears with which to [illegible]

But the [illegible] words, these signals of struggle
these sounds [illegible] cannot be free
until the [illegible] with [illegible]
[illegible]

[illegible]

[illegible]

[illegible]

[illegible]
[illegible] and ends of erotic love poetry [illegible]

Glossary

Aesthetic
Those qualities of beauty which give pleasure and inspiration.

Allegory
Symbolic tale, often with a moral message, in which figures and objects described in the story represent certain qualities (such as evil, truth, etc.). In some spiritual allegories, the characters represent religious figures or doctrines. Other allegories create fantasy characters which represent actual historical figures and events in their lives.

Ballad
Narrative poem (i.e., it tells a story) which deals with folklore or legend, often containing supernatural elements and featuring dialogue. Originally meant to be sung, ballads have a regular rhythm, usually with repeating lines or a chorus.

Comedy (as in drama)
Not necessarily humorous; however, there is always a happy ending (misunderstandings are cleared up, conflicts resolved, and the potential for evil and harm is averted) which involves the union of one or more pairs of lovers and their marriage.

Devotional
Used to describe poetry or prose written for purposes of religious or spiritual praise or meditation.

Dramatic monologue
Poem where only one voice (and viewpoint) is heard, but in which the author's own (often very different) opinion is implicit.

Elegy
Commemoration of someone who has died; poem or other form of writing which expresses grief and mourning and finally moves towards some kind of resolution or comfort.

Epic
Heroic narrative which tells of unusual adventures, travel, or feats of bravery and war.

Genre
Identifiable type or form of literature; for example, novel, drama, poetry. Within poetry itself, different genres can be found, such as epic, lyric, and so forth.

Irony

It is difficult to provide a concrete definition of irony, as it relies on tone to succeed. It is primarily a form of criticism or mockery in which the very opposite meaning or message to what is written or spoken is communicated. It is often used to create a 'double' sense of communication, in which a distance is deliberately created between a character's perspective and that of the author. (See, for example, Chaucer's 'The Pardoner's Prologue' [pp. 4 – 6] or Browning's 'My Last Duchess' [p. 92]).

Lyric

Expressive and gentle poem or song praising a specific object or scene, or describing a mood or emotion; often concerned with beauty or love.

Metaphor

An image in which an object or figure is described as something else as an implicit form of comparison, which is not meant to be understood literally; for example, 'the sun was a gold coin on the horizon'.

Metaphysical

School of poetry associated with the seventeenth-century writers Donne, Herbert, Marvell and others. Particularly known for its clever wit and inventive and unusual ideas and images, it features comparisons known as 'conceits', which are striking or original rather than accurate.

Metre

The rhythmic shape of a line of poetry, identified by the number of stressed (or emphasized) syllables.

Mock-heroic

Often used for satiric or humorous purposes, this involves describing a trivial or ordinary subject or event in an inappropriately grand and lofty style.

Modernism

Movement in literature and art which sprang up at the beginning of the twentieth century. It swept away many of the 'rules' of art and culture, and set out to create inner realities and visions, experimenting with new forms of representation in the process. Poetry increasingly relied on association rather than explanation, with words being used for their evocative qualities, rather than as means of communication and explanation.

Narrative

Form of writing which tells a story with a distinct plot; the focus is on events, not description.

Pastoral

Literature or poetry which provides an often artificial and utopian view of rural or outdoors life. It involves a very stylized representation of nature, and always draws on imagery of spring or summer. The object is to create an atmosphere of beauty rather than realism.

Polemic
Piece written with an explicit (and often strongly worded) political or ideological message.

Romance (as in drama)
Possesses characteristics of both tragedy and comedy; suffering and loss force deluded or weak characters to recognize their faults, at which point magical elements transform or reverse tragic events (those believed to be dead are restored, spells are broken, lost children are found, and so forth). The ending invariably involves marriage, symbolizing restoration of family and society.

Satire
Writing which mocks or criticizes something by means of exaggeration or exposure. The difference between satire and irony (see above) is that irony says the opposite of what is intended to be understood, whereas satire describes its object accurately, but unflatteringly, by highlighting its flaws. The effect is often humorous. (See also Mock-heroic above.)

Simile
Imagery which takes the form of an explicit comparison by using the words 'as' or 'like'; for example, 'She runs like the wind, but he is as slow as a tortoise'.

Sonnet
Carefully crafted 14-line poem, with a strict rhyme scheme and metre. The lines are either divided into three sets of four lines each, plus a rhyming couplet, or into an eight-line section (the octave, which usually describes the topic or sets out the argument) followed by six lines (the sestet) which reflects on the subject of the octave. The last two lines usually sum up the argument of the poem or state the speaker's final message.

Tragedy (as in drama)
Tragic events and actions befall characters either through their own weakness or sin (their 'fatal flaw') or through the twists of 'fate'. The narrative moves inevitably towards the death of the hero and/or heroine (as well as many of the other characters), after which a new sense of resolution is found. The Greek philosopher Aristotle argued that the purpose of tragedy was to evoke emotions of pity and fear in the audience, and then to provide a catharsis (outlet) for these feelings.

Vernacular
Local or indigenous language. Throughout the centuries, the revival or flowering of vernacular languages has been associated with national and cultural pride.

Acknowledgements

The editors and publishers gratefully acknowledge permission to reproduce copyright poems in this book. Every effort has been made to trace copyright holders, but where this has proved impossible, the publishers would be grateful for information which would enable them to amend any omissions in future editions.

Lionel Abrahams: 'Note in Prosy Verse'. Printed by permission of the author.

Tatamkulu Afrika: 'The Handshake'. Printed by permission of the author.

John Agard: 'Poetry Jump-up' from *You'll Love That Stuff,* Cambridge University Press. Reprinted by permission of the Caroline Sheldon Literary Agency.

Maya Angelou: 'Still I Rise'. Reprinted by permission of Virago Press.

W. H. Auden: 'Roman Wall Blues', 'Lullaby', and 'In Memory of W. B. Yeats' from *Collected Poems* by W. H. Auden. Reprinted by permission of Faber and Faber Ltd.

Kofi Awoonor: 'The Weaver Bird' from *The Penguin Book of Modern African Poetry* edited by Gerald Moore and Uli Beier. Reprinted by permission of the author.

Shabbir Banoobhai: 'last poem for the year'. Reprinted by permission of the author.

Eva Bezwoda: 'A Woman's Hands' published by Renoster Books. Reprinted by permission of Lionel Abrahams, publisher.

Bertolt Brecht: 'Questions from a Worker who Reads' (translated by Michael Hamburger) from *Bertolt Brecht Poems 1913 –1956.* Reprinted by permission of Reed Consumer Books Ltd.

Dean Brogden: 'april 1993'. Printed by permission of the author.

Gwendolyn Brooks: 'We Real Cool' © 1991 Gwendolyn Brooks. Published in 'Blacks', 1991, by Third World Press, Chicago, Illinois, USA. Reprinted by permission of the author.

Sterling Brown: 'Children's Children' from *The Collected Poems of Sterling A. Brown,* edited by Michael Harper. © 1980 Sterling A. Brown. Reprinted by permission of HarperCollins Publishers, Inc.

Dennis Brutus: 'Letter to Camden'. Printed by permission of the author.

Sally Bryer: 'Ingrid Jonker' from *Breaking the Silence: A Century of South African Women's Poetry* edited by Cecily Lockett and published by Ad. Donker.

Guy Butler: 'Near Hout Bay'. Reprinted by permission of the author.

Roy Campbell: 'The Zulu Girl' from *Selected Poems* by Roy Campbell. Reprinted by permission of Francisco Campbell Custadio and Ad. Donker (Pty) Ltd.

Sydney Clouts: 'Poetry is Death Cast Out'. Reprinted by permission of David Philip Publisher (Pty) Ltd.

Lisa Combrinck: 'To the Reader' from *Essential Things: Anthology of New South African Poetry* edited by Andries Oliphant.

Jeni Couzyn: 'The Red Hen's Last Will and Testament to the Last Cock on Earth' from *Life by Drowning, Selected Poems,* Bloodaxe Books, 1983. Reprinted by permission of the author and Bloodaxe Books.

Jeremy Cronin: 'Faraway City, there' from *Inside* by Jeremy Cronin published by Ravan Press, 1983. Reprinted by permission of Ravan Press (Pty) Ltd.

E. E. Cummings: 'anyone lived in a pretty how town' and 'next to god of course america i' from *The Collected Poems 1913 – 1962* by E.E. Cummings. Reprinted by permission of W.W. Norton & Company, Ltd.

Jennifer Davids: 'For Albert Luthuli (21.7.67)'. Reprinted by permission of David Philip Publisher (Pty) Ltd.

Ingrid de Kok: 'Mending' from *Boston Review*, June/August 1993. Reprinted by permission of the author; 'Small Passing' from *Familiar Ground* by Ingrid de Kok published by Ravan Press, 1988. Reprinted by permission of the author and Ravan Press (Pty) Ltd.

Anthony Delius: 'Deaf-and-Dumb School'. Reprinted by permission of Peter Delius.

Modikwe Dikobe: 'Khoikhoi-Son-of-Man' from *Dispossessed* by Modikwe Dikobe published by Ravan Press, Johannesburg, 1983. Reprinted by permission of the author and Ravan Press.

H. D.: 'Helen' from *The Collected Poems of H. D.* Reprinted by permission of Carcanet Press, Ltd.

T. S. Eliot: 'Journey of the Magi', 'Preludes' and 'Marina' from *Collected Poems 1909 – 1962* by T.S. Eliot. Reprinted by permission of Faber and Faber Ltd.

L. Ferlinghetti: 'Constantly Risking Absurdity' from *A Coney Island of the Mind.* Reprinted by permission of New Directions Publishing Corporation.

Robert Frost: 'Mending Wall' and 'The Road Not Taken'. Reprinted by permission of Henry Holt and Company, Inc.

Nikki Giovanni: 'For Carol'.

Erika Gouws: 'Kaap van Goeie Hoop'. Printed by permission of the author.

Geoffrey Haresnape: 'Pruning a Mulberry in Autumn'from *The Slug Newsletter* 25 and 'In and Around the Yacht Basin – Simon's Town'. Reprinted and printed by permission of the author.

S. Heaney: 'Follower'. Reprinted by permission of Faber and Faber Ltd.

Li Ho: 'On the Frontier' from *Poems of the Late T'ang* (translated by A. C. Graham), Penguin Classics. © 1965 A. C. Graham. Reprinted by permission of Penguin Books Ltd.

Langston Hughes: 'Mother to Son' and 'The Negro Speaks of Rivers'. Reprinted by permission of David Higham Associates Ltd.

Antonio Jacinto: 'Letter From a Contract Worker' from *The Penguin Book of Modern African Poetry* edited by Gerald Moore and Uli Beier.

Wopko Jensma: Poem 3 from 'Not Him' from *Sing for our Execution* published by Ravan Press, 1973. Reprinted by permission of Ravan Press (Pty) Ltd.

Fhazel Johennesse: 'A Young Man's Thoughts Before June 16th' from *The Rainmaker.* Reprinted by permission of the author.

Ingrid Jonker: 'The Child who was Shot Dead by Soldiers at Nyanga.' Reprinted by permission of Anna Jonker.

Solly Kaplinski: 'Story-telling in the Singular'. Reprinted by permission of the author.

'Kilaben Bay Song' (translated by Perce Haslan) from *The New Oxford Book of Australian Verse.*

Thomas Kinsella: 'Sacrifice' from *New Poems 1973* by Thomas Kinsella, published by The Dolman Press, Dublin, Ireland. Reprinted by permission of the author.

Philip Larkin: 'Talking in Bed'. Reprinted by permission of Faber and Faber Ltd.

Denise Levertov: 'What Were They Like?' from *To Stay Alive* by Denise Levertov.

Douglas Livingstone: 'Dust' from *The London Magazine.* Reprinted by permission of the author.

Lorde, Audre: 'Coal'.

Claude Mackay: 'If We Must Die' from *Selected Poems of Claude Mackay.*

Archibald MacLeish: 'Ars Poetica' from *Collected Poems 1917 – 1982.* © 1985 The Estate of Archibald MacLeish. Reprinted by permission of Houghton Mifflin Company.

Valente Malangatana: 'Woman' from *The Penguin Book of Modern African Poetry* edited by Gerald Moore and Uli Beier.

Don Mattera: 'Remember'. Reprinted by permission of the author.

Gcina Mhlophe: 'Say No'.

Edna St. Vincent Millay: 'I, Being Born a Woman and Distressed' from *Collected Poems,* Harper Collins. © 1923, 1951 Edna St. Vincent Millay and Norma Millay Ellis. Reprinted by permission of Elizabeth Barnett, literary executor.

Ruth Miller: 'Honey' and 'Blue-mantled Mary'. Reprinted by permission of Lionel Abrahams on behalf of Mrs Pat Campbell and the estate of Ruth Miller.

Mbuyiseni Oswald Mtshali: 'Men in Chains' and 'An Abandoned Bundle'. Reprinted by permission of the author and Ad. Donker (Pty) Ltd.

Tu Mu: 'The Gate Tower of Ch'i-an City' and 'To Judge Han Ch'o at Yang-chou' from *Poems of the Late T'ang* (translated by A. C. Graham), Penguin Classics. © 1965 A. C. Graham. Reprinted by permission of Penguin Books Ltd.

Charles Mungoshi: 'A Letter to a Son' from *Zimbabwean Poetry in English.* Reprinted by permission of Mambo Press.

Augustinho Neto: 'The Grieved Lands' from *The Penguin Book of Modern African Poetry* edited by Gerald Moore and Uli Beier.

Arthur Nortje: 'In Exile'.

Richard Ntiru: 'The Gourd of Friendship' from *Poems of Black Africa* edited by Wole Soyinka.

Essop Patel: 'In the Shadow of Signal Hill'. Reprinted by permission of the author.

Sylvia Plath: 'You're' and 'Pheasant'. Reprinted by permission of Faber and Faber Ltd.

William Plomer: 'A Transvaal Morning' from *Collected Poems* by William Plomer. Reprinted by permission of Jonathan Cape.

Henry Pote: 'To a White Child' from *Zimbabwean Poetry in English*. Reprinted by permission of Mambo Press.

Ezra Pound: 'In a Station of the Metro' and 'The River Merchant's Wife' from *Collected Shorter Poems* by Ezra Pound. Reprinted by permission of Faber and Faber Ltd.

Reynolds, Malvina: 'What Have They Done to the Rain?'

Adrienne Rich: '"I am in Danger — Sir"'; from *The Fact of a Doorframe: Poems Selected and New, 1950 - 1984* by Adrienne Rich. © 1984 Adrienne Rich and W.W. Norton & Company, Inc.

Roethke, Theodore: 'Elegy for Jane'. Reprinted by permission of Faber and Faber Ltd.

Damian Ruth: 'Sunday Morning Breakfast'. Printed by permission of the author.

Helen Segal: 'The Sea is all Male' from *Breaking the Silence: A Century of South African Women's Poetry* edited by Cecily Lockett and published by Ad. Donker.

Sipho Sepamla: 'Hurry up to it!' and 'The Loneliness Beyond'. Reprinted by permission of the author.

Wally Mongane Serote: 'Alexandra', 'City Johannesburg', For Don M. — Banned' and 'That's Not My Wish'. Reprinted by permission of the author and Ad. Donker (Pty) Ltd.

Mutiswayo Shandu: 'Bye Bye, Overcoat' from *Quarry 80–82*.

Rushdy Siers: 'Sets of Two and their Silence' from *Essential Things: an Anthology of New South African Poetry* edited by Andries Oliphant. Reprinted by permission of the author.

Stevie Smith: 'Not Waving but Drowning' from *The Collected Poems of Stevie Smith,* Penguin Twentieth Century Classics. Reprinted by permission of James MacGibbon, executor.

Wole Soyinka: 'Capital' from *Poems of Black Africa* edited by Wole Soyinka.

Dylan Thomas: 'And Death Shall Have No Dominion' and 'In my Craft or Sullen Art' from *Selected Poems* by Dylan Thomas. Reprinted by permission of David Higham Associates Ltd.

Mao Tse-Tung: 'Lou Mountain Pass' from *Poems of Mao Tse-Tung* (translated by Hua-ling Nieh Engle and Paul Engle).

Chris van Wyk: 'Memory' and 'On Learning Sotho'. Printed and reprinted by permission of the author.

Stephen Watson: 'In Exile' from *In This City* and 'The Rain that is Male' from *Return of the Moon*, both by Stephen Watson. Reprinted by permission of the author.

William Carlos Williams: 'This is Just to Say' and 'The Dance' from *Collected Poems*. Reprinted by permission of Carcanet Press, Ltd.

David Wright: 'On the Margin'. Reprinted by permission of V. J. Beatson, literary executor.

Index